D1608375

HAPPY BIRTHDAY
UNCLE GREG ~
HOPE THIS BOOK
GIVES YOU LOTS
OF TRAVEL
ENTHUSIASM!

Golfing Florida's BEST

Golfing Florida's BEST

Rob Armstrong

PELICAN PUBLISHING COMPANY
Gretna 2001

Library of Congress Cataloging-in-Publication Data

Armstrong, Rob, 1949-
Golfing Florida's best / by Rob Armstrong.
p. cm
Includes index.
ISBN 1-56554-732-2 (alk. paper)
1. Golf courses—Florida—Guidebooks. 2. Golf courses—Florida—Directories. I. Title.
GV982.F5 A74 2001
796.352'06'8759—dc21
00-069205

Printed in Singapore
Published by Pelican Publishing Company, Inc.
1000 Burmaster Street, Gretna, Louisiana 70053

For mother, dad, and
Barbara with love and thanks

CONTENTS

ACKNOWLEDGMENTS

Putting together this book has taken nearly a year and has involved countless people in its research, planning, organization, logistics, and final preparation. Not to mention all those golf professionals, enthusiastic amateurs, friends, and colleagues who have given generously of their time and knowledge to help me come up with the final list of courses.

As with all of my books, I could not have written this one without the help, encouragement, support, and love of my wife, Barbara. She drove thousands of miles through Florida with me, played a majority of these golf courses, offered her keen insight, and edited the first drafts of the manuscript. Likewise, Murray and Freda Armstrong, my mother and father—avid golfers still, in their mid-eighties—have always been there with love, sound advice, and support.

Once again, my thanks to the wonderful people at Pelican Publishing Company. I will be forever indebted to my publisher, Dr. Milburn Calhoun, for having the faith and confidence to undertake another book project with me. Linda Moreau, former publicist, and Frank McGuire in sales are fine, dedicated professionals to work with. Erin Best, my editor on this project, demonstrated a keen insight and an adroit touch with the manuscript. And Nina Kooij, Editor in Chief, is the best editor in the book business—sharp-eyed, intelligent, clever, and enormously skilled. Working with her has been my good fortune as a writer.

Listing all the individuals who have helped me gather and synthesize the information needed in an undertaking like this one is impossible. The following people went out of their way to share their insights, point me in the right direction, and offer advice. I am extremely grateful to Jason Powell and Tom Derringer Jr. at Marsh Creek Country Club, Mary Hafeman and Jim Grimes at Ponce de Leon Golf Club, Rich Whelan at Jacaranda West Country Club, Ed and Margaret Travis and Charley Stine at *Florida Golf News*, Cathy Harbin at World Golf Village, Cindy Cockburn at Westin Innisbrook Resort, Rene O'Connor at Doral, Karen Hutchens at Sandestin, and Randy Stamitoles at Bay Point. Sadly, Marsh Creek Golf Director Hugh McCracken lost his battle with cancer before this book became a reality.

My friends and colleagues were warm and generous with their advice, support, and encouragement through the months this project was on the drawing board. As always, my warmest thanks to my closest personal friends, Tom Taylor, Sheila Vidamour, Wen and Yaling Lin, Kal and Betsy Lee, and Alex and Mea Gillies. I am indebted to my former colleagues at CBS News and on Capitol Hill, Larry McCoy, Howard Arenstein, David Jackson, Diane Lane, Jamie DuPree, and Kia Baskerville. And deep appreciation to my friends and colleagues at Flagler College, William and Pam Procter, Bill Abare, Caroline Dow, Doug Covert, Virgil Moberg, and Laurin Bosse.

INTRODUCTION

Golf is to Florida as thoroughbred horse racing is to Kentucky and skiing is to Switzerland. But this has not always been the case; back in the mid-1700s, when golf was becoming fashionable in the British Isles, Florida was, for the most part, an inhospitable, largely uninhabited, semi-tropical swamp interrupted occasionally by dense forests of pines, oaks, cypress trees and the like. During the American Civil War, Florida was the deepest of Dixie, with little of the state populated at all south of a line from Jacksonville in the east to Pensacola in the west.

As the nineteenth century entered its final two decades, the full promise of Florida was still just the dream of such visionaries as industrialist Henry Flagler. Flagler, more than any other individual, opened Florida's Atlantic seaboard and began the unprecedented growth and development that has evolved into the modern state. Flagler built a railroad down the east coast of Florida, clearing the way for businesses, workers, and a flood of tourists from Jacksonville to Key West. Along the rail line, Flagler built a series of ultra luxurious hotels, including such architectural landmarks as the Ponce de Leon and Alcazar Hotels in St. Augustine, the Ormond Beach Hotel in Ormond Beach, the Royal Ponciana and Breakers Hotels in Palm Beach, and the Royal Palm Hotel in Miami. Flagler's first hotel, the Ponce de Leon in St. Augustine, opened in 1888, the same year golf came to the United States. Nine years later, in 1897, a golf course was constructed at his Breakers Hotel, the first course in Florida.

Those early days of golf in Florida reflected the same prejudices and exclusivity as golf in the rest of the United States. It was a sport for rich, white people. Even the earliest municipal and public golf courses, often supported in part or in full by local tax dollars, were highly segregated. Private country clubs almost always excluded African Americans, often excluded Jews, and usually treated women as second class citizens. For the most part, such overt racism, bigotry, and sexism have vanished, although I regret to report that some vestiges of the past lurk alarmingly near the surface in several areas.

In retrospect, golf in Florida was a slow starter. Aside from a few private clubs and a handful of public courses, golf gradually crept into the state and eventually arrived with a bang and a flourish. The wonderful Scottish golf course architect, Donald Ross, was commissioned to design a few Florida courses in the early part of the century, such as the municipal golf course in Palatca and the Ponce de Leon Golf Course in St. Augustine. But the courses were not inundated with players. Equipment—shoes, clubs, and golf balls—was expensive and hard to come by. And for most of the year, Florida is excruciatingly hot, especially when you're walking and carrying your clubs.

It wasn't until the years leading up to World War II that golf enjoyed a significant spike in public interest, owing primarily to a few traveling professionals who put on exhibitions, challenged local players, and made the game a show. Legends of the game like "Slammin'" Sammy Snead, Jimmy Demaret, and Byron Nelson traveled up and down the east coast demonstrating their skills and hustling for a few bucks. During the war and immediately thereafter, golf caught the attention of such entertainment stars as Bob Hope, Bing Crosby, and Jackie Gleason. They talked about it in their performances, on the radio, and over a new electronic medium called "television."

The 1950s saw the first wave of what was to be the Florida golf boom. And as air conditioning became more widely available and motorized golf carts burst on the scene, Florida golf was off to the races in the 1960s and 70s. Resorts devoted to golf were the rage. Real estate developers were quick to capitalize on the notion of "golf course communities" in which houses were constructed around golf courses. By the 1980s, Florida was one of the fastest growing states in the Union, and golf was one of the biggest businesses in the state. The trend-line has been almost vertical ever since.

Twenty-first century Florida is golf heaven. The state has something for virtually every golfer. There are courses to challenge players of every skill level, courses to satisfy every taste, courses to accommodate every budget. In addition, there is world-class instruction and abundant practice facilities. Every year thousands of people move to the Sunshine State primarily because of the golf. Tens of thousands of others visit and play. You rarely see a television ad, travel brochure, Internet pop-up or other promotion for the state where you don't see somebody with a golf club in his or her hand.

If there is any doubt about the fact that the golf business in the Sunshine State is expanding faster than Tiger Woods' follow-through, just consider that while this book was being researched, more than a score of new golf courses opened and another score entered the planning and construction phase. The sheer number of golf courses is staggering. Determining which courses to include or omit proved to be a daunting task. Nonetheless, I have sought to present a representative, if occasionally arbitrary and highly subjective, list of courses you can play.

I began by omitting all private clubs—any private, semi-private, or resort course that required special conditions for visitors, such as staying at the resort connected to the course or limiting visitors to guests of members. While that narrowed the list considerably, it still left far more courses than could be accommodated in this space.

So I turned to intangible considerations. I went through all of the published lists of the state's best and most popular courses I could find, including *Golf Magazine, Golf Digest, Golf for Women,* and *Florida Golf News.* I talked to dozens of local golf pros and knowledgeable golfers about the courses with which they were familiar. Then I played every course included in the book and dozens of others that were not included for various reasons. What I looked for in each course was what nearly every player looks for: design, condition, and playability of the course, staff attitude, service, course maintenance, management, and the overall look and feel of the place.

The list turned out to be eclectic, to say the least. It includes such PGA, Senior PGA, and LPGA tournament venues as the Blue Monster at Doral, the TPC at Tampa Bay, Westin Innisbrook's Copperhead Course, The Slammer & The Squire at World Golf Village, and LPGA International's Champions Course. It covers some of Florida's most talked about and written about courses, including El Diablo, Pine Barrens and Rolling Oaks at World Woods, the Raven and Burnt Pines at Sandestin, Greg Norman's Great White at Doral, Lagoon Legend at Bay Point, Emerald Dunes, and the South Course at PGA Golf Club.

It also includes classic, traditional designs such as Charles Clarke's El Campion at Mission Inn, Robert Simmons' Atlantis Country Club, Dean Refram's Saddlebrook Course, and Willard Byrd's Club Meadows at Bay Point. It discusses some of Florida's newest and most adventurous designs, such as Arnold Palmer's North Hampton, Fred Couples' Kelly Plantation, the Dye Course at PGA Golf Club, and the Diamond Players Club Claremont.

A who's who of the best golf course architects is represented as well, including the following: Tom and Jim Fazio, Pete Dye, Jack Nicklaus, Arnold Palmer, Greg Norman, Gary Player, Dick Wilson, Robert von Hagge and Bruce Devlin, Rees Jones, Mark McCumber, Ron Garl, and Bobby Weed.

A few words about prices; the range represented in this book is from unbelievable bargains to signing up for a second mortgage. In general, courses charge more during the high season (which is usually from about Thanksgiving until April or May) than in the low season (which is generally the summer). Many resorts offer golf packages with reduced rates for resort guests. Some offer senior citizen discounts. Some reduce their prices for residents of Florida or residents of the county in which they are located.

The problem in writing a book of this nature, as I discovered with my earlier volumes, *Golfing in Ireland* and *Golfing the Virginias* is that virtually every golfer you encounter has a favorite or group of favorite golf courses. In other words, a list like this is an invitation to have people disagree with me, and I fully expect that. Every published list varies. Sometimes heated and lively discussions ensue whenever the subject comes up. Such disagreement is healthy and worthwhile. What follows are profiles of fifty of the best public and daily-fee golf courses you can call up, make a tee time, and play in the state of Florida. I hope you hit them long and straight!

Golfing Florida's BEST

Avoid the water and the bunkers at the par-three #10 at Atlantis Inn & Country Club.

ATLANTIS COUNTRY CLUB & INN

190 Atlantis Boulevard, Atlantis, Florida (From I-95 take exit 47 and go west on 6th Avenue South for about 2 miles; turn left on Congress Avenue and go south for about 1 mile; turn right at JFK Drive.)
Phone: (561) 968-1300

Architect: Robert Simmons Year opened: 1972

Course rating/Slope rating:

Gold—71.5/129 Blue—69.1/122
White—67.5/117 Red—70.9/123

Every serious golfer has one or more favorite courses. Sometimes they are the shrines of the game, like St. Andrews or Pebble Beach, but as often as not they are courses that have fond personal memories associated with them. One such course for me is Atlantis. I have been playing it for many years, and it has a certain feeling of comfort for me. It has always been kept in superb condition; it's always been friendly and welcoming; it's always made me feel good when I walk into the pro shop or step onto the practice green. It was one of the first full-length courses my wife, Barbara, played when she was just learning the game. It was the first course on which somebody's cellular phone rang in the middle of my backswing.

Atlantis isn't the longest course in Florida. It's only 6,610 yards from the back tees. But it is a wonderful layout, hardly a surprise in that architect Robert Simmons was an associate of Dick Wilson, the same Dick Wilson who designed Doral's Blue Monster. In fact, there's a similar feeling in the design of the two courses. Naturally you've seen the Blue Monster on television, but Atlantis is the same kind of old-fashioned, traditional golf course. It's tight. There's abundant water and sand. It's cut through a dense forest. The greens are subtle, tough, and well protected. Three of the four par fives are reachable in two; there's a nice mix of par fours; and the four one-shot holes can reach up and wrest a good round from your grasp with bogies and worse.

For women, it's an especially good test at 5,242 yards from the forward markers. "I still have to hit every club I carry," said Barbara after her last round there, remembering how far her golf game had advanced in a decade. She noted that the first time she played Atlantis, she didn't hit the ball far enough to get into much trouble. Now she says, "Go a few yards off the fairway and you're in jail."

The course opens with a gentle dogleg right par five followed by a long, tight par four, the toughest hole on the course for women. These holes give you a good feel for what's to come. The next two holes are short, tricky par fours. On #3 most players use something other than a driver, as a stream intersects the fairway about 90 yards from the green and can be reached by a big tee shot. The ideal tee shot lands about 120 yards from the green. On #4, the green is hooked to the left behind a stand of trees. Your tee shot has to stay far enough to the right to avoid the lumber and open up the elevated, well-bunkered green.

Number 6 is the toughest hole on the course for men, a dogleg left with a blind tee shot that plays around the forest. Driving precision is rewarded more than brute strength or sheer length. If you can't see the green on your second shot, par can be very elusive.

The side finishes with a tight par five that can be reached in two shots. A lake is in play to the left from about 150 yards away from the green up to the left side of the putting surface. The entrance to the green is very narrow with towering pines intruding on the right and bunkers all around. For women it's a huge three-shot hole playing 467 yards from the Red Tees.

The inward side opens with a pretty and challenging par three. It's a visually intimidating hole with a lake that laps along the left up to the elevated, undulating green. The green, itself, is wide and shallow. While it's not a forced carry, the water is in your field of vision almost constantly.

The 12th hole is a splendid par five. A big drive can find the water hazard that intersects the fairway about 220 yards from the green. A drive short of the hazard, a lay-up second over the hazard, and a short iron to the flag sets up a good scoring opportunity. A brazen effort to reach the hole in two that falls short and catches the enormous, deep bunker in front of the green can test the nerves of even the best players. A quartet of par fours follows, the toughest of them #16. Trees tightly hug the left side of the fairway and water is in play down the right, starting at the bend of the dogleg. The elevated green is small and well protected.

Number 17 is a wonderful, challenging par three with water between the tees and the green, angled in such a way that it can come into play to the left front of the putting surface, which is sandwiched between a pair of looming bunkers.

Your round at Atlantis wraps up with a big par five that will be a three-shot hole for almost everybody. Trees and out-of-bounds guard the left length of the hole. About 100 yards from the green, the hole is choked by a long thin bunker on the left and a sand trap that's overhung by a gnarled, bent old tree to the right. The big elevated green is bunkered on all sides and the embankment at the front virtually guarantees that short shots will not roll onto the putting surface.

Walk off the 18th green having played Atlantis to your handicap, and you can be well satisfied. Over the years, players have said that the course is far more difficult that one would guess from looking at the scorecard. It's demanding. It requires all of your concentration and skill, but it is a joy to play. Play it once and you'll want to play it again; play it twice and you'll be hooked.

Atlantis Country Club & Inn

HOLE NUMBER	Ra	Sl	1	2	3	4	5	6	7	8	9	OUT	10	11	12	13	14	15	16	17	18	IN	TOT
GOLD	71.5	129	494	404	365	363	147	402	419	170	525	3289	164	382	515	361	343	435	385	172	564	3321	6610
BLUE	69.1	122	461	386	331	316	131	380	368	151	488	3012	147	357	468	331	321	405	355	138	526	3048	6060
WHITE	67.5	117	446	375	275	300	120	345	340	135	475	2811	135	340	445	318	315	382	335	120	500	2890	5701
MEN'S HCP			9	3	13	11	17	1	5	15	7		18	6	10	14	12	2	8	16	4		
PAR			5	4	4	4	3	4	4	3	5	36	3	4	5	4	4	4	4	3	5	36	72
RED	70.9	123	439	361	264	248	103	338	280	110	467	2610	110	330	402	269	265	376	325	102	453	2632	5242
WOMEN'S HCP			5	1	11	13	15	7	9	17	3		18	10	6	12	14	2	8	16	4		

BAY POINT YACHT & COUNTRY CLUB

3900 Marriott Drive, Panama City, Florida (From U.S. Highway 98 go south on Thomas Drive about a mile; turn left onto Magnolia Beach Road and follow signs to the resort.)
Phone: (850) 235-6950

Club Meadows Architect: Willard Byrd Year opened: 1972
Lagoon Legend Architects: Robert von Hagge and Bruce Devlin Year opened: 1986
Club Meadows course rating/Slope rating for men:
Blue—73.3/126 White—70.7/120 Green—68.2/116

Club Meadows course rating/Slope rating for women:
Red—73.0/124 Gold—68.0/118

Lagoon Legend course rating/Slope rating:
Orange—75.3/152 Blue—73.0/148 White—70.7/144
Green—70.1/135 Red—69.8/127

The Bay Point Yacht & Country Club is a first rate golf destination. In addition to a pair of marvelous golf courses, it offers all of the other resort amenities you'd expect, including water sports, boating, swimming, tennis, and top notch restaurants. Panama City has long been a Gulf Coast playground, tourist Mecca, and haven for golfers. It's a friendly, laid-back town and Bay Point is a friendly, laid-back resort.

Bay Point's two golf courses are a study in contrasts. One is user-friendly; the other lies in wait like a mugger in the alley. One is traditional, even old-fashioned; the other is modern, even avant-garde. One is gentle; the other is brutal.

The older of the two Bay Point courses, Club Meadows, was commissioned in 1970 and took two years to build. It's a lovely, traditional design, carved through dense forest. It's tight. It's fair. It's charming. It's fun to play. The greens and tees are close together. The greens are small. The bunkering is well designed. It's layout is reminiscent of other traditional courses from the 60s and 70s by such outstanding golf course architects as Ed Ault, George Cobb, Ellis Maples, and Robert Trent Jones, Sr.

The second and newer Bay Point course, Lagoon Legend, can be described as nothing less than *X* golf. It is golf's answer to snow boarding, line skating, hang gliding, and full-contact martial arts. Its USGA slope ratings are the highest of any golf course in the continental United States, and from the back tees, it will humble even the best touring pros. It ranks with the Cashen Course at Ballybunion, Ireland—a monster of a links golf course designed by Robert Trent Jones, Sr.—as the toughest track I've ever played. Neither is terribly long, but as Randy Stamitoles, one of the assistant pros at Bay Point noted, "Difficulty isn't necessarily determined by length."

In short, both the golf and the resort as a whole make Bay Point an outstanding place for a vacation.

The beautiful but dangerous par-three 13th hole at Bay Point's Club Meadows requires a forced carry across a pond.

CLUB MEADOWS

I liked Club Meadows from the moment I drove up and a fellow, whose name tag identified him as Papa Joe, put my bag on a golf cart and started regaling me about what a wonderful golf course I was going to play. His enthusiasm was infectious. When my first 15-yard putt on the practice green found the bottom of the cup, I knew this was a special place. By the time I stood on the #1 tee and looked down the narrow chute of fairway lined by towering ancient trees, I was in a wonderful frame of mind for golf. Everything about the place announces that it is a mature, traditional golf course. The staff treats even a first-time visitor as if he/she has been a member for years.

Club Meadows is a fine test for women players. There are two sets of women's tees, each offering a challenging and fair look at the course. Tee placement is well considered and clearly done with care. Women whose handicaps are in the teens or lower should move back and play the Red Tees, which measure more than 5,600 yards. Other women will have a fine, enjoyable time from the Gold Tees, which check in at just under 5,000 yards.

Your introduction to Club Meadows is a pair of shortish par fours. The first is a dogleg left. Two problems: A short tee shot will almost certainly find the approach to the green obscured by trees and there's a lake within driving distance straight ahead where the dogleg bends. Play something other than a driver to the 150-yard stake and give yourself a straight shot at the green. The second is a mirror image of the first—a dogleg right. This hole favors a left to right shot and if you can work your tee shot around the bend in the dogleg, you'll be in ideal position to approach the green.

The third hole is a solid par-three with a huge bunker directly in front of the green. It's a tough hole for women in that it requires a long accurate shot to clear the sand and find the putting surface. (The women's Red Tees measure 141 yards; the Golds are 138 yards.)

The outgoing nine features two good par fives. Even moderate hitters can think about reaching the 5th hole in two. The driving zone is generous, but the hole gets increasingly narrow the closer you get to the green. A lake is in play down the right for the last 200 yards to the green. The ninth is a long, tight three-shot hole with forest lining both sides of the fairway. Your tee shot must avoid a pair of fairway bunkers on the left. The small green, which slopes from back to front, is brushed by oaks on the right and guarded by a bunker on the left.

Number ten is a long, demanding par four, with a pond—not visible from the tees—in play on the right from about 170 yards away from the long, thin, multi-level green. The eleventh is a tight par five, especially off the tees. Forest on both sides renders the landing area very narrow. The elevated green is guarded by three big bunkers and a pond on the right. It's possible for long hitters to get to the green in two, but the shot must be precise or risk finding the myriad hazards.

The best par three on Club Meadows is #13, a short, but dangerous little hole, with a forced carry over water for everybody. Three large bunkers surround the putting surface, and there's precious little bail-out room anywhere.

A pair of lovely par fours follows. The fourteenth is a demanding dogleg left. You drive through a chute of trees to a narrow landing area. The elevated green is angled to the left behind a gaping bunker. The fifteenth is a severe dogleg left with a tight landing area from the tees. Your drive must be long enough and right enough to prevent your view of the green from being blocked by the forest that defines the left length of the hole.

Your round wraps up with a difficult duo. The seventeenth hole is three-shot par five that's replete with trouble. A canal runs most of the left length of the hole and a lake comes into play at the right front of the large elevated green. A quartet of sand traps surrounds the long, thin putting surface. Number eighteen is a dogleg right, par four. Your drive must split the fairway bunkers at both sides of the hole's elbow. The approach to the green is incredibly narrow. The green, itself, is angled to the right behind a lake and guarded by a pair of bunkers as well.

There's very little about Club Meadows that I didn't like, save for the fact that I hooked my drive into the canal on #17, but that's hardly the fault of the golf course. It's the kind of course that grows on you. By the time you leave it, it's like leaving an old friend. And once you've gone, it lingers in your memory.

LAGOON LEGEND

Let's say it right up front. The Lagoon Legend golf course is no place for beginners. In fact, if you're not a pretty good player you're well advised to leave this monster for another day. That said, Lagoon Legend—which has gotten more favorable ink and top national ratings than almost any golf course in Florida—is a simply spectacular design. Robert von Hagge and Bruce Devlin were commissioned to build a tough golf course. They obviously approached their mission with zeal. But they also managed to come up with a golf course layout that verges on being a work of art.

The rich fabric of the tapestry results from an amalgam of man-made and natural elements. Man's manipulation of sand, water, and exaggerated contours work in sophisticated harmony and rhythm with the forests and marshes that nature put there. Water is in play on sixteen holes. More than fifty-five bunkers have been constructed, one of them in excess of 180 yards.

Unlike some deliberately difficult golf courses which punish good shots and deliver punitive lies or penalties when they are not deserved, the extreme difficulty of Lagoon Legend is not unfair, tricked up, artificial, or unplayable in any way. When I saw the slope ratings, including the awesome 152 for the back tees, I expected some convoluted layout that would be part theme park and part moonscape. My fears proved unfounded, although the vast expanse of waste bunker that sits menacingly in front of the first tees is enough to make even the boldest players a bit squeamish.

Lagoon Legend opens with a long par five. Once safely over the desert-like bunker you must negotiate your way through a trough of mounds and bunkers. Your approach is a forced carry over water to a smallish two-tiered green.

The second hole also features a giant waste area in front of the men's tees. The forward markers are spared the carry. This par four is a dogleg right with a steep downhill approach to a long, undulating green that's angled to the left behind a pond. The closer you get to the water the more severely the fairway slopes toward it. The water guards the left side of the green and a big bunker guards the right.

At Bay Point's Lagoon Legend, the short, treacherous par-four 10th is a severe dogleg right, with the green tucked behind a marshy lake.

Club Meadows

HOLE NUMBER	Ra	Sl	1	2	3	4	5	6	7	8	9	OUT	10	11	12	13	14	15	16	17	18	IN	TOT
BLUE	73.3	126	402	397	197	405	513	183	419	404	542	3462	443	532	398	153	403	387	181	533	421	3451	6913
WHITE	70.7	120	363	375	167	372	480	160	384	379	509	3189	409	499	370	132	378	353	155	503	384	3183	6372
GREEN	68.2	116	325	335	145	350	451	142	362	360	480	2950	386	475	349	100	345	340	134	485	355	2969	5919
MEN'S HCP		15	11	9	1	13	17	3	5	7			2	14	10	18	8	12	16	6	4		
PAR			4	4	3	4	5	3	4	4	5	36	4	5	4	3	4	4	3	5	4	36	72
RED	73.0	124	306	320	141	338	441	128	340	351	465	2830	375	449	334	89	291	332	123	470	341	2804	5634
GOLD	68.0	118	268	276	138	305	413	110	252	396	421	2579	315	437	292	81	288	296	118	415	268	2510	5089
WOMEN'S HCP		9	5	15	1	13	17	11	3	7			2	8	10	18	14	12	16	4	6		

Lagoon Legend

HOLE NUMBER	Ra	Sl	1	2	3	4	5	6	7	8	9	OUT	10	11	12	13	14	15	16	17	18	IN	TOT
ORANGE	75.3	152	542	405	450	208	442	569	381	226	378	3601	376	193	512	300	434	402	192	519	392	3320	6921
BLUE	73.0	148	515	382	427	178	399	549	356	189	356	3351	359	172	497	283	394	361	170	472	362	3070	6421
WHITE	70.7	144	502	370	401	165	387	531	336	168	340	3200	341	154	481	267	349	329	157	448	340	2866	6066
GREEN	70.1	135	477	314	387	132	356	517	296	142	321	2942	307	132	469	249	303	279	139	425	314	2617	5559
MEN'S HCP		5	7	1	11	13	3	15	17	9			6	18	10	12	2	16	14	8	4		
PAR			5	4	4	3	4	5	4	3	4	36	4	3	5	4	4	4	3	5	4	36	72
RED	69.8	127	439	295	321	101	318	469	289	118	256	2606	278	103	399	213	290	269	129	385	270	2336	4942
WOMEN'S HCP		3	13	5	15	11	1	7	17	9			4	18	12	10	14	16	8	6	2		

The par four 3rd gives you a bit of a breather. Number 4 is a long watery par three. There's bail-out room to the right, but beware of the long, deep bunker behind the bail-out area that's invisible from the tees. On the par-four 5th hole, your tee shot must avoid the long fairway bunker about driving distance on the left. The fairway is a furrow between steep mounds, and while there's no sand at all around the big green, there's a steep drop-off to the right from about 100 yards out and the green is perched above the grassy valley. In addition, there's a deep indentation in the middle of the putting surface, creating a three level challenge.

A lot of players use less than a driver on the short par-four 7th, which tightens dangerously between bunkers and mounds the closer you get to the wide thin, green. The multi-level green, itself, is guarded by three bunkers in front and two in the rear.

The long par-three 8th hole is called "Molloy's Revenge." I have no idea who Molloy was, but he must have been one vengeful fellow. The long, tough hole plays uphill to a green that measures some 44 yards in length. It's a visually intimidating golf hole, with a lake to the right and front of the tees, bunkers all around the plateaued green, and parts of the putting surface obscured. The direction and velocity of the wind off the Gulf of Mexico, along with the placement of the flag, will have a profound impact on club selection.

The side finishes with a dogleg right par four with water everywhere. Keep your tee shot to the right of the huge fairway bunker, but remember that even a moderate drive can find the lake through the fairway. A tee shot just short of the steep hills on the right will set up a good second shot. The wide, shallow two-tiered green, however, is fronted by water and demands a high, soft approach.

On the back nine, watch out for the short, treacherous par fours. Number 10 is one of them, an extreme dogleg right to a green that juts out into the lake that extends the entire length of the hole. Your drive is to a very small, hilly landing area. Hit it too long and you're in sand, moguls, or deep rough; hit it too short and trees will block your view of the green. Your second shot is no bargain either. A short shot will find the water and weeds in front of the green; an approach that's too bold can find the water and weeds in the back.

The 13th hole is the shortest par four on the Lagoon Legend course. It can be an easy birdie or par, but scores of players every week slink away with double- and triple-bogeys. Most players use a mid- to long iron to come up short of the hazard that intersects the fairway and surrounds the small island green. The entrance to the green is framed by giant old trees. The margin for error is almost zero.

Number 15 is the third of the short par fours on the back. There's water in play off the tee. The fairway is elevated. The green sits in a little basin, angled to the left behind an enormous bunker. Both your tee shot and your approach require surgical precision.

Lagoon Legend finishes with three extraordinary golf holes. They are as breathtaking to look at as they are heart stopping to play. Number 16 is unique and controversial. It is a completely blind par three. You can see the flag fluttering in the breeze, but you can't see the putting surface, which is obscured by marsh grass, reeds and shrubs. A bunker—also invisible from the tees—sits behind the green. The tee provides a spectacular view of the bay.

Number 17 is a par five that even moderately long hitters can reach in two, although the approach to the green requires a forced carry of more that 100 yards across a lake. The green itself is fronted by the lake and backed by a two wide, deep sand traps. Where you come to rest in the hilly, contoured landing area will play heavily into your decision about your second shot. A good drive, mid-iron, and wedge is the safe combination.

The par-four 18th is the signature hole at Lagoon Legend, an extreme dogleg left, almost a horseshoe. All but the forward markers tee off across an expanse of marsh and water that renders the fairway an island. The yardage guide recommends putting your tee shot just to the right of the bridge leading to the green. The shallow green is then back across the same marsh and water.

What a golf course! What a test! One little lapse of concentration and this monster will eat you alive. A Bay Point member with whom I happened to play another course in the area said there's only one piece of advice: "Take plenty of golf balls!" If you play it within five strokes of your handicap, you can feel well satisfied. If you don't, you have a lot of company. At the very least, if you're a moderate to good player, Lagoon Legend is an absolute must on your Florida Gulf Coast or Panhandle itinerary.

Number 6 at Baytree National Golf Links is a tight par four with an elevated green.

BAYTREE NATIONAL GOLF LINKS

8270 National Dr., Melbourne, Florida (Take exit 73 east from I-95 about a mile; turn right at the entrance to Baytree on Wickham Rd. and follow signs to the clubhouse.)
Phone: (407) 259-9060

Architect: Gary Player Year opened: 1994

Course rating/Slope rating for men:
Black—74.0/135 Gold—71.6/129
Blue—69.7/123 White—66.5/114

Course rating/Slope rating for women:
White—71.5/128 Red—68.4/121

Gary Player does not design ordinary golf courses. From his tough, demanding mountain marvel at Hawthorne Valley, West Virginia, to Blackmoor in what was once a rice plantation near Myrtle Beach, South Carolina, to Raspberry Falls which meanders through the hills of Virginia horse country near Leesburg, Gary Player is a design artist. Some golf course architects are predictable; play one of their courses and you've played them all. Not Player. There's nothing cookie-cutter, one-dimensional, or prefabricated about a Player golf course. Each one is unique in its texture and temperament.

In the case of Baytree National, Player has selected water and sand as the key props for his golfing stage. Player was a shot-maker and his golf courses uniformly demand shot-making to score. In most cases, he will leave the golfer with a reasonable approach to the green, if the preparatory shot has been well executed. On the other hand, his designs will punish shots that stray from the fairway; shots that stray too far will usually result in penalty strokes as well.

As one of the foremost sand players ever, the South African champion always takes great pains with the placement and construction of his bunkers. In the case of Baytree National, he has combined traditional greenside and fairway sand bunkers, grass bunkers, mounding and natural wetlands in a most appealing and most demanding way.

The opener is a gentle handshake, but it ends there. Two of the first four holes are fine one-shotters. Number 2 is a medium-long par three. The shot must carry an expanse of marsh to an elevated green with perilously little bail-out room. For women, it's a short hole—only 93 yards—but nonetheless demanding. The par-three 4th extends more than 200 yards from the back markers and just shy of 110 from the forward tees. The hole is superbly well bunkered and presents a visually intimidating challenge from the three back sets of tees. You are required to play through a chute of palms and scrub oaks. The further back your markers are, the narrower the hole appears. Everybody hits across an expanse of marsh grass and palmettos.

The par-five 5th is a solid three-shot hole for all but those who hit the ball like Tiger Woods, with water along most of the left side of the hole just waiting to snag a shot that drifts too far that way. The long, thin green—typically well bunkered—is button-hooked behind a little stretch of the lake.

Numbers 6 and 7 are very solid, tight par fours. The 7th, with its contoured well- protected green, is rated the toughest hole on the course for men. The par-five 8th is a pretty golf hole, bordered by pines and palms with water on the right as you tee off. The landing area is generous, but the lake narrows and angles across the fairway near the green. That water does not come into play from the tee, but presents a dilemma on your second shot—to play up to it or try to clear it.

The long par-four 9th is the toughest hole on the course for women. The biggest problem is an expanse of wetland in front of the green. Many women, and some men, must consider whether to hit a second shot lay-up or try to clear the marsh.

The back side opens with a pair of par fours. Number 10 is a difficult, medium length dogleg right. Your tee shot must stay to the left side of the fairway or the palms and scrub oaks that define the dogleg will block your approach to the green. The left side of the green is protected by a large, menacing waste-bunker, with smaller sand bunkers on the right. The eleventh hole is a short par four with all the trouble near the green, which is fronted by water and a series of sand traps.

The par-five 13th is fairly straight, though the shot to the green can be tricky. A grassy basin sits in front of the green, preventing most run-up shots from reaching the putting surface. A horseshoe arc of bunkers surrounds the putting surface with the exception of a small opening in front. The best approach to this green is high, with a soft landing.

Number 14 is a tough dogleg left par four. It's a risk-reward hole with the option of playing to the fairway to the right, or biting off an expanse of marsh on the left and getting closer to the green. The one-shot 17th is a cute hole with water off the tee and an enormous bunker arching around the front, right, and back of the green. Some women may find it a bit easy from the red markers at only 78 yards.

Number 18 is rated the second toughest hole on the course for both men and women. It is a Gary Player signature hole, requiring precision both from the tees and on the approach to the green. Typical of Gary Player, the only truly safe approach is straight at the green. There's water left and back, and sand left back and right of the putting surface. Your tee shot can cut across the marsh to the left and leave only a short iron to the pin, or you can play more safely to the right and leave a longer approach. Be aware, however that a shot that's too long can go through the fairway and into the marshy hazard and a shot that drifts left-to-right can easily find the lake.

Baytree National Golf Links is a superior test of the game. The greens are fast and true. The course is well maintained and uniformly in excellent condition. It is a wonderful example of Gary Players' architectural prowess, and a worthwhile stop if you find yourself anywhere near Melbourne.

Baytree National Golf Links

HOLE	Ra	Sl	1	2	3	4	5	6	7	8	9	OUT	10	11	12	13	14	15	16	17	18	IN	TOT
BLACK	74.0	135	421	194	367	203	555	364	406	545	411	3466	389	372	193	543	416	447	554	209	454	3577	7043
GOLD	71.6	129	394	164	348	190	534	354	389	499	381	3253	372	352	173	521	367	414	543	193	369	3304	6557
BLUE	69.7	123	357	132	317	178	499	327	370	480	359	3019	358	326	153	511	334	375	490	162	353	3062	6081
WHITE	66.5(m)/71.5(w)	114(m)/128(w)	319	117	257	122	464	285	349	466	345	2724	293	283	131	428	309	343	435	129	328	2679	5403
MEN'S HCP		3	17	15	7	9	11	1	13	5			4	14	18	8	12	6	10	16	2		
PAR			4	3	4	3	5	4	4	5	4	36	4	4	3	5	4	4	5	3	4	36	72
RED	68.4	121	286	93	227	107	403	247	312	425	295	2395	257	261	119	413	286	297	408	78	289	2408	4803
WOMEN'S HCP	13	17	11	15	5	7	9	3	1			14	16	12	4	8	6	10	18	2			

The long, tight 6th hole is the first of a quartet of par fours that wrap up the front nine at Black Bear Golf Club.

BLACK BEAR GOLF CLUB

24505 Calusa Blvd., Eustis, Florida (East of Eustis take 44A to Lake Norris Rd., turn north less than a mile to the clubhouse sign.)
Phone: (352) 357-4732 or (800) 4-BEAR-18

Architect: P. B. Dye   Year opened: 1995

Course rating/Slope rating for men:
Bear Paw—74.7/134   Gold—73.8/133
Black—71.8/127   White—69.5/124

Course rating/Slope rating for women:
Brown—72.4/126   Green—70.5/121

The winding road up to the clubhouse at Black Bear reveals a golf course that has the hilly, mounded, relatively treeless look of a classic Scottish or Irish links. Your eye beholds a wee bit of England's Royal St. Georges, Scotland's Royal Dornoch, and Ireland's Waterville. Of course, your eye has been deceived. There is no linksland as traditionally defined in central Florida. (Links are coastal golf courses built on hard, sandy, non-agricultural land that buffers habitable and arable soil from the sea.) Nonetheless, at Black Bear the firm, hard-packed soil on which the course is built, soil that is given to tight lies and plenty of roll, has a surprisingly authentic feel to it, especially if the weather has been fairly dry.

Black Bear is a solid, straight-forward test. What you see is pretty much what the course has to offer. It features abundant hills, mounds, and grass bunkers with the result that a flat stance is the exception, especially if you stray from the fairway. As you might expect from architect P. B. Dye, sand is plentiful. On the other hand, water is largely absent, save for the finishing hole where a small lake borders the right side of the fairway up to the front of the green. There is a pond at the back and side of #10 green and to the side of the tees on #11, but save for an extremely errant shot the hazard should be no factor at all.

The greens range from big to gigantic and from merely difficult to breathtakingly tough. They are kept fast, putt true, and feature both extreme contours and artistic subtleties, although unlike classic links greens—which are often impossible to hold—these hold well and will reward accurate shots.

Black Bear is among the most woman-friendly of the courses owned by the Legends Group of Myrtle Beach, South Carolina—long but fair from either of the two forward sets of tees. Women whose handicaps are in the low 20s or less should consider playing the Brown Tees. At 5,428 yards, it is a fine challenge. For men with handicaps in the low teens or single digits, consider playing the Gold Tees. It's 6,825 yards and a grand test. If you aren't up for that kind of work-out, the Black Tees will provide a splendid day of golf at just under 6,400 yards.

The course opens spiritedly and never eases up. Number 1 plays from an elevated set of tees down a trough-like fairway between hills and bunkers. The huge, multi-level green is tucked behind a pair of hills that constrict the entrance to the putting surface. The 2nd is a long par five with a portion of the fairway split by a patch of heavy rough that separates the upper portion of the short grass from a lower level. Number 3 is a downhill par-three to a long, saddle-shaped green that's sloped away from you. The green is nearly 45 yards from back to front, so club selection is critical depending on pin placement.

For women, the long par-five 4th plays more like a par six. From either set of forward markers it stretches more than 450 yards and requires three big shots to find the green in regulation. The par-three 5th is just the opposite—a relatively short, easy hole for women and a long, difficult test of skill and accuracy from any of the men's markers.

Three lovely, challenging par fours follow. The outgoing side finishes with a long uphill par four that is rated the most difficult hole on the course. Big old oak trees stand menacingly on either side of the tees and one big tree looms directly in front of you as you look up the fairway. The only options are to thread the needle between the trees or hit a high shot over the leafy impediment. The well-bunkered green is big, hilly, and canted severely from back to front.

The par-four 10th features a blind tee shot down a trough with steep mounds and berms along both sides. In front of the huge, multi-tiered green is a grassy catch basin that's invisible on your approach, but which prevents run-up shots from reaching their target.

Number 13 is a long, par-four featuring a pair of huge waste-bunkers along most of the left length of the hole. The best place to aim your tee shot is at the 150-yard pole in the middle of the fairway. From there you can reasonably approach the extremely long (about 45 yards from back to front) thin green. Most of the perils of this green are invisible from the fairway because of a steep hill and bunker in front. There are sharp inclines along the right-front and left-rear that will channel stray shots into the enormous sand trap that bounds the back left quadrant or into a steep faced grass bunker on the right-front. It is one of the toughest greens on the golf course to approach, and it is extremely easy to hit right through the green.

The long, tight par-five 14th features a blind tee shot and a blind second (for all but the longest of ball strikers) to a thin, little elevated green that's *J*'ed to the left, up a steep incline, tucked behind hills and bunkers. To open the approach to the green, keep your second shot to the right side of the fairway; anything left of center will render your approach blind as well.

Club selection is paramount on the short par-three 15th hole. The long, slender green measures just under 50 yards from front to back. It sits amid a field of bunkers that look extremely intimidating from the tees. Club selection can vary tremendously depending on pin placement and wind; what might be a pitching wedge or sand wedge on a day when the pin is up and the wind is helping can be a 6- or 7-iron or more if the pin is back and the wind is in your face.

A long par five followed by a long par four will demand all of your shot-making skill. The par-four 17th is rated the second toughest hole on the course. The operative word is long. I played it one day when the wind was directly in my face and was humbled by it. "Driver, driver, 8-iron on a day like this," grinned the young assistant pro, Chris Libby, when I lamented my triple-bogey. "Maybe even driver, driver, 5-iron."

The par-four finisher offers a good scoring opportunity to wrap up your round. The only potential difficulties are the lake that caresses the front-right portion of the green and a nasty little sand trap that sits directly in front of the putting surface. The green is another one of architect P. B. Dye's exercises in extremes. It stretches more than 55 yards from front to back and, while it is thin as my belt, it features four separate levels.

If your match is tied, or you can't quite get enough of the place, there's a cute little par-three 19th hole (aside from the clubhouse bar) on which any final disputes can be decided. It plays across the lake that borders the 18th from a hillside tee to a hillside green.

Black Bear Golf Club

HOLE NUMBER	Ra	Sl	1	2	3	4	5	6	7	8	9	OUT	10	11	12	13	14	15	16	17	18	IN	TOT
BEAR PAW	74.7	134	401	537	186	543	197	390	386	394	429	3463	425	213	395	405	579	138	524	462	398	3539	7002
GOLD	73.8	133	388	529	180	541	190	383	386	369	420	3386	423	207	391	372	577	131	513	439	386	3439	6825
BLACK	71.8	127	342	489	156	520	177	358	361	369	385	3157	396	187	365	364	549	107	470	413	386	3237	6394
WHITE	69.5	124	342	453	156	498	147	331	330	323	385	2965	364	168	360	331	469	107	457	413	341	3010	5975
HCP			15	7	11	13	3	5	9	17	1		12	4	14	8	10	18	16	2	6		
PAR			4	5	3	5	3	4	4	4	4	36	4	3	4	4	5	3	5	4	4	36	72
BROWN	72.4	126	324	413	150	464	115	315	307	278	362	2728	312	164	323	312	451	95	390	323	330	2700	5428
GREEN	70.5	121	302	403	136	451	92	278	288	270	341	2561	310	148	315	294	382	79	380	308	267	2483	504428

A beach-like bunker extends some 365 yards around a lake on Diamondback Golf Club. The 18th green sits above the rocky embankment in the distance.

DIAMONDBACK GOLF CLUB

6501 S.R. 544E, Haines City, Florida (From I-4 take exit 23 and go south on U.S. Highway 27 for about 10 miles; turn left onto State Route 544E and go east for about 6 miles; the entrance is on the left.)
Phone: (863) 421-0437 or (800) 222-5629

Architect: Joe Lee   Year opened: 1995

Course rating/Slope rating:

Gold—73.3/138   Blue—71.3/132
White—69.3/126   Red—70.3/122

The first thing you see when you walk into the pro shop at Diamondback is a diamondback. There's a Plexiglas case with an imposing, if mercifully very dead, rattlesnake in it. The skilled taxidermist displays the coiled serpent as menacing, glowering, and fierce, a reminder of the wildlife that still inhabits the forests and marshes of central Florida. It's a heart-stopping sight, a five foot reptile with the girth of a strong man's arm, the tell-tale pattern in brilliantly articulated camouflage colors down its back, the distinctive rattle at the tail, and a huge triangular head poised to strike. "They found him when they were clearing the land for the course," said head pro Sean Camacho. They found a number of others too, but none as big as this guy.

Standing on the first tee reveals the dense vegetation that once covered the whole area—towering pines, scrub oaks, wax myrtles, palmettos, and wild grasses. Enough of the plant life remains that if your shot strays too far from the fairway you might as well reload and fire again, because a ball in the woods is probably lost.

Diamondback is a tight, demanding par 72. Architect Joe Lee used what nature put there—rolling hills, pine forests, and natural swamps—to create the basic fabric of the course. He added sand and a couple of man-made lakes to create further texture. The result is a stimulating and enjoyable golf course. A measure of Lee's success is the fact that the course looks and feels very mature, as if it had been there since long before 1995.

The 1st hole gets you right into the feel of the golf course. It's is a long par five dogleg left. Big hitters need to use caution from the elevated tees so as not to hit through the fairway at the bend of the dogleg. Around the corner, which is guarded by a big bunker on the left, a wedge of marsh intersects the fairway. Your lay-up is downhill. The green is well bunkered. That's followed by a solid pair of par fours with fairways tightened and intensified by forest, wetland, and strategically placed bunkers.

Number 2 is a medium-length dogleg left par four that's very tight off the tee with woods defining the bend in the dogleg to the left and a big bunker right. It's uphill to the green from the landing area. On the short par-three4th, a long, thin sand trap is in play most of the length of the hole.

The toughest hole on the course for men and women is the long, tough par-five 5th that requires three shots from almost all players. It's a *J*-shaped hole—straight most of its length until you approach the green. The hole bends to the right where you see a small pond. Your lay-up second must stay well to the left of the lake to set up a makable short-iron to the flag. The well-bunkered green is uphill, above the lake and demands a high, soft approach.

A trio of par fours takes you to the turn. Number 7 is a short, demanding dogleg right. Your tee shot must avoid the trees that line narrow lane to the landing area, but you must avoid hitting so far that you find the big bunker visible beyond the trees. This is a wonderful scoring hole for women. At only 204 yards from the forward markers, your tee shot can be placed directly in front of the bunker that sits in front of the slightly elevated green. Number 8 features a lobe of marsh intruding into the fairway in front of the tees. A lake is in play down the left side from about 180 yards out, and the green is offset and angled behind the lake whose stony bank forms a bulkhead in front of the green. The 9th is an uphill dogleg right, playing to a plateaued green.

After a stop for an iced drink, it's back into the forest with a pair of downhill holes. The inward side is the hillier of the two. Like the front, the back nine opens with a par five playing from elevated tees. The 11th hole tees off downhill, across a patch of marsh. Trees on the right and a bunker on the left about driving distance define the point where the hole turns gently to the right and starts uphill to the green.

On #12, men tee off across a marsh; women do not. There's a drop-off along the right side of the fairway that feeds into deep rough and a waste area. The hole bends to the right and plays up to a hilltop green that's framed by trees and bunkers.

A solid downhill par three is followed by a pair of hilly par fours. Number 14 is short and plays uphill all the way. Number 15 is a difficult, long dogleg right. Your uphill tee shot must land between the big bunker on the left and the Spanish moss-draped oaks on the right. The hole then plays downhill to a turtleback green that sits behind a marshy area and is sandwiched between a pair of bunkers.

The lovely 16th is one of Diamondback's signature holes. A waterfall is visible from the tees at the end of the lake on the left side. Architect Lee has created one of the biggest beach-like bunkers in Florida. It forms a golden strand around a lake that's in play on both #16 and #18. The beach bunker itself is some 365 yards long (no kidding, this is not a typographical error). The par-five 16th plays to the crest of a hill, then downhill and around the bend to the elevated, two-tiered green, which is angled behind another gaping bunker.

Number 17 is an attractive and good-sized par three—from hillside tees to a hilltop green—that will let you catch your breath before you tackle the splendid finisher.

The 18th is a demanding way to head to the clubhouse. It's a par four dogleg right that plays over a hill. Your approach shot must avoid the lake, with architect Joe Lee's beach bunker shimmering like a scene from *Key Largo* along the left, and be long enough to reach up to the hillside green. Simply getting aboard the huge putting surface does not ensure an easy two-putt.

What a pleasure! The greens are receptive and true. The topography demands shot-making accuracy and presents a feast for the eye. There's a great deal of sand and water to contend with. And there are enough trees to keep Paul Bunyan busy. From the opening hole to the last putt, Diamondback is first rate. It is both aesthetically pleasing and a superb challenge for players of all playing levels. It is an easier course for women than for men. If you're a low handicapper looking for a real test, buckle your seat-belt and play it from the tips.

Diamondback Golf Club

HOLE	Ra	Sl	1	2	3	4	5	6	7	8	9	OUT	10	11	12	13	14	15	16	17	18	IN	TOT
GOLD	73.3	138	540	388	395	142	553	180	365	354	420	3337	541	378	413	192	358	414	524	207	441	3468	6805
BLUE	71.3	132	520	372	349	133	522	147	343	342	399	3127	507	358	385	171	336	398	496	177	404	3232	6359
WHITE	69.3	126	495	328	323	124	502	125	317	325	378	2917	473	338	357	138	325	368	468	154	386	3007	5924
MEN'S HCP		3	11	5	17	1	15	13	9	7			6	12	4	18	14	2	10	16	8		
PAR			5	4	4	3	5	3	4	4	4	36	5	4	4	3	4	4	5	3	4	36	72
RED	70.3	122	425	318	255	116	427	114	204	241	330	2430	427	304	260	100	314	330	440	124	332	2631	5061
WOMEN'S HCP	3	9	5	17	1	15	13	11	7				2	14	10	18	12	8	4	16	6		

There's a 90-foot drop from the back tees to the 2nd green (foreground) at Diamond Players Club Clermont. The long par-four 3rd (background) plays into a valley, then steeply uphill to the green.

DIAMOND PLAYERS CLUB CLERMONT

2601 Diamond Club Drive, Clermont, Florida (From Florida Turnpike take exit 272 and go west on state route 50 about a mile to the entrance on the right; from state route 27, go east about 3 miles on state route 50 to the entrance on the left.)
Phone: (352) 243-0411   E-mail: info@dpcgolf.com

Architect: Terry LaGree   Year opened: 1999

Course rating/Slope rating:
Black—73.7/138   Gold—71.5/126
Blue—69.4/123   White—67.0/115
Green—69.7/114

To baseball fans the world over, Todd Stottlemyre is known as a Major League pitcher, a superstar. But in Florida, his name comes up more and more frequently when the conversation turns to his other passion, golf. Stottlemyre and a group of investors—most that have baseball connections—are the nucleus of a golf corporation that owns the Diamond (that's baseball diamond) Players Clubs. They own three courses with more planned for the areas around Major League Cities. The flagship of the fleet is the Diamond Players Club Clermont.

The golf course is the first full eighteen hole layout by a young architect named Terry LaGree and it is an awesome opening salvo in what is destined to be a stellar design career. The club's own literature touts it as "Florida's mountain golf course," which is quite a feat in that there are no mountains in the state. Nonetheless, there is an area in central Florida north of Orlando that is anything but flat. And it is on a tract of that hilly terrain that the boys of summer commissioned Terry LaGree to perform his design artistry. What he did was nothing less than a grand slam homer.

The Diamond Players Club Clermont is one of the most unusual, fascinating, atypical golf courses in Florida. LaGree used the natural contours of the land to construct each hole. Some of those are extremely difficult—as mountain golf holes are wont to be—but good shots are rewarded. On the other hand, even slightly errant shots can suffer ignominious consequences that result from the pull of gravity and particularly inhospitable terrain.

Every hole makes some use of the elevation changes that define the topography, 190 feet of changes in elevation over all, including the par-three 2nd with a 90 foot drop from tee to green. Everywhere you turn the eye is met by the unusually hilly Florida landscape. The outgoing side is a par 35, featuring three par threes; the back nine has only one par three and one par five, playing to a par 36. Seven unique par fours make up the bulk of the inward side.

Architect LaGree wastes no time with handshake holes. In fact, the first four holes on this par 71 track are daunting. Standing on the elevated, terraced tees on #1 reveals a long par five with a blind tee shot. The huge green is on a hill with a forbidding bunker that sits like a crater to the front left of it.

Club selection is critical on the par-three 2nd with its 90 foot drop from the highest of the terraced hillside tees to the putting surface. The hill is so severe in places that only portions of the putting surface are visible. Club selection is tricky, in that you must consider the elevation change, the wind speed and direction, and the pin placement.

Number 3 requires a precise drive across a yawning maw of waste area into a little valley. The green is steeply uphill from the landing zone. It looks like a short par four on the scorecard, but it plays substantially longer, and the putting surface is not visible on most approach shots although you can see the flag stick.

The par-four 4th is a severe dogleg left with the fairway perched above a canyon that is loaded with all manner of trouble—sand, scrub brush, and water. It's a risk-reward hole, but trying to carry too much of the abyss will almost certainly result in a penalty stroke. The perils don't end with your drive. The approach to the green is extremely thin with a bunker up the hill to the right and ball-eating vegetation down the hill to the left. It is rated the toughest hole on the course for women.

Two local members with whom I played told me that some of the extremely long hitters try to drive the green on the short par-four 5th. Most regular players hit something other than a driver and try to put their tee shots just inside 100 yards from the green and try for an up-and-down birdie.

The next three holes, a par five sandwiched between a pair of par threes, will give you a bit of a breather before you head up the hill to the clubhouse. The par-four 9th is the toughest hole on the course for men. The key is to keep your tee shot far enough to the left that you have a straight uphill approach to the elevated green. There's nothing but trouble and woe to the right. Beware of the optical illusion created by architect LaGree. As you look up the hill on your approach your eye tells you that all you have to do is crest the hill and you'll be putting. In reality there's a good 20 yards between the crest of the hill and the putting surface.

Number 10 sets the stage for the back nine. It is a devilish short par four on which accuracy is everything. The tees are terraced from the top of a hill, playing onto a ledge between a long high ridge to the left and a drop-off to the right. The fairway ends at a grassy shelf about 50 yards in front of the green, which is in a basin well below fairway level.

You need driving precision on the demanding par-four 11th. It's a blind dogleg right, but just beyond the 150 yard marker, the fairway ends. If you happen to run off the edge of the fairway you'll face a severe downhill shot that can verge on the unplayable. The green is some 70 feet below the level of the fairway. An enormous long scalloped bunker guards the right front of the green.

The elevated tees on the par three 14th look through a *V*-shaped notch created by dunes to the right and left. It's a semi-blind tee shot; only a portion of the putting surface is visible.

Number 15 is a *J*-shaped dogleg left. You drive from a terraced series of hillside tees down into a valley with an uncharacteristically small landing area. The key is to avoid the enormous waste area along the left side of the hole. A handful of sand traps in various sizes and depths guard the approach to the hillside green.

Number 18 is one last hill to climb to conclude your round. A long drive is needed, but to have a decent scoring opportunity you must avoid the deep bunkers that litter the right and left sides of the fairway. It's a tough, uphill hole for women, who face 330 yards from the forward markers to the green. The elevated, undulating green is guarded on the left by a gaping bunker.

When you finish and you survey the course from the hilltop clubhouse you know you've played one of the most unique golf courses in the state. There's little wonder why it was nominated as one of the country's best new public golf courses in 2000.

Diamond Players Club Clermont

HOLE	Ra	Sl	1	2	3	4	5	6	7	8	9	OUT	10	11	12	13	14	15	16	17	18	IN	TOT
BLACK	73.7	138	555	250	398	445	385	190	556	230	425	3434	340	430	538	461	173	375	420	305	435	3477	6911
GOLD	71.5	126	535	205	370	420	360	175	525	181	395	3166	330	410	510	435	160	365	405	300	415	3330	6496
BLUE	69.4	123	525	185	355	400	340	155	495	165	353	2973	315	385	490	405	135	345	385	285	390	3135	6108
WHITE	67.0	115	485	155	325	375	310	135	465	145	310	2705	300	365	470	390	125	325	370	255	360	2960	5665
MEN'S HCP		7	13	9	3	11	17	5	15	1			10	8	16	2	18	14	4	12	6		
PAR			5	3	4	4	4	3	5	3	4	35	4	4	5	4	3	4	4	4	4	36	71
GREEN	69.7	114	440	110	295	315	280	105	435	115	255	2350	245	345	420	360	110	300	310	235	330	2655	5005
WOMEN'S HCP	5	13	11	1	9	17	7	15	3				14	4	12	2	18	10	8	16	6		

The par-four finishing hole on Doral's Blue Monster ranks among the most famous golf holes in the country.

DORAL GOLF RESORT AND SPA

4400 NW 87th Avenue, Miami, Florida (From I-95 take highway 826 west for about 14 miles; exit onto NW 36th Street for about 1 mile; turn right onto NW 87th Avenue and the main entrance is on your left.)
Phone: (305) 592-2000 x2105 or (800) 713-6725

Blue Course Architect: Dick Wilson Year opened: 1961
Red Course Architect: Robert Von Hagge Year opened: 1962
Gold Course Architect: Robert Von Hagge/Bruce Devlin Year opened 1968
Silver Course Architect: Robert Von Hagge/Bruce Devlin Year opened: 1984
Great White Course Architect: Greg Norman Year opened: 2000

Blue Course rating/Slope rating:
Gold—74.5/130 Blue—72.2/125
White—69.7/118 Red—73.0/124

Red Course rating/Slope rating:
Gold—70.2/121 Blue—69.9/118
White—67.6/114 Red—70.6/118

Gold Course rating/Slope rating:
Gold—73.3/129 Blue—70.7/124
White—68.7/120 Red—71.4/123

Silver Course rating/Slope rating:
Gold—72.5/131 Blue—70.9/128
White—68.7/123 Red—67.1/117

Great White Course rating/Slope rating:
Gold—75.1/133 Blue—72.5/128
White—69.4/116 Red—70.7/130

Doral Golf Resort and Spa—just Doral, to almost everybody in Florida and most of the rest of the golfing world—is golf Nirvana. For my money, Doral is certainly among the top handful of golf resorts in Florida, a state that is always well represented in every major golf publications' listing of such facilities. There are folks who don't agree. Some people are obviously using a different yardstick than mine. My top priority is the golf; not just the "big name" course or the signature course of the facility, but the whole package. Does the star course deserve its reputation? How are the secondary golf courses? How are the golf courses maintained, from greens to tees to sand to rough to ancillary plantings and shrubbery? How are the practice facilities? How are guests treated? How knowledgeable are the grounds crews? How's the pro shop staff? What's the attitude of the starters and rangers? Doral scores well in every category.

Doral is a full service resort mega-complex with golf at its very heart and soul. Start with five top-notch, beautifully maintained golf courses, two of which, the famous Blue Monster and Greg Norman's soon-to-be-famous Great White, are simply world class. Add the internationally acclaimed Jim McLean Golf School, acres of practice facilities, a superior pro shop, and an array of golf clothing stores. Then throw in well appointed rooms and suites, good restaurants, a sports bar, more exercise equipment than you'll find in Arnold Schwartzenegger's garage, a 35-acre spa, the Blue Lagoon water recreation park, the Arthur Ashe Tennis Center, and assorted other facilities.

The complex started simply in 1959, when Doris and Alfred Kaskel bought some twenty-four hundred acres of swamp in West Miami and envisioned putting a golf course and a hotel there. Their friends thought they were nuts and argued that the land was only fit for gators, 'skeeters, and snakes and hardly the place for a golf club and resort. The Kaskels persisted and the Doral Hotel and Country Club opened its doors in 1962 with not one, but a pair of eighteen hole golf courses. That same year the Kaskels invited some of the country's top pro golfers to play in what they called the Doral Open Invitational. The players liked it. The golf press liked it. The fans and spectators liked it. A tradition was born. And the Kaskels had trumped the skeptics.

In the early 1990s, the Kaskel Family sold their facility to KSL Recreation Corporation, which undertook a thirty million-dollar facelift on the old place and pointed it toward the new millennium. Among their early moves was to commission PGA champion Raymond Floyd to redesign the Gold Course and the Blue Monster. They hired PGA champion Jerry Pate to rework the Silver Course. And their long range plans included razing the old White Course and getting golf legend Greg Norman to design a new golf course, the like of which had never been seen before in south Florida.

BLUE COURSE

Doral's Blue Course is known around the world by the intimidating moniker the Blue Monster. Every golf fan from Miami to Moscow, Florida to Finland, has seen this golf course on television; they have witnessed it humble some of the greats of the game with unforgiving bunkers and relentless water; they have cheered as it has rewarded its winners with barrages of birdies and the trappings of being the best. It was home to the Doral-Rider Open from 1982 until 2000, the third oldest PGA Tour tournament, a rite of spring each March which drew huge television audiences especially up north where the chill of winter still lingered. Starting in 2001, the name changed to the Genuity-Doral Championship.

Dick Wilson, a golf course designer in the classical school of Dr. Alister MacKenzie, Harry Colt, and A. W. Tillinghast, was the original architect at the Blue Monster, starting work back in 1960. The game, like the mood of the nation, was different back then. Golf fanatic Dwight Eisenhower was still President. Golf was a game for rich, white folks. Golf course care meant little more than cutting the grass, pulling the weeds, and raking the sand traps. Air conditioning was just coming into general use. Alan Shepard hadn't even considered hitting a golf ball on the moon.

Number 5 on the Red Course at Doral is a risk-reward par five with a severe dogleg left around a lake and a well-protected green.

Tiger Woods wasn't born. Architect Wilson was well steeped in golf's traditions but was considered an innovator. One of his trademarks was huge bunkers with grassy islands in them.

Over the years, the Blue Monster was redesigned and modified, to mounting criticism from both visiting amateurs and touring pros. In 1996, PGA star and three-time Doral winner Raymond Floyd was brought in to restore the Blue Monster to its traditional stature, to make it what it once was. In 1999 Doral's highly regarded golf professor, Jim McLean, oversaw the retrofitting of the course's bunkers, a project designed to give the course the same 1960s feel it had under the aegis of Architect Dick Wilson.

Is there any wonder that passionate golfers feel a little tingle when they stand on the first tee, the tight par five opener with bunkers on the right and trees lining the fairway? I could almost hear the excitement of the gallery, the voice of the television commentators. I knew the pros would probably reach the slightly elevated green in two and I'd be lucky to find it in regulation. I knew that they'd split the middle with ease, while I prayed quietly—even though my only gallery was my wife and the starter—oh, God, don't let me slice it into the trees.

I'd obviously heard the TV pundits tell me what an easy scoring hole the short par-four 2nd is, but I somehow had difficulty believing it when I saw the fairway narrow to less than 25 yards between the bunkers. The right fairway bunker is one of those Dick Wilson-type hazards with a trio of grassy oases in the desert.

About the time I'd managed to calm my nerves on the two opening holes, the 3rd jolted me back to the reality, reminding me why the course is called the Blue Monster. Number 3 is a long par four, a risk-reward dogleg right around a lake. The big belting pros know that the further they hit it the wider the landing area becomes. I stood on the tee knowing that the harder I swung the greater the likelihood I'd find the water to the right or the deep rough or sand to the left. I knew that if I safely found the short grass I would then hit to a plateaued green with the water lapping at the front right and an especially severe drop-off to the left.

By this point, I was fully aware that the rough is kept longer than most resort golf courses. I could only imagine how it is for the tournament.

The par three 4th is the toughest of the one-shot holes for men, 236 yards from the gold tees over water to an elevated green guarded in back by a pair of sand traps. For the pros it's considered a pivotal hole, where a birdie can set the stage for things to come. For me, the immediate concern was keeping my golf ball dry. (For women it is long—149 yards from the red tees—but is rated the number 15 handicap hole and the placement of the Red Tees makes the pin fairly accessible. My wife, Barbara, who parred it with ease, said she didn't find it any big deal. I quietly wrote down my bogey and moved on.)

I thought I could catch my breath on the short dogleg left par four 5th, but then I got a look at the green, surrounded by five snarling, hungry greenside bunkers. "They're thinking birdie here," say the TV guys during the tournament. My only thought as I played my second shot was don't put it in the sand! For most women it plays like a par five, requiring a lay-up in order to hit a high, soft shot over the sand to the green.

I was delighted to find a pair of manageable par fours next, leading to the long, tough par-five 8th. The hole is a gentle dogleg left, with the green hooked back to the right, behind a corner of lake. While the pros contemplate going for it in two, I stood there looking at the twin water hazards—the lake that juts into the fairway on the left and the second lake on the right—and hoped for a dry landing somewhere in between. The lay-up area looked about as big as a bridge table.

The outgoing side at the Blue Monster finishes with a delightful par three, the shortest one-shot hole on the course. It's a forced carry over water to a green that's pitched fairly severely back to front. Even though the hillsides were devoid of spectators, the leader board posted no name but last year's winner, and the TV cameras were nowhere to be seen, I couldn't help but feel a little of the electricity of what has gone before on that spot.

The exhilarating back nine opens with a brutally long crescent-shaped par five that arcs to the left around a lake. The 10th green is sandwiched between sand on the right and the water on the left with only the tiniest of openings in front.

Number 11 is a short, treacherous par four with a bunker splitting the center of the fairway that gives players three options for getting to the green: lay it up short of the sand, hit it long and to the right (there's all of 21 yards of fairway over there), or play it to the left of the fairway sand trap.

I could hardly imagine players like Tiger Woods playing the 12th as a two-shot hole. It looked like it went on forever when I peeked at it from the back tees. It is one of the longest par-fives on the PGA Tour, a massive 603 yards from the tips down to a merely brutal 492 yards for women playing the Red Tees. It's fairly straight until you get down near the green where the hole bends slightly to the right. For pros and amateurs alike, there is only one place to be if you expect to score on this monster hole, and that's in the short grass.

That's followed by the longest par-three at Doral. From the championship Gold Tees #13 requires a 245 yard shot to reach the plateaued green. At 173 yards from the Red Tees, is a demanding hole for women. "What are you hitting?" I asked my wife. "Driver," she said. "It's the only thing that will get me there."

If the course hadn't quickened my heart rate to this point, the last four holes certainly got my adrenaline pumping. I looked at the par-three 15th green with the permanent camera platform towering behind the putting surface and the echoes of yesterday's cheers still somehow lingering. I hoped for a par or birdie to set up the famed trio of par fours to come.

Number 16 is steeped in PGA Tour history. On March 16, 1980, it was the second hole of a sudden death playoff in what was then the Doral Eastern Open. Raymond Floyd chipped in for a birdie to beat Jack Nicklaus. Then six years later Andy Bean defeated Hubert Green after a four-hole playoff that started on #16 and ended on the same hole. I could feel the history, but certainly not the pressure of a PGA Tour playoff as I looked down the sand-lined fairway. The bunker to the left is another of the Dick Wilson-style sand traps with islands of grass in it. The key for the amateur is to avoid the trouble and leave a clear shot at the well-protected, elevated green. The bunkers around the green have also been restored to the unique configuration favored by Architect Wilson.

The 17th is a demanding, long hole that plays to an extremely long thin mesa of green, just short of sixty yards from back to front and only about fifteen yards wide at its narrowest point. The camera tower behind the green looked down in silence as I plunked my second shot into the sand. I could hardly contemplate how humiliating and humbling it must be to do something like that on national television.

Standing on the tee at #18 on the Blue Monster is a unique experience. My wife likened it to worshiping at one of the shrines of the game. "This is a dream game of golf," she said with more than a touch of reverence. "It's what you've seen on television year after year. If you never get another opportunity you can always say 'I've been there.'" It ranks among the most famous golf holes in the world. It's right up there with the rocky, coastal 18th at Pebble Beach, the Road Hole, #17, at St. Andrews Old Course, and the island green at the 17th hole at TPC at Sawgrass. On the left there's the lake with the signature Doral fountain shooting jets of water into the air, the palm studded lakeside bunker that looks like a small strip of beach in front of the green, and the green itself perched at the water's edge with gaping bunkers to the right and rear.

Such PGA stars as Jack Nicklaus, Lee Trevino, Nick Faldo, Tom Kite, Ben Crenshaw, Raymond Floyd, Jim Furyk, and Greg Norman have all walked up the 18th fairway on a March Sunday to claim the trophy and the check at this classic golf course. Jim Furyk's finishing round of 65 in 2000 was electrifying. Three-time winner Greg Norman holds the 18-hole tournament record—62 in 1990 and 1993—and in '93, Norman also carded the 72-hole record 265. We've all seen the crowds surrounding the famous 18th green, breathlessly awaiting the final putt. Once having played it, the average amateur can but envy the skill of those masters of the game who have tamed the Blue Monster.

Blue Course

HOLE	Ra	Sl	1	2	3	4	5	6	7	8	9	OUT	10	11	12	13	14	15	16	17	18	IN	TOT
GOLD	74.5	130	529	376	409	236	394	442	428	528	169	3511	551	363	603	245	443	175	372	419	443	3614	7125
BLUE	72.2	125	504	346	382	215	367	415	407	502	158	3296	528	336	583	229	416	156	346	397	414	3405	6701
WHITE	69.7	118	481	321	357	184	342	390	387	475	144	3081	507	312	563	212	388	140	322	369	387	3200	6281
MEN'S HCP		11	17	1	3	13	5	9	7	15			10	18	8	2	6	16	14	12	4		
PAR			5	4	4	3	4	4	4	5	3	36	5	4	5	3	4	3	4	4	4	36	72
RED	73.0	124	390	272	305	149	288	348	345	422	117	2636	455	283	492	173	316	110	277	311	339	2756	5392
WOMEN'S HCP	9	17	5	15	13	1	3	7	11				4	18	10	2	8	14	16	12	6		

RED COURSE

The original Red Course was designed by Robert Von Hagge to be the companion to the Blue Course in the early days of the Doral Hotel. It is shorter than the championship track and plays to a par 70. The layout features 4 par fives, 6 par threes, and 8 par fours. My wife noted that the par threes require as much or more from women than even the Blue Monster, with three of them playing in excess of 150 yards, which is extremely demanding from the forward markers.

Doral's Red Course is a mature, visually soothing course. Yet at the same time it is a golfing challenge that requires shotmaking and course management. There's water in play on thirteen holes, an abundance of stately trees, and strategically placed sand. If the Red Course were anywhere other than in the shadow of the towering peaks that are the Blue Monster and the Great White Course, it would be well worth a special detour. As it is, it is often treated as a poor relative in books and articles. Such denigration is unfair, because it's a wonderful golf course.

As with all the Doral courses, it is immaculately maintained. The greens are a little slower than the Blue Monster, but they are receptive and true. The rough is not cut quite as high as the Blue Monster, but it was never intended to be as tough a course. The sand is superbly tended. The tees and fairways are kept in lovely condition, exactly as you would expect from a first rate operation.

I love the opening hole on the Red Course. It looks benign enough from the tees but reveals itself the further you play. It's a long par five, dogleg right. The landing area is generous, but then the hole narrows and ultimately funnels uphill to a long, elevated, multi-tiered green that looks like a grassy lane between yawning bunkers on both sides. From the fairway, a false front—the level below the putting surface—makes the green appear even longer and more alpine than it is. Your tee shot is blind. Your second must avoid a lake along the right around which the dogleg bends.

The next two holes let you catch your breath in preparation for the tight par-four 4th. Sand traps line both sides of the fairway and your tee shot must stay left of center to avoid being blocked out by the gnarled old trees that guard the right edge of the hole. The further you hit it, the smaller the landing area.

Number 5 is the toughest hole on the Red Course. It's a par five with a severe dogleg left around a lake. It's almost a horseshoe around the water. It's a risk-reward hole that requires every player to consider how much, if any, of the lake to try to carry. The approach to the green, and the green itself, is protected by a series of bunkers along the left side, including one enormous sand trap with grass islands and palm trees studding it.

The par-three 6th is a spectacular one-shot hole that has water on three sides. It demands a forced carry to a tri-level, highly contoured green, with precious little bail-out room anywhere. The green is big enough that it's fairly easy to hit, but unless you get close to the flag, it can send you away with three or more putts very easily.

The outgoing side closes with a short, straight, very tight par four. Most of the trouble is up near the green. The putting surface is cupped by a *Y* shaped sand trap with its tail extending down the left side of the fairway.

The back side on the Red Course opens

with a pair of par fives sandwiching a par three. Number 10 is long with water guarding the green. At 462 yards from the red markers, for most women it requires three wood shots to get on in regulation.

Number 13 is a narrow par four, compressed between a pair of lakes that parallel the fairway right and left. The par three 14th is a visually stimulating hole with water left, right and rear and a menacing sand trap guarding the front of the green. Number 15 is a risk-reward par four dogleg left around a lake with the fairway choked by sand right and water left at driving distance for most players. The well-protected green—with sand and water left and a quartet of small bunkers right and rear—demands a precise shot to avoid the trouble.

Two fine par fours take you back home. Number 17 is a short dogleg right playing to a small, elevated, well-protected green. And the finishing hole is long, with a green that's all but surrounded by bunkers. There's a narrow little neck of grass in front if you want to try a run-up shot, but it's only about as wide as a bowling lane.

I find Doral's Red Course both charming and immensely satisfying. It is a tougher, more demanding track for women than for men, mostly because of the length. At a par 70, the Red Course is 5,096 yards from the women's tees. Consider that the Blue Monster, which is a par 72, is less than 300 yards longer from the red markers. For men, the difference the Red and the Blue courses is nearly 1,000 yards from the gold markers.

Of the par threes, my wife, Barbara, said, "You stand on the tee and can see the trouble in front, and there always seems to be trouble in front. But you get the feeling that if you hit the shot crisp you should be able to convert it into a par or birdie."

Of the par fours she noted, "There's a lot of trouble at the outer limits of your reliable clubs. So you end up hitting a lot of lay-up shots to avoid the trouble, which leaves you struggling to save par or settling for bogey. It's almost impossible to get on in regulation because of the amount of trouble around almost every green."

For men and women alike, if you're visiting Doral and you've played the Blue Monster and the Great White, make the wonderful Red Course your next choice.

Red Course

HOLE	Ra	Sl	1	2	3	4	5	6	7	8	9	OUT	10	11	12	13	14	15	16	17	18	IN	TOT
GOLD	70.2	121	561	191	370	381	497	146	397	190	345	3078	515	189	501	354	175	388	196	347	403	3068	6146
BLUE	69.9	118	556	188	365	376	492	141	392	185	340	3035	510	184	496	349	170	383	191	342	398	3023	6058
WHITE	67.6	114	510	175	344	322	453	123	358	168	320	2773	486	170	473	322	150	368	168	318	368	2823	5596
MEN'S HCP		3	13	9	5	1	17	7	15	11			4	16	2	12	18	8	10	14	6		
PAR			5	3	4	4	5	3	4	3	4	35	5	3	5	4	3	4	3	4	4	35	70
RED	70.6	118	492	162	323	308	408	106	325	151	300	2575	462	156	432	296	129	337	120	301	288	2521	5096
WOMEN'S HCP	3	13	11	5	1	17	7	15	9				4	16	2	12	18	8	10	14	6		

Water is in play on all five of the par threes on Doral's Gold Course. There's little bail-out room here on #12.

GOLD COURSE

Doral's Gold Course was originally the design of Bruce Devlin and Robert Von Hagge. It was redesigned in 1995 by PGA Tour champion Raymond Floyd, three-time winner of the Doral-Ryder Open. The Gold Course is fairly typical of Florida golf courses and not dissimilar to Doral's Silver Course. It's relatively short, playing to a par 70, featuring three par fives and five par threes. Water and sand provide the bulk of the hazards. The big greens are well contoured. Despite being short, the Gold Course is no pushover. It was the site of the 1999 PGA Qualifying School and gave the wannabe touring pros all they could handle. It is not a tricky course; what you see is what you get. If you can put your shots in play, you can score.

The opening hole sets the stage. It's a par-four dogleg right. A tee shot that is too long can easily make its way through the fairway into the pond that defines the bend in the dogleg. The long green is guarded by a pair of bunkers—right and left front.

Number 2 is the only par five on the outward side, a short dogleg left around a lake. For men it's a risk-reward hole. For women, the lake is largely taken out of play and the dogleg is straightened by the placement of the Red Tees. The slightly elevated green is hard to approach because of three big bunkers.

The 4th is a long, watery, crescent-shaped dogleg left playing around a lake. This par four is the toughest hole on the Gold Course. The perfect tee shot splits the two fairway bunkers, leaving an approach to a green that is sandwiched between a bunker to the right and a lake to the left.

Two straight par fours and a par three lead to a fine pair of holes with which to conclude the front nine. Number 8 is a splendid golf hole. It's a par four dogleg right around a lake. A corner of the lake extends into the middle of the fairway in front of the green setting up a tricky approach. The 9th hole is a lovely par three that requires a forced carry over water. If you find the putting surface it's a good birdie hole. If you miss the green it can be an easy bogey or double.

Like traditional courses of the British Isles, the Gold Course does not return to the clubhouse. The front side plays out; the back plays in. The inward side starts with a tough par four that arcs to the left around a lake. Another lake to the right pinches the fairway directly in front of the contoured green.

Water is a key design element here. Number 12 is a lovely, watery par three It is followed by two par fours—one short, one moderately long, both with water in play down their left sides.

The Gold Course doesn't cut you much slack on the concluding holes. Number 17 is a fine par three that's long and tough. It's an especially long hole for women, playing 164 yards from the red markers. The green does provide room for a run-up shot. The signature hole on the Gold Course is the 18th. It's a medium-length par four that's lined with big old trees on both sides and features an island green.

As with the other Doral golf courses this one is well maintained and manicured. The greens are fast and contoured. The sand is tough. It is a fine example of traditional golf course design and it is a pleasure to play.

Gold Course

HOLE	Ra	Sl	1	2	3	4	5	6	7	8	9	OUT	10	11	12	13	14	15	16	17	18	IN	TOT
GOLD	73.3	129	406	517	415	440	433	414	199	417	196	3437	387	579	153	350	422	173	517	187	397	3165	6602
BLUE	70.7	124	373	482	387	420	413	393	168	394	176	3206	365	547	136	333	404	159	498	179	382	3003	6209
WHITE	68.7	120	347	467	369	388	364	343	146	374	150	2948	349	522	123	307	380	124	478	170	356	2809	5757
MEN'S HCP		11	7	9	1	3	13	15	5	17			10	2	18	12	4	16	6	14	8		
PAR			4	5	4	4	4	4	3	4	3	35	4	5	3	4	4	3	5	3	4	35	70
RED	71.4	123	327	422	333	338	331	328	123	328	122	2652	304	489	94	287	341	102	466	164	280	2527	5179
WOMEN'S HCP			7	17	9	1	5	11	13	3	15		4	6	16	18	10	8	14	12	2		

The signature hole on the Silver Course at Doral is the par-three 14th, with a small island green.

SILVER COURSE

The Silver Course was originally designed by Bruce Devlin and Robert Von Hagge in 1984 and given a face-lift by PGA Tour champion Jerry Pate in 1998. It is a fairly typical south Florida golf course in that the greens are highly contoured, there is abundant sand, and all but three holes have water in play. Most of the greens are to some degree elevated or plateaued. While it does not quite fall within the definition of a "target" golf course, it rewards accurate approach shots and punishes shots that stray. It is relatively short, playing to a par 71.

The opening hole presents a nice howdy-do to the Silver Course. It's a straight par four with water on the left and steep mounds on the right. You get down to serious business on #2, a short par five on which even medium hitting men will think about going for it in two. Women, on the other hand, face a solid three-shot hole that plays 420 yards from the forward markers. The key here is avoiding trouble off the tee—water to the left, a threatening out-of-bounds on the right, and strategically placed bunkers that compress the fairway as you near the elevated green.

The 3rd hole is rated the toughest on the card for both men and women. A par four, it's only a little shorter than the par five you just played. Your tee shot has to remain far enough left that your view of the big plateaued green isn't blocked out by palms.

Number 6 is a par three with a pond between the tees and the big elevated green. That leads to three short par fours that set up good scoring opportunities as you make the turn. Number 7 has water down the entire right length. In front of the green, the lake balloons into the fairway, providing a watery grave for any approach shot that comes up short. The 8th plays to a plateaued green with big sand traps on both sides. Number 9 is a pretty but tight and demanding hole. There's a big fairway bunker scooped out of a hillside about driving distance down the right. And while many players might opt for something other than a driver here, your tee shot must be hit far enough that you can play a soft shot to the elevated green that's perched behind a small pond.

Number 10 is the only par five on the back nine. It's long and straight. Keep it in the fairway. That's followed by a pair of par fours. Number 12 is tight, tight, tight with water to the right and out-of-bounds to the left. Strategically placed bunkers create a chute through which you approach the green. The straight 13th has water along the right length of the hole. The green is offset to the right with a tongue of the lake lapping into the fairway in front of the putting surface, and a gaping hillside bunker that guards the left. It's one of the toughest greens on the course to approach.

The par three 14th is the signature hole on the Silver Course. The green is an island with a single palm tree at the rear of it. Unlike other well-known island greens—such as the 18th at the neighboring Gold Course, the 17th at the TPC at Sawgrass, or #16 at the Golden Horseshoe's Gold Course in Williamsburg, all of which are substantial—this one is small and looks like about the size of my desk top from the tees. If you're not a little nervous standing on the tee you're a strong person. The reality is that almost as many tee shots find the water as find the putting surface. Bring your *A* game to this little gem.

The round finishes with a quartet of varied and interesting par fours. Number 15 is tight and demanding, with water down the right and the out-of-bounds line precariously close to the left edge of the fairway. The 16th also features water down the right with a wedge of the lake carved into the fairway in front of the green. Number 17 plays to a domed green with closely shaved slopes on all sides that will reject shots that fail to find the putting surface. And the 18th is a pretty finisher with the splendid clubhouse as a backdrop.

My wife, Barbara, said that at Doral in general and on the Silver Course in particular, she felt that the designers went "out of their way to make women feel welcome." And she added that nowhere did she have the impression that women were an afterthought in the architectural scheme.

The Silver Course is several blocks from the main Doral campus. The beautiful clubhouse is a welcome oasis while you wait for the shuttle to come and take you back to the resort.

Silver Course

HOLE	Ra	Sl	1	2	3	4	5	6	7	8	9	OUT	10	11	12	13	14	15	16	17	18	IN	TOT
GOLD	72.5	131	402	485	469	174	509	164	375	363	375	3316	523	200	360	437	155	372	378	413	403	3241	6557
BLUE	70.9	128	382	451	422	159	497	145	337	343	365	3101	512	180	350	395	139	357	368	400	395	3096	6197
WHITE	68.7	123	330	440	390	130	440	124	303	316	308	2781	484	161	326	364	95	333	335	353	357	2808	5589
MEN'S HCP		5	7	1	11	3	13	9	17	15			6	8	18	2	14	12	10	4	16		
PAR			4	5	4	3	5	3	4	4	4	36	5	3	4	4	3	4	4	4	4	35	71
RED	67.1	117	261	420	335	121	399	101	250	246	237	2370	413	145	278	314	85	271	265	296	301	2368	4738
WOMEN'S HCP			7	3	1	13	5	15	11	9	17		6	16	18	2	14	12	10	4	8		

The view from the 18th green on Greg Norman's Great White Course at Doral reveals oasis-like fairways playing between coquina waste areas studded with hundreds of palm trees.

GREAT WHITE COURSE

There are those unenlightened non-golfers who suggest that Florida needs another new golf course like Washington needs another lawyer or Nashville needs another guitar player. But in February, 2000, a new supernova was born in the galaxy of golf course superstars. Greg Norman—winner of more than 80 international titles, including two British open championships and a trio of Doral victories—was commissioned to create a new golf course on the patch of real estate where Doral's old White Course and executive length Green Course used to be.

What he did on that tract is nothing short of spectacular. He not only created a new course, but made a foray into an entirely new genre of golf course design. It's an amalgam of Norman's experience growing up in Australia, playing in Europe and Asia. His design draws on the modern techniques of such architects as Pete Dye, Tom Fazio, and Jack Nicklaus, and from the classical work of such design legends as Harry Colt, Sir Guy Campbell, Dr. Alister Mackenzie, and even "Old" Tom Morris. The result is a post-modern tapestry of unique textures, colors, and contours working in harmony to synthesize a rich and wonderful work of art.

Of course, they call it the Great White Course after Greg Norman's nickname—the Great White Shark—but it could just as well be called Doral's newest monster. It's a par 72, with three par threes and two par fives on the outgoing side, for a par 35. On the back nine, brace yourself! There are three par fives and two par threes, for a par 37.

At the heart of the design is the fact that there is very little traditional long grass rough surrounding the fairways and greens. Instead, Norman has bounded his fairways with water, marsh, and acres of coquina waste areas studded with hundreds upon hundreds of mature palms, oaks, and black olive trees. (Coquina is indigenous to Florida, a gravelly combination of pebbles, seashells, shell shards, and sand. In the waste areas you may ground your club and remove loose impediments, unlike traditional sand hazards.)

Norman has littered his creation more than 220 pot bunkers, which appear like little punctuation marks. Where there's no coquina there's water—some 20 acres of lakes. He used four different types of grass, Zoysia, Tidwarf Bermuda, Tifeagle, and GN-1—a Bermuda hybrid developed in Australia at Norman's own turf company.

The temperament of the course is unique as well. Norman is quoted as saying the dominant flavor is that of the Southwest. No doubt, there are elements of desert golf like you find in Arizona or southern California. But there are also touches of Scottish and Irish links. And there are places that are pure Florida with water, palms, marsh, and sand. Norman has varied the elevation and size of his greens from huge to tiny and from steep hilltop putting areas to flat, fairway-level greens without bunkers or hazards, reminiscent of early 20th century British parkland courses.

There are a lot of "new" golf courses that strive for uniqueness and instead manage only to be artificial, contrived, or punishing only for the sake of cruelty itself. This golf course is nothing short of a masterpiece—tough but fair, unusual but in keeping with the traditions of the game, stark but beautiful, absolutely original but without elements that are forced or ill-fitting.

Norman and his associates have also factored in the Florida weather. The other four Doral courses are relatively sheltered by mature trees. The open nature of the Great White Course means that the wind has little or nothing to stop it. As with the links of Scotland and Ireland, as with the barren deserts of the American southwest, the direction and velocity of the wind will have a profound impact on club selection and course management. This is not an accident.

The par five 1st hole launches you down a green fairway with coquina waste areas on both sides. The elevated green is guarded by an octet of pot bunkers, five on the left and three on the right at staggered intervals. The embankment around the long, thin, plateaued green is tightly mowed and designed to reject any shot that doesn't make it to the putting surface.

A long par four is then followed by a short par-four risk-reward dogleg left. Players must decide how much of the lake, with it's rocky bank, to cut across.

Number 4 is the first of Norman's four spectacular one-shot holes. Your tee shot is over water to a green that provides precious little bail-out room. A lake guards the front and left of the small, irregularly shaped green and an expanse of coquina guards the right. Norman has taken pains to give every player a similar look at the hole from each set of tees. The low-handicap men playing the back tees face a 195-yard carry; women playing the red tees have 63 yards. The bottom line for both is the same: don't miss the putting surface.

The 6th is the shortest of the par threes on the Great White Course, but the green is domed on top of a high hill. The grass on the banks that surround the putting surface are slick and tightly cut. The first time I played it, what I thought was a perfect tee shot landed by the flag in the center of the green, took one big hop and was rejected down the slope in the back into the waste area. The result was a profoundly difficult bogie.

Number 8 is a solid par three with the elevated, multi-tiered green sitting on an island, although there is ample room between the water and the putting surface. The big difficulty here is that if you miss the big green the odds are really good that you'll find one of the twenty-one pot bunkers that surround it.

The side finishes with a lovely but treacherous dogleg left par four. Water plashes along the entire left length of the hole. The long, thin green is protected on the right by a trio of deep pot bunkers. The boulders that define the banks of the lake also define the left side of the green.

On finishing the 9th my wife, Barbara raved about the design and the care Norman took with the placement of the women's tees. "It's tough," she said. "There's so much trouble right up to the greens that you really have to be on the money with every shot."

Norman uses his pot bunkers to create a unique texture around the greens. For example on the 10th hole—a medium length, straight par four—he has positioned a pair of pot bunkers at greenside to the right, one a few yards further away from the putting surface in the middle, and a trio of them at about a 45 degree angle to each other about 20 yards in front of the left side of the green. The vista from the fairway is enough to strike fear in your heart as you hit your approach.

Number 11 is another brilliant, beautiful, and demanding par three. Water and the rocky banks of the lake play from tee to green to the left and caress the left side of the green. Paying homage to such links-like designs as the Royal and Ancient Golf Club at St. Andrews, Norman has created an enormous green that is shared with the 13th and 17th holes.

On the long, tight par-five 12th, Norman has split the fairway in front of the green with a pair of pot bunkers—one about 150 yards from the green and the other about 100 yards out—creating a number of options for your approach.

Number 13 is narrow enough to test your nerves. There's water down the left side, coquina and palms down the right. The hole plays back to the huge shared green. Number 14 is huge. It's 602 yards from the championship gold tees and a massive 519 from the forward markers. "This plays like a par seven," said my wife peering down the double dogleg. Norman created the par-four 15th in the style of old-fashioned English parkland gold courses—no bunkers around the green, the small, oval putting surface at virtually the same level as the fairway.

That sets up a spectacular threesome of finishing holes. The 16th may be the best of Norman's artistry with one-shot holes, both challenging and fair to all players. It requires a forced carry over water to the putting surface. The dogleg left par-four 17th, features a collection of palms down the left side that will give you pause before you try to cut off much of the corner. At the same time the lake down the right will keep you mindful of not drifting too far in the other direction. A handful of pot bunkers waits to draw in your drive like a poker player trying to fill an inside straight. The green is again part of the shared complex that also completes holes #11 and #13.

If the 18th on Doral's Blue Monster holds sway as one of the most famous holes in golf, it's a good bet that it will soon share that mantle with #18 on the Great White Course. Greg Norman, the architect, has created a hole that's worthy of the best shot-making of Greg Norman, the PGA Tour champion. It's a short par five that will offer a multitude of options, provided you hit a long drive that stays in the fairway. Then you must decide whether to go for it in two shots and risk finding the trouble around the green—including water, coquina waste area, and a mine-field of pot bunkers—or do you hit a lay-up into the ribbon of fairway that is a grassy peninsula in the coquina.

I just love this golf course. I've been asked in numerous interviews about my favorite golf courses and I'm always hard pressed to name just one. There's the traditional majesty of Cherry Hills in Englewood, Colorado, or Winged Foot in New York's Westchester County. There's the Cascades, the mountain marvel at Virginia's Homestead in Hot Springs. There the magnificent links at Old Head and Lahinch in Ireland. But all of a sudden, as the new century of golf dawns, a new contender for *la crème de la crème* is born.

Great White Course

HOLE	Ra	Sl	1	2	3	4	5	6	7	8	9	OUT	10	11	12	13	14	15	16	17	18	IN	TOT
GOLD	75.1	133	513	455	360	195	572	168	474	177	434	3348	402	203	548	412	602	481	194	452	529	3823	7171
BLUE	72.5	128	493	422	350	179	525	149	435	161	416	3130	347	170	524	374	577	445	174	413	498	3549	6679
WHITE	69.4	116	458	392	320	142	487	125	399	132	404	2859	347	128	481	344	547	397	123	383	476	3226	6085
MEN'S HCP		7	9	5	11	1	15	13	17	3			18	12	10	16	4	14	8	2	6		
PAR			5	4	4	3	5	3	4	3	4	35	4	3	5	4	5	4	3	4	5	37	72
RED	70.7	130	366	334	259	63	445	75	314	84	349	2289	299	95	413	282	519	339	79	345	366	2737	5026
WOMEN'S HCP		5	9	7	13	3	17	11	15	1			12	18	8	14	2	10	16	4	6		

Putting out the signature par-four 5th at Eagle Harbor.

EAGLE HARBOR GOLF CLUB

2217 Eagle Harbor Pkwy, Orange Park, Florida (Take exit 3 south of Jacksonville from I-295 and go south on highway 17 for about 7 miles. Turn right into the development, go about a mile, and left into the clubhouse parking lot.)
Phone: (904) 269-9300

Architect: Clyde Johnson Year opened: 1993

Course rating/Slope rating for men:
Blue—73.3/138 White—71.5/131
Green—69.5/125

Course rating/Slope rating for women:
Green—71.8/124 Red—69.8/121

Eagle Harbor is tucked back in a pleasant residential community south of Jacksonville. It has the feel of a fine private country club. The pace is relaxed. The people who greet you, tend to your clubs, sign you in, and take your green fees treat you more like a member than a daily fee player. Head pro Marion Detlefsen sums it up succinctly: "More than anything, this is your friendly, neighborhood golf course. It's fair. Typical north Florida golf, with lots of water. And we try to keep it in pretty good shape."

Eagle Harbor's management succeeds on all fronts. It is a pretty golf course, carved through a pine forest with plenty of strategically placed bunkers. Water is evident or in play on fourteen holes. The greens vary in size and are well maintained and true, if not lightening fast. The fairways are narrow, but for the most part the rough is kept short enough that it renders only minimal punishment for shots that stray from the short grass.

Your introduction to the course is a pair of par fours. Number 1 is a slight dogleg left with a lake in play on the right near the green. The 2nd is short, inviting a fairway wood or long-iron off the tee. The large, well-contoured green is guarded by a big bunker to the left front.

Number 4 is the first of Eagle Harbor's one-shot holes and requires a forced carry across a waste bunker that extends from the front of the red markers to a few yards short of the putting surface.

The 5th is a demanding par four. It's long and tight, with a green that is surrounded by a horseshoe-shaped bunker and a lake. Neither really comes into play unless your approach is wildly long. However it makes for a pretty piece of real estate. For women, on the other hand, it plays only 303 yards from the forward markers and presents a good scoring opportunity.

Number 6 is a picturesque par three with a forced carry across a marsh that caresses the front edge of the green. This is an exceptional hole for women in that the red markers sit on a peninsula that juts out into the marsh.

The last three holes on the front are a challenging way to send you to the back nine. Three pars or better to close the outgoing side should please almost anybody. Number 7 is a long par five. Your lay-up second must be kept far enough left to take a stand of pines out of play and give you a good look at the flag. The green itself is hooked behind water, sculpted out of a hillside that rises to the right. The 8th features water down the right side from tee to green. "There's a lot of room to the left, but you see about every third golfer find that water," said a local member with whom I was playing one pleasant spring day. In fact, all four of the players in front of us found the lake to the right. Number 9 is a great golf hole and it is rated the toughest at Eagle Harbor. It's a long par four with a narrow strip of bunker surrounding the elevated putting surface. The bunker and the green are surrounded on three sides—front, right, and back—by a lake.

Men can take a breather on next two holes. For women, #11 is a 412 yard par-five monster that requires three solid shots to have any hope of a birdie putt. Number 13 is one of PGA pro Marion Detlefsen's favorite holes on the course. "It's a real good par three, with lots of natural areas around it," she said. "It's a tough little hole." Your tee shot must clear an expanse of marshy wetland, although there is bail-out room all around the putting surface. The backdrop is a forest of pines behind the green. That pine forest hugs the right side of the fairway on the par-four 14th, requiring a tee shot that stays far enough left that you can see the green on your second.

If the heart of Eagle Harbor is the trio of holes that wrap up the front nine, the soul of the course is the four finishers.

The road home starts with #15, the longest par three on the course. An extremely long bunker protects the front and right side of the large green. The area in front of the green tends to be soft and a bit spongy, punishing a shot that fails to carry all the way to the putting surface. The 16th is a long par-four dogleg right. Water is in play along the left from about midway down the fairway all the way to the green. The green is one of the toughest on the course to putt with an abundance of breaks and contours.

Alan Slaughter, superintendent from the time the course opened in 1993 likes #17. "It's one of the most picturesque holes out here," he said. It's a par-four dogleg left with the toughest green on the course to approach. The elevated green is like an hourglass laid on its side, with a precariously narrow waist, and drop-offs in front and in back. A low-handicap member with whom I was playing one day hit a low shot onto the putting surface that rolled at least twenty yards off the back. He tried to flop his next shot near the pin only to have it hop once and squirt a good fifteen yards off the front. He rescued a double-bogey.

Number 18 is the hardest hole on the side for women and no pushover for men. It's a long par five. The fairway is compressed between a pair of lakes. Your lay-up second must be precise to avoid a Maginot Line of bunkers—a trio of pot bunkers about 50 yards in front of the green and an enormous gaping greenside sand trap in front of the putting surface.

Eagle Harbor is one of those courses that most local players know well and often try to keep their own secret preserve. However, word is rapidly spreading about this fine, challenging track, and the secret won't be safe for long.

Eagle Harbor

HOLE	Ra	Sl	1	2	3	4	5	6	7	8	9	OUT	10	11	12	13	14	15	16	17	18	IN	TOT
BLUE	73.3	138	432	385	515	178	415	165	552	372	393	3407	377	518	358	167	417	202	420	420	554	3433	6840
WHITE	71.5	131	393	355	497	165	395	152	527	366	380	3230	352	493	348	150	402	186	368	380	523	3202	6432
GREEN	69.5(m)/71.8(w)	125(m)/124(w)	345	327	472	150	358	143	502	313	325	2935	322	472	327	135	382	167	340	345	490	2980	5915
MEN'S HCP		5	15	11	17	3	9	13	7	1			18	16	10	14	4	12	2	8	6		
PAR			4	4	5	3	4	3	5	4	4	36	4	5	4	3	4	3	4	4	5	36	72
RED	69.8	121	285	283	420	115	303	87	433	268	258	2452	280	412	280	117	292	136	266	307	438	2528	4980
WOMEN'S HCP		7	15	9	17	11	13	5	3	1			14	4	10	8	12	18	16	6	2		

The par-four opening hole on El Diablo sets the stage for a round of golf that takes you across a hilly, verdant course representing some of architect Jim Fazio's best work.

EL DIABLO GOLF AND COUNTRY CLUB

10405 N. Sherman Drive, Citrus Springs, Florida (From I-75 take exit 67 and go east on State Road 484 for about 20 miles to the town of Dunnellon; turn left onto Highway 41 for about 6 miles to the entrance to Citrus Springs on the left; go about 1 mile and follow the signs.)
Phone: (352) 465-0986

Architect: Jim Fazio   Year opened: 1998

Course rating/Slope rating for men:
Gold—75.3/147   Blue—73.7/136
White—71.7/130   Gray—68.7/121

Course rating/Slope rating for women:
Gray—73.0/124   Red—69.8/117

When I started researching this book, El Diablo was not on my short list of Florida's best golf courses. But the more players and club pros I talked to, the more the name kept cropping up in conversation. Virtually everyone who had played it raved about it. They were taken with its beauty and design, as well as its "golfability." The fact is, El Diablo is worth a long detour for the sheer pleasure of playing it. The course may well rank as Architect Jim Fazio's best work to date.

General Manager Nathan Pyles said proudly, "When you're playing, you'll notice that every hole on the course is completely different than the next. When it was designed, we did that for a purpose: so you'll remember this golf course." The goal has been met, and then some. It etches itself in your memory, imposes itself on your subconscious. It's unique. It's beautiful. It meanders through a forest of pines and oaks, and possesses a maturity that makes you think it's been there for a long time. While there was a lot of earth moved in building El Diablo, there's nothing artificial here. Fazio succeeded brilliantly in creating a golf course that works superbly with nature.

His use of mounds, sand, marsh, and water combine to form a delightful amalgam. Nearly 80 feet of elevation change is incorporated into the design, unusual for a flat state like Florida. But in addition to the overt and obvious, it's the subtleties of the design that make the course so very good. Fazio left a dozen or more trees in play in places you would not expect them—forming a canopy over tees, shading and arching over putting surfaces, standing guard like leafy sentries at the entrance to greens. Flowers and ornate shrubs hit your eye serendipitously—around greens, beside tees, under trees. Boulders are in evidence on several holes as if nature put them there and Fazio decided not to tinker with it. The placement of the forward markers is done with exacting care, giving women an almost identical look at every hole as the pros playing the tips.

There's very little out of bounds at El Diablo, which means that when you hit it into the trees you play it if you can find it—quite a trick sometimes. "If you hit it in the woods, you're in trouble," said Pyles. In addition, there are myriad waste areas. You may ground your club and remove loose impediments when you find yourself in them, but the best playing tip is to avoid them.

The course opens with a beautiful par four on which you drive through a chute of trees. The well-bunkered green is downhill from the landing area that sets up an approach across a little mounded and contoured valley.

Number 2 is a gentle double-dogleg par five that's a three-shotter for almost everybody. The hole bends to the right about driving distance and then hooks back to the left at the green. Keep your second shot far enough right to open up the two-tiered green, which is tightly guarded by sand on the left and a stand of pines and oaks on the right.

The lovely par-three 3rd plays through a chute of moss-laden trees and across a waste area. The trees—including a towering oak that crowds the line from tee to green—frame the putting surface, which is protected by bunkers and plantings.

If the golf course doesn't have your attention by now, it's time to concentrate. The next hole is a long par four with a split fairway in front of the green that sits at the base of a small hill. The optimal drive is to the upper shelf on the left side of the split. Your drive on the hilly, par-five 5th is over an intimidating stretch of waste area to the crest of a ridge, where the hole doglegs to the right and starts downhill. A grassy knoll splits the fairway in front of the green. The green is protected on the right by an embankment that drops off sharply into a pair of bunkers and by a waste area to the rear.

The outgoing side finishes with a trio of long par fours. Number 7 is fairly straight with a blind, uphill tee shot; your approach is downhill to a two-tiered green which is angled to the left. A menacing trio of bunkers that start about 100 yards from the green run right up to greenside. The downhill 8th is a dogleg left. A mossy, towering old oak overhangs the right front of the putting surface. And #9 is a great finisher for the front nine. Your drive is to the base of a hill where the hole doglegs left and begins to climb to the long, thin green.

The back nine is every bit as hilly and forested as the front. Number 10 is a long straight downhill par four. A lone pine tree stand like a soldier at the left front side of the green and a trio of bunkers guards the right. A pair of oaks stands within a couple of steps of the back right collar of the green as well.

General Manager Nathan Pyles said, "The 11th is our signature hole. Uphill. Par four. Got a lot of character to it." That's an understatement. It's a breathtaking golf hole. Your drive is across a small lake that is pretty but shouldn't really come into play. The fairway is tight leading up to a green that has been sculpted and molded from a hillside with an embankment arcing around about three-quarters of it.

Number 12 is a short par five dogleg right. If you're thinking of going for it in two you'll either have to play your tee shot to the right or play a left-to-right approach to get around the trees that are leaning into the fairway. If you're laying up you'll have to leave your second shot well short of the bunkers and waste area Architect Jim Fazio has placed in front of the two-tiered green.

A downhill par three and a pleasant little par four lead to a demanding short one- shot hole. Number 15 plays downhill to a smallish green. A lone deep, nasty pot bunker sits directly in front of the putting surface. "It used to be six feet deeper," said General Manager Nathan Pyles with a grin. He rejected the suggestion that it was raised because it was littered with the parched bones of those who couldn't get out.

The 16th is one of the tightest par fours on El Diablo. Hit your straightest club here, not your longest. The hole is downhill off the tee and then back up to an elevated two-tiered green. The putting surface is extremely well protected with trees that overhang the sand at the right. One of those strategic trees that Fazio left in play is at the front right edge of the green and a huge waste bunker studded with wild grasses brushes the left.

An uphill par five leads to the par four 18th. There's a generous landing area, but then the hole compresses incrementally the closer you get to the elevated green. Bunkering protects the right side from about 150 yards out and a series of hills guard the left.

In the final analysis, there's a lot more that's divine than devilish about El Diablo. It is a brilliant design, a marvelous golf course to play, and a real bargain. As this volume goes to press, another eighteen holes in an old quarry on the same tract of land is in the early stages of development. Again the architect is Jim Fazio, and the new holes promise to be a wonderful companion to El Diablo.

El Diablo

HOLE	Ra	Sl	1	2	3	4	5	6	7	8	9	OUT	10	11	12	13	14	15	16	17	18	IN	TOT
GOLD	75.3	147	441	582	205	405	529	180	409	407	408	3566	457	392	541	181	373	187	396	532	420	3479	7045
BLUE	73.7	136	427	576	198	377	510	169	392	390	398	3437	436	373	501	166	332	155	337	508	403	3211	6648
WHITE	71.7	130	392	526	171	369	498	154	368	360	378	3216	408	359	478	145	315	134	341	478	358	3016	6232
GRAY	68.7(m)/73.0(w)	121(m)/124(w)	366	476	138	353	470	131	341	306	327	2908	393	333	449	127	291	102	312	431	308	2746	5654
HCP			3	7	13	11	15	17	5	9	1		4	12	10	18	16	14	6	8	2		
PAR			4	5	3	4	5	3	4	4	4	36	4	4	5	3	4	3	4	5	4	36	72
RED	69.8	117	333	445	115	303	429	113	309	292	302	2641	372	307	428	110	260	81	278	401	266	2503	5144

Emerald Bay's short par-four 14th is a risk-reward hole. The more of the lake you cut across, the shorter your approach shot.

EMERALD BAY

4781 Clubhouse Drive, Destin, Florida (From I-10 take exit 14 and go south on US Highway 331 for about 15 miles; turn right onto State Route 20 and go about 15 miles; turn left and cross the Mid-Bay Toll Bridge; at U. S. Highway 98 turn left and go east about 2 miles to the entrance to Emerald Bay.)
Phone: (850) 837-5197

Architect: Robert Cupp   Year opened: 1991

Course rating/Slope rating:
Gold—73.1/135   Blue—71.3/127
White—68.9/120   Red—70.1/122

The resort communities of Fort Walton Beach, Destin, and Sandestin share a narrow strip of land between the Gulf of Mexico and Choctawatchee Bay. On that strip of land, or within an easy drive, are a dozen or more good golf courses. Chronicling the best of them is an exercise in subjectivity, guaranteed to generate lively debate among locals and regular visitors who play these courses frequently. For my money, Emerald Bay has maintained a respected place among the area's best for a decade. The year after it opened, *Golf Digest* named Emerald Bay one of the "best new courses" in the country. The standard that brought it that recognition still stands.

Emerald Bay is a superior test of the game, wending its way among the pines, and along the banks of the shimmering bay. The course features small to medium greens that are generally well protected. You must keep your tee shots in play or you can take a penalty stroke on almost every hole. Long hitters will have an advantage on several holes—two of the par fives are reachable for the big boomers in two shots and three of the par fours are in excess of 400 yards from both the Gold and Blue Tees. Average players will find comfort in the fact that architect Robert Cupp has blended in a nice mix of par three holes and included four very short par fours that, while demanding, will provide good opportunities for pars and birdies.

Women will find ample scoring opportunities. My wife Barbara noted, "There are enough par fours that let women hit an iron to the green on their second shot that it's fun." But she added that the par fives are very long for most female players. "A couple of them make you hit two big woods and a long-iron or even a nine-wood to get on in regulation," she said.

The two par-four opening holes play parallel to each other and provide a nice introduction, but when you cross the street and face the first one-shot hole you find yourself in the thick of Cupp's design. Number 3 is a short but demanding par three with a wide, shallow green. A mound on the right side hides a portion of the putting surface from the tees.

A trio of tight par fours follows. The short 4th plays down a tree-lined chute with out-of-bounds close at hand on both sides. It requires less than a driver. The kidney-shaped green is guarded by a bunker directly in front and is divided from front to back by a ridge. Number 5 is rated the toughest hole on the course. It's long, with water down the left which narrows into a channel that intersects the fairway and curls around the right side of the green. The 6th is a severe dogleg right. Water extends down the right length of the hole. Your tee shot needs to be long and straight or you'll leave a risky approach shot to the green.

Number 7 is a substantial par five with water down most of the left length. One of the best holes on the course is the lovely long par-three 8th. You tee off across a lake to a long, thin, hillside green. It's huge, angled to the right, and measures some 45 yards from front to back. For women this is an especially tough hole—146 yards from the Red Tees. There's a little bail-out room to the left front.

You make the turn with a long par five, followed by the longest par four on the course. Big hitters will be rewarded on these two holes. The par-four #11 is a dogleg left with a blind tee shot. A wedge of pine forest and a pair of big bunkers define the bend in the dogleg. Your tee shot must be long or to the right in order to give yourself a look at the flag on your approach.

Number 12 is the longest par three on the course. Men must play through a frame of trees and over a bit of marshy wetland to reach the green. It's rated the eighth hardest hole on the course, which is understandable for men, but it's not that hard for women. Women have an unimpeded shot at the putting surface and face little trouble. In fact, the hole presents an excellent scoring opportunity from the forward markers.

The extremely long par-five 13th is an alley between the trees. The entrance to the green is compressed by bunkers. That leads to the very pleasant par-four 14th. You drive over a marsh but you need to be aware of the hidden hazard on this short hole. A lake forms the point at which the hole bends to the left, but you can't see it from the tees. The ideal drive is straight, aimed at the tallest of the pines visible through the fairway, which leaves you a straight approach to the green that's perched on a hillside beside the lake.

Choctawatchee Bay forms the backdrop for the next two holes. Number 15 is another long par four. Avoid the hillside bunkers to the right. You drive to the crest of a small hill and then play your approach downhill to the green. It's a pretty hole, with the bay behind the green. The 16th is a spectacular par three right on the shores of the bay. The views are breathtaking. It's a photo op if you have a camera along. Take a lingering look back at the bay from the 17th tees and then head to the clubhouse. The penultimate hole is a short par four with water down the right side. Men face a forced carry across a patch of wetland from tees that are almost on the bayside beach. Women do not have the forced carry, but everybody must negotiate the ample bunkers and hills that guard the green.

The finisher is a moderate par five that the big hitters will consider going for in two. It can be an easy par or birdie, or a produce humiliatingly big numbers. Your tee shot is fairly open, but it must avoid the three bunkers on the right side of the fairway. A canal intersects the fairway about 200 yards from the green and then proceeds to form a water hazard that plays up the right all the way to greenside.

Emerald Bay isn't going to leave you gasping for air, but you have to hit some good golf shots to score on this scenic and pleasant course. Add in the magnificent views, the lovely surroundings, and the pleasant attitude, and the place is a winner.

Emerald Bay

HOLE	Ra	Sl	1	2	3	4	5	6	7	8	9	OUT	10	11	12	13	14	15	16	17	18	IN	TOT
GOLD	73.1	135	398	410	135	293	396	425	566	200	528	3351	455	349	229	611	358	466	166	328	512	3474	6825
BLUE	71.3	127	377	385	126	282	381	411	540	193	510	3205	446	327	213	600	325	405	149	315	496	3276	6481
WHITE	68.9	120	344	362	106	271	358	374	481	176	476	2948	390	311	201	532	300	379	132	296	478	3019	5967
HCP			11	3	15	17	1	5	7	9	13		2	14	8	6	10	4	16	18	12		
PAR			4	4	3	4	4	4	5	3	5	36	4	4	3	5	4	4	3	4	5	36	72
RED	70.1	122	296	312	97	256	344	334	448	146	426	2659	335	295	103	460	258	320	120	216	418	2525	5184

The enormous bunker guarding the 12th green at Emerald Dunes is typical of what you can expect on this lovely Tom Fazio course.

EMERALD DUNES

2100 Emerald Dunes Drive, West Palm Beach, Florida (From the Florida Turnpike take the West Palm Beach-Okechobee exit and turn right; go west on Okechobee Blvd. about a mile and follow the signs.)
Phone: (561) 687-1700 or (888) 650-4653 E-mail: edunes@aol.com

Architect: Tom Fazio Year opened: 1990

Course rating/Slope rating for men:
Gold—73.8/133 Blue—71.7/129
White—69.7/125 Green—67.3/120

Course rating/Slope rating for women:
Green—72.2/126 Red—67.1/115

Even before they started moving dirt at the Emerald Dunes construction site, when all that was there on that tract of land just west of the Florida Turnpike was scrub and sand and palmettos and swampland and snakes, the course was envisioned to be a cut above the ordinary. The pre-opening publicity proclaimed it a whole new type of daily fee golf course. From the day it opened Emerald Dunes has lived up to those early expectations. Everything about the place is first class.

The Spanish-style clubhouse with its red tile roof looks like an exclusive private country club. The service—from the guys who load your bag onto the golf cart to the pro shop staff to the starters—is gracious and knowledgeable. The grounds crews are polite and courteous. All that, even before you take a look at Tom Fazio's brilliant piece of design work.

The golf course is delightful, tough, and fair. It's not for beginners. The tees and fairways are kept in pristine condition. The greens are tournament quality—receptive, fast, and true. The bunkers are well-maintained. In all, there is very little not to like about Emerald Dunes.

Architect Tom Fazio leads you onto the course with three solid, long holes that afford good scoring opportunities if you keep your shots in the fairway. If there is a key to Fazio golf courses, in general, it is to keep the ball in play. Seldom is a long shot that drifts right or left rewarded as much as a shorter shot that finds the short grass.

Number 1 is a short par five. It's tight with water and bunkers along the right. On the left, there's enough room among the trees and mounds that only an extremely errant or unlucky shot will yield a penalty. This is a good chance for long hitters and even some not-so-long hitters to get on in two. For women it's hard. At 365 yards from the forward markers, it's a three shot hole for all but the LPGA Tour.

The 2nd is a long, tight, dogleg right with the long thin green angled to the right behind a big bunker. Number 3 is a medium length par four that is pinched, about driving distance, by a pair of bunkers on the right and trees on the left. Now that you've been introduced, the handshake's over and architect Tom Fazio will test your skill and shot-making ability for the next fifteen holes.

Walk over the hill behind the 3rd green and you find a lovely little par three. It's short, but presents all players with a forced carry across an expanse of water. There's room to bail out to the left but the green is highly contoured and can offer some devilishly hard putts.

Number 5 is a mammoth par five, with water in play down the entire left length. A slight left-to-right tee shot is an advantage here. Your lay-up second must avoid the bunker on the left side about 80 yards from the green which is offset to the left behind a wedge of the lake. The hole is called Waterloo, a Napoleonic reference to the fact that it can easily be where a proud player comes face to face with ignominious defeat.

It doesn't get any easier on the next two par fours. The 6th is a demanding dogleg right with water down the left side and a beach-like bunker that sits at lakeside, from about 100 yards out, to the elevated green. The green has a drop-off to the left that guarantees a sand shot and another to the right that feeds into a deep grass catch basin. Number 7 is a risk-reward dogleg left around a lake. The fairway is above the lake and is canted toward it. A long, mean bunker guards the left front; a pair of menacing bunkers lie in wait to the right for those who try to avoid the water to the left.

The men's tees on the sandy par-three 8th are bracketed by tall palm trees. Sand traps are in play along most of the left length of the hole with an enormous bunker in the shape of a surreal star guarding the long, thin two-tiered green on the left.

Number 9 is rated the toughest hole on the golf course. It's a long, severe dogleg left with water down the right length and hills to the left. The ideal tee shot comes to rest between the right and left fairway bunkers. There's bail-out room to the left if you feel you're in danger of finding the water in front of the green.

Stop at the clubhouse for a cold drink, a sandwich, or a Valium and then brace yourself for some of the best golf in south Florida. The back nine opens with a hilly, rocky par four that bends slightly to the right and plays uphill to an elevated green. As with several holes on Emerald Dunes, architect Tom Fazio has been fairly generous with the size of the landing area for your tee shots, but he narrows the holes like a noose the closer you get to the green. Take enough club on your approach.

A short par five followed by a short par four offer a chance to get your score in line, although neither hole could be characterized as easy. Then comes the long dogleg left par-four 13th that's a crescent around a lake. A bunker runs most of the left length of the hole and forms a buffer between the rough and the water. Right-center is the place to put your tee shot.

The one-shot 14th is a visually deceptive hole. The putting surface sits on a mesa above a lake to the right. From the tees, the front-right bunkers appear to be greenside, but they are, in fact, separated from the green by a grassy depression that's a good ten yards wide. The result is that the green appears closer than it is. Architect Fazio has given you a little room to bail out to the left, but on this hole there are two absolutes: Don't be short and don't be right.

Number 15 is another risk-reward hole, a long par-four dogleg right around a lake. It's a blind tee shot, trees blocking the view of the green. The landing area is tight. Your tee shot has to end up left enough to give you a clear look at your target. Club selection will depend on pin placement as the extremely thin, multi-level, elevated green is more than 50 yards from front to back, with dunes and hillside bunkers to the left and a steep drop-off to the right.

As if the previous holes haven't been spectacular enough, the trio of finishers at Emerald Dunes are tremendous. Number 16 is a par three with a forced carry across water, sand and rocks for men. Architect Fazio has taken the water pretty much out of play for women from the forward markers. The green is pear-shaped and two tiered with the stem-end of the pear higher than the fat part of the pear. The 17th is truly memorable. It's an extremely tight par five in the shape of an inverted, elongated *S*. Your tee shot has to avoid a quartet of fairway bunkers—two right and two left. Your lay-up second must thread its way between trees that compress the fairway to about the width of a two-car garage. Your approach is to a lakeside green that's got bunkers to the left and right front. The putting surface is pitched sharply from left to right.

You then climb to the top of a waterfall to tee off on the finishing hole from a series of island tees that sit among cascades, pools, and gurgling, plashing waters. Your tee shot must reach the point at which the dogleg bends to the left to give you a look at the enormous 60-yard long green. The runway to the putting surface is extremely thin, squeezed by hills to the left and sand and water to the right.

From the first tee, down all the demanding fairways to all the difficult greens, to the spectacular finishing holes, the golf course is a slam-dunk winner. The long and the short of Emerald Dunes is that it is a wonderful, challenging golf course that should be on your "must play" list any time you happen to be in south Florida. It is not to be missed.

Emerald Dunes

HOLE	Ra	Sl	1	2	3	4	5	6	7	8	9	OUT	10	11	12	13	14	15	16	17	18	IN	TOT
GOLD	73.8	133	501	408	400	169	555	430	415	199	474	3551	417	479	333	395	212	422	181	580	436	3455	7006
BLUE	71.7	129	478	393	380	155	530	370	389	181	420	3296	392	472	315	366	190	393	165	550	419	3262	6558
WHITE	69.7	125	451	370	355	130	492	338	368	150	393	3047	373	449	298	345	166	380	150	544	368	3073	6120
GREEN	67.3(m)/72.2(w)	120(m)/126(w)	420	310	335	120	442	320	346	130	370	2793	345	424	271	311	153	336	128	502	330	2800	5593
HCP			11	13	9	17	3	7	5	15	1		6	12	14	10	16	4	18	8	2		
PAR			5	4	4	3	5	4	4	3	4	36	4	5	4	4	3	4	3	5	4	36	72
RED	67.1	115	365	260	244	90	400	230	250	100	290	2229	272	375	222	303	129	307	100	424	317	2449	4678

Grand Haven's signature hole is the par-three 8th, which plays to an island green.

GRAND HAVEN

2001 Waterside Parkway, Palm Coast, Florida (From I-95 take exit 91C, go east on Palm Coast Parkway to Colbert Lane, turn right and go south to the Grand Haven entrance and follow the signs)
Phone: (904) 455-2327

Architect: Jack Nicklaus Year opened: 1998

Course rating/Slope rating:
Black—74.9/135 Gold—72.8/131
Blue—71.5/126 White—68.3/120
Red—70.4/123

When Jack Nicklaus was at the apex of his game, he played his best on tough golf courses—Winged Foot, Cherry Hills, and Royal Troon. As a golf course architect, Jack Nicklaus has incorporated many of the elements he liked as a player into his golf course designs. Grand Haven represents some of Jack Nicklaus' best design work. It's moderately long with well-protected greens, challenging fairways, inventive tee placements, and it's kept in championship condition.

The fact that it sits in the heart of a residential development in Palm Coast—between Daytona Beach and Jacksonville—makes it less crowded than many other courses closer to the cities. That doesn't mean that Grand Haven is empty. It gets plenty of play, especially in the high season—late winter and early spring. But for a golf course of this caliber tee times are generally available. Add to that a management philosophy and style based on friendliness, courtesy, and helpfulness and Grand Haven is worth a special trip to play it.

Hampton Golf, which bought Grand Haven in the summer of 2000 and which owns three other golf courses in northeast Florida, has a corporate goal of providing country club amenities for upscale daily fee players. The ownership transition was not hard for Grand Haven, which had a wonderful, friendly attitude—from the pro shop to the grounds crew—from the day it opened. There is good reason that Grand Haven is a favorite, even among members of exclusive clubs in Jacksonville, Ponte Vedra, and St. Augustine.

Your introduction to the course is a lovely par four. The approach is to a large, contoured, slightly elevated green that slopes from left to right. Deep bunkers guard the front. Through a tunnel, under a road and you find a solid par five. The 2nd tees are tucked behind a corner of the lake that plays down the left length of the hole. The green is angled to the left so that the lake forms a hazard at left front of the elevated putting surface.

Number 3 is a fine risk-reward par four, the toughest hole on the course. The risk is to determine how much of the marsh in front of the tees you want to cut across. The fairway is substantial, but the more marsh you bite off, the shorter your approach to the well-protected green. A second marshy area intrudes in front of the green and requires a forced carry for most approach shots.

The next three holes—a pair of par fours sandwiching a par three—offer good scoring opportunities. Number 4 is long, with all of the trouble on the left side. A pond and a gigantic bunker guard the left front of the multi-level green. The is a very pleasant one-shot hole with a wetland menacing you along the right length of the hole. The green is on a hillside with the bunker to the right well below the putting surface and the bunker to the left well above it. Number 6 is a nice, short par four.

When Jack Nicklaus was the long hitting Golden Bear of yesteryear, he loved holes that let him strut his stuff off the tee. Nicklaus, the player, would have liked Grand Haven's 7th hole. He might have even gotten there in two shots. For almost everybody else it's a three shot hole that plays 575 yards from the back tees, uphill all the way. Water is in play along the right from about the mid-way point up to the green. The highly contoured green is perched above the fairway, with the hill in front poised to reject any approaches that come up short. A devilish cluster of bunkers will catch almost any shot that drifts short and right. Two long shots do not guarantee an easy approach and on in regulation does not secure an easy par or birdie.

The par-three 8th hole is Grand Haven's signature hole. A series of terraced tee boxes overlook an island green. The hole is not particularly long, but it can be an exercise in terror, especially if there's a fresh ocean breeze blowing in from the east.

Number 9 is a fairly straight par four that provides good scoring opportunities and a refreshing way to make the turn. A bunker in front of the green creates something of a split fairway, which will not affect a shot going for the flag and the elevated green, but will have a strategic impact on players needing to lay up.

The back nine opens gently, with a dogleg right par four around a lake. Keep your tee shot left and you'll have a relatively easy approach shot. That said, be aware that the lake caresses the front right side of the green, which is angled to the right along the shore.

Play the tight par five and then cross the road to face the short, but tricky par-four 12th. Most members use something other than a driver on this hole. It's a dogleg right with a forced carry over marsh to a fairly constricted landing area. A giant waste bunker guards the left side of the hole, and marsh and pine forest run along the right. The entrance to the small green is pinched by a giant bunker on the left and an extension of the marshy hazard on the right.

The 14th is a delightful par three, with trees to the left, marsh and trees to the right and a giant old oak overhanging the middle tee box. The small green is among the most contoured on the course and the putting surface is partially obscured from the tees by a mound and a steep-faced bunker.

The par-four 15th is the second hardest hole on the course. It opens with an uphill tee shot. The elevated green is fronted by a large, deep bunker. The pine forest along the right comes ever more dangerously into play the closer you get to the green.

Number 16 is a fine, tight par four with an uphill plateaued green and waste bunkers studded with marsh grass along the left side. Forest of pines and palmettos protects the right. The green is sloped left to right and guarded by deep bunkers in front and is the most elevated green on the course.

A long par three with a well-bunkered turtleback green takes you to the 18th tees. It's a short par five dogleg left, with a lake in play along the right as you tee off. Your shot to the green will encounter a line of giant old trees on the left. If you're going for it in two, you'll likely have to clear the trees; if you're laying up, stay far enough to the right to take the trees out of play.

Grand Haven is fun. It's a challenging, fair golf course. And if you're visiting northeast Florida for any length of time, it's a course you'll probably want to play more than once. It's Jack Nicklaus architecture at its very best, with a wonderful, friendly, knowledgeable staff to make the experience even more enjoyable.

Grand Haven

HOLE	Ra	Sl	1	2	3	4	5	6	7	8	9	OUT	10	11	12	13	14	15	16	17	18	IN	TOT
BLACK	74.9	135	406	500	436	464	189	384	575	156	437	3547	400	520	345	434	175	471	430	222	525	3522	7069
GOLD	72.8	131	381	480	421	443	174	376	557	137	416	3385	372	496	323	410	150	460	406	194	499	3310	6695
BLUE	71.5	126	361	471	399	417	165	357	525	124	391	3210	352	486	308	384	142	433	383	182	483	3153	6363
WHITE	68.3	120	307	458	357	376	144	261	494	103	370	2870	342	469	279	351	116	373	339	157	466	2892	5762
MEN'S HCP		15	11	1	5	17	13	3	9	7			10	6	16	8	18	2	4	14	12		
PAR			4	5	4	4	3	4	5	3	4	36	4	5	4	4	3	4	4	3	5	36	72
RED	70.4	123	255	409	320	321	107	220	412	77	313	2434	310	418	239	312	100	322	304	129	417	2551	4985
WOMEN'S HCP			13	9	1	3	17	15	5	7	11		8	4	18	10	14	2	12	16	6		

This enormous, serpentine green at Kelly Plantation Golf Club is shared by #11 (in the foreground) and #7 (in the background). The dark patch of grass between the two flags hides a deep pot bunker in the middle of the putting surface.

KELLY PLANTATION GOLF CLUB

307 Kelly Plantation Dr., Destin, Florida (From I-10 take exit 14 and go south on US Highway 331 for about 15 miles; turn right onto State Route 20 and go about 15 miles; turn left and cross the Mid-Bay Toll Bridge; at U. S. Highway 98 turn right and go west about 1/2 mile to the entrance.)
Phone: (850) 650-7600 or (800) 811-6757

Architect: Fred Couples Year opened: 1998

Course rating/Slope rating:

Couples—74.2/146 Plantation—72.0/138
Palmetto—68.4/128 Magnolia—70.9/124

Kelly Plantation is amazingly mature for its age. It has the feel of a much more established golf course. It's a beautiful course on the banks of Choctawhatchee Bay, the design of PGA star Fred Couples. This long, difficult track is cut through dense pine forests, with eleven lakes in play, along with nature preserves and wetlands that are home to all manner of birds and coastal wildlife. (The scorecard warns you to steer clear of alligators and poisonous snakes, not that a smart golfer should need such a warning.) Chilled apples are provided on the 1st and 10th tees.

The practice facilities are excellent. There's a large tiered driving range and target greens. There are two big practice greens for chipping and putting.

The course itself is a fair challenge for players of all levels, and it's an especially good test for women. Architect Couples has provided an excellent look at the course from the forward tees, which play to 5,170 yards. The par threes demand length and accuracy from women players, all of them measuring in excess of 100 yards.

The course is superbly maintained. The greens are highly contoured. They're firm and fast, but not blistering. The bunkers tend to be large and deep. It's a par 72, but the unconventional back nine features three par threes, three par fours, and three par fives.

Architect Couples provides only one handshake hole, the short par four opener. Then it's down to serious business. The 2nd is a long, tight par five dogleg left with marsh down the left length of the hole and a forest of pines, oaks and palmettos down the right. The green is well bunkered and sloped from back to front.

The par-three 3rd, with an undulating green tucked behind a gaping bunker, leads you to the signature hole at Kelly Plantation. With Choctawhatchee Bay shimmering through the pines along the left and a lake to the right, the par-four 4th is a lovely golf hole. The left side of the elevated, bowl-shaped green is guarded by a giant bunker, separated from the bay by a bulkhead. The Mid-Bay Bridge runs right behind the green and rises to the sky as it spans the water.

A backward glance from the 5th tees provides a superb panorama of the bay and the bridge. The golf is stimulating too. It's a long, demanding par four. Number 6 is a par five that big hitters can think about reaching in two shots. The key here is to avoid the fairway bunkers that litter the hole from tee to green. Your drive is slightly uphill and the approach to the green is gently downhill. Two towering pines on the left and four on the right frame the entrance to the elevated putting surface.

Number 7 is another visually pleasing hole with water to the right and dense forest to the left. The hole shares an enormous, serpentine, highly contoured green—with a deep, nasty pot bunker in the middle of it—with the 11th hole, but you can't see that from the fairway.

Head to the turn with a long par three and a solid par four. The 9th has water down the left length. The green is hooked to the left behind the lake. A bunker sits to the right of the water and in front of the putting surface. There's almost no successful way to play a bump-and-run approach shot here. The green itself is diabolical. A ridge intersects it front to back. While the effect is to create two levels, the left level slopes toward the water and the right mesa slopes to the right and front. The key is getting your approach on the proper side of the ridge.

Number 10 is a three-shot par five for almost all players, unless of course you hit the ball as far as the guy who designed it. A marshy hazard—invisible from the fairway—lurks in front of the elevated green, and unless you are in position to carry all the way to the putting surface, a lay-up short of the hazard is paramount.

Your drive on #11 is up to the crest of a hill. Your approach is to that huge, snaky green shared with #7. Don't be so bold that you find that pot bunker in the middle of the putting surface. The 13th is another par five that long hitters can consider going for in two. The landing area is fairly tight and a lake is in play from about 200 yards in to the multi-tiered green, but it's a good scoring hole.

Number 14 is a long par four, a gentle crescent-shaped hole that arcs to the right around a lake. The green is on a hillside above the water, with a sand trap between the putting surface and the lake. Two par three holes with a par four between them lead to the demanding finisher. Number 18 is a long, extremely tight par five. From the tees, your eye is engaged by a huge bunker that sits up a hill in front of you. You must either play short of it or clear it on your drive. The hole bends to the right near the green. The approach to the long, thin, multi-tiered putting surface is guarded by water and a cluster of sand traps. Three careful shots will produce a rewarding finish; stray from the fairway and the result can be most disappointing.

While I've been a fan of Fred Couples, the PGA Tour champion for years, Kelly Plantation is the first course I've played by Fred Couples the architect. I enjoyed it thoroughly. In fact, if this course is a benchmark, I shall eagerly seek out any other course that bears Couples' name.

Kelly Plantation Golf Club

HOLE	Ra	Sl	1	2	3	4	5	6	7	8	9	OUT	10	11	12	13	14	15	16	17	18	IN	TOT
COUPLES	74.2	146	373	560	165	401	443	548	410	194	439	3533	550	411	240	525	446	150	447	207	590	3566	7099
PLANTATION	72.0	138	348	537	154	378	394	496	381	170	368	3226	521	392	189	507	412	133	414	178	549	3295	6521
PALMETTO	68.4	128	328	497	146	324	366	491	343	160	349	3004	513	359	156	488	393	128	389	169	519	3114	6118
HCP			13	1	17	3	9	11	5	15	7		2	12	14	8	4	18	10	16	6		
PAR			4	5	3	4	4	5	4	3	4	36	5	4	3	5	4	3	4	3	5	36	72
MAGNOLIA	70.9	124	257	432	109	302	329	380	313	117	317	2556	425	320	119	407	355	91	333	124	440	2614	5170

The par-three 8th features a gigantic bunker studded with marsh grass that runs from tee to green on the Arnold Palmer-designed Legacy Golf Club at Lakewood Ranch.

LEGACY GOLF CLUB AT LAKEWOOD RANCH

8255 Legacy Blvd., Bradenton, Florida (Take exit 40 from I-75 and go east on University Parkway less than three miles to the entrance on the left.)
Phone: (941) 907-7067

Architect: Arnold Palmer Year opened: 1998

Course rating/Slope rating for men:
Black—73.7/143 Gold—72.1/140
Silver—69.6/134 Copper—66.6/129

Course rating/Slope rating for women:
Copper—71.4/132 Jade—68.2/125

Legacy Golf Club is one of the most popular, most talked-about golf courses in southwest Florida. Not only is it a superb golf course, it is a much-needed daily-fee facility in a part of the state where most of the best courses are private and exclusive.

It is a brilliant design by "The King", himself. The people who run it—Troon Golf—are among the best golf facility managers in the country. The service is spectacular, from the cart guys to the groundskeepers. The course is kept in wonderful condition. The greens are fast and true. The bunkers are impeccably maintained. The huge practice green and practice area is delightful. In short, Legacy is a first rate golf experience from the minute you drive up to the bag drop until you drain your final beverage at the 19th hole after your round.

While this Arnold Palmer design is long, difficult, and demanding, it is a fair test of the game for average to expert players. (Raw beginners would be well advised not to tackle the course until they get their games under control.) The layout puts a premium on accuracy off the tee and precision approaching the greens. Trouble is everywhere. Water or marshy wetlands are in play on thirteen holes. Sand traps and waste bunkers appear on virtually every hole.

Legacy opens with a very solid par four with water down the right length of the hole, mounds and forest down the left. It's a dogleg right with a huge, irregularly shaped green sandwiched between the water and a gaping, steep-faced bunker.

A three shot par five that plays to a large, well-bunkered green takes you to the 3rd, a treacherous short par four. Everybody drives over water. The lake extends down the right side of the hole. The green—shaped like a three-leaf clover on multiple levels—is nestled behind huge bunkers. Most players will use something other than a driver here. The key shot is the approach.

Number 4 is a long, watery par-three with the lake forming an *L*-shaped border to the highly contoured *L*-shaped green. Architect Palmer has given players a little bail-out room to the right front. But any shot that comes up short or left will be wet; most shots that are too long will find sand.

The par-four 5th is long and tough, the toughest hole on the course. For women it's nearly 360 yards from the forward tees. "A couple of good woods are the only way to get on in regulation," said my wife, Barbara, sizing up the test. The design presents a generous landing area from the tees, but the long thin green is angled to the left with water and marsh caressing the left front and bunkers squeezing the entrance at the right. Keep your tee shot to the right in order to give yourself the maximum amount of green to work with.

The par-five 7th can be a great scoring hole or send you into paroxysms of gloom. It's a three shot hole for all but the mightiest ball strikers. Your tee shot has to avoid a gaping fairway bunker about driving distance. Your second shot must avoid the lake to the right, which intrudes into the fairway about 100 yards from the green. The green itself is multi-tiered.

Numbers 8 and 9 are fine turning holes. The former is a par three with a forced carry over a waste bunker that runs from tee to green. The green is small and shallow with trouble behind it for shots that come in too hot. The 9th is a dogleg right par four with a lake in play on the right from tee to green. The further you hit your tee shot the less water you'll have to carry to the green.

You start the back side with little decompression time. Number 10 is a long, trouble-filled par-four dogleg right. Your tee shot has to split the fairway that's framed by a lake on the right and a giant pine in the middle of a waste area on the left. The ideal tee shot is aimed at the right fairway bunker at the turn of the dogleg. The approach is across another waste area that fronts the green and wraps around the right side of it.

It doesn't get any easier on the next hole, which is a nightmare for players who are uncertain of their ability to hit and aim their tee shots. The short par-four 11th looks like a cluster of grassy islands in a sea of sand. The hole offers several different ways to play it. One option is to play to the left, to an oasis of fairway in the middle of a desert of waste area. Another option is to go straight at the flag and try to clear the waste area, leaving a very short approach. Some really big hitters even try to drive the green. "You see as many big numbers as you do birdies," said one of the young assistant pros.

Arnie the architect sets up a lovely trio of holes to follow. Number 12 is a sandy par three. The long thin green is 40 yards from front to back. The 13th hole is a short par four dogleg right with water bordering both sides of the fairway most of the way from tee to green. And the 14th is a long dogleg right par five with sand in play off the tee and water in play near the green.

Number 15 is a delightful, but treacherous golf hole. It's a short par four that likely will not require a driver. Shot placement is paramount. Play your tee shot to the right, aimed at the lake, and avoid the waste area that is visible between you and the green. Your approach is a forced carry across water to a highly contoured green. For the faint of heart, there's bail-out room to the left of the putting surface, over the waste area.

Heading home, the 16th offers a good scoring opportunity. It's a long par four. Once you've safely negotiated the mounded fairway, the long thin green is one of the easiest on the course to approach. Number 17 is a medium length par three that plays to an island green. Palmer has presented you with a bunker that looks like a small beach in front of the putting surface. There's enough room behind the green to catch a shot that's a bit too bold.

The finishing hole is a long par four, surrounded by waste areas. Long hitters can play straight at the flag along the grassy runway between the bunkers. Short hitters will have to play to a little island to the right, leaving them a long, tough approach to the green all over waste area. The green is enormous—just short of 50 yards from back to front. Wrap up with a par or birdie here and you can be well satisfied.

My wife was impressed with the intelligent and challenging way in which architect Palmer placed the women's tees. Women with handicaps in the mid-teens or lower should consider playing the Copper Tees—one back from the forward markers.

Legacy Golf Club is a winner on all fronts. You can tell a lot about the dynamics, attitude, and playability of a relatively new facility by what the people who pay to play it have to say and how much repeat business the place gets. The people who have been paying to play Legacy over and over again have nothing but good things to say about it. I join them in those accolades.

Legacy Golf Club at Lakewood Ranch

HOLE	Ra	Sl	1	2	3	4	5	6	7	8	9	OUT	10	11	12	13	14	15	16	17	18	IN	TOT
BLACK	73.7	143	454	539	380	205	447	397	543	180	428	3573	530	369	189	398	565	379	441	151	472	3494	7067
GOLD	72.1	140	418	519	367	187	417	376	524	165	399	3372	501	336	172	383	540	361	425	139	455	3312	6684
SILVER	69.6	134	361	487	339	174	411	335	472	127	369	3075	459	328	140	359	502	329	378	129	409	3033	6108
COPPER	66.6(m)/71.4(w)	129(m)/132(w)	316	463	296	145	358	305	439	117	330	2769	411	265	105	326	456	313	359	101	360	2696	5465
HCP			5	11	9	7	1	17	13	15	3		8	10	18	14	4	12	6	16	2		
PAR			4	5	4	3	4	4	5	3	4	36	5	4	3	4	5	4	4	3	4	36	72
JADE	68.2	125	300	403	270	123	317	289	419	92	284	2497	401	258	84	251	414	271	314	82	314	2389	4886

At LPGA International's Champions Course, a watery grave awaits any shot that comes up short on the one-shot 17th.

LPGA INTERNATIONAL

300 Champions Drive, Daytona Beach, Florida (From I-95 take exit 87C onto LPGA Blvd., and go west about a half mile; the entrance gate is on the left and follow the signs to the clubhouse.)
Phone: (904) 274-LPGA

Champions Course Architect: Rees Jones Year opened: 1994
Legends Course Architect: Arthur Hills Year opened: 1998

Champions Course Rating/Slope rating for men:
Black—74.0/134 Blue—72.0/130
White—70.1/124 Gold—67.1/118

Champions Course Rating/Slope rating for women:
White—75.6/146 Gold—72.4/131
Red—68.9/122

Legends Course Rating/Slope rating for men:
Black—74.5/138 Blue—72.6/134
White—71.3/128 Gold—69.1/122

Legends Course Rating/ Slope rating for women:
White—77.3/144 Gold—73.8/132
Red—70.2/123

It was back in 1950 that a group of women who played golf for a living—including such stars as Patty Berg and Babe Didrikson Zaharias—launched a fledgling organization that became known as the LPGA. Many skeptics, mostly men in the world of golf, did not expect the Ladies' Professional Golf Association to survive into the next decade, much less into the next millennium. Well, today, after more than a half century, the LPGA is going strong. It is headquartered in Daytona Beach.

Adjacent to the home of the LPGA are two championship golf courses, a study in contrasts. The older of the two is the work of architect Rees Jones. He created the long, challenging Champions Course in the spirit of British and Irish links, with few trees, copious mounds and contours, and firm turf that encourages booming drives. Four years later, architect Arthur Hills carved and massaged the Legends Course from a pine forest, calling on marsh, palmettos, and dense woods to provide natural hazards. One has an open look; the other is tight. Both will challenge players of every caliber. And, as you might expect from their collective name and their proximity to LPGA Headquarters, both are especially good tests of the game for women. In fact, the Champions Course rated as one of the country's most woman-friendly golf courses by *Golf For Women* magazine.

CHAMPIONS COURSE

The first tee at architect Rees Jones' Champions Course tells you what you can expect—water, sand, and enough mounds to remind you of Ballybunion. Rees Jones is not a designer who likes tricks or illusions. He puts it all out in front of you. He tightens almost every hole with hills, berms, mounds, and ridges. His greens tend to be big with lots of subtle breaks and not-so-subtle contours. The opener—a short par four—has a serpentine fairway with mounds and bunkers to the right and a lake along the left. The green is slightly elevated.

Two par fours sandwich a par three to get you well into the Champions Course. All three holes present good scoring opportunities. The 5th is the second toughest hole on the course, a very solid par five. The approach to the green is pinched by three gaping sand traps to the left and the lake to the right. There's no let up as you drive around the lake to the 6th tees. What you face is a short but demanding par three that requires a forced carry across the same lake that caressed the 5th green.

Number 8 is one of the prettiest holes on the outgoing side, a short par four playing to a green that has a wee neck of grass in the front. Two enormous bunkers arc around the right and left sides of the putting surface.

The long par-five 9th hole demands that you thread your way between severe mounding and bunkers on both sides of the fairway to make your way to the green. It is an arduous trek for most women, playing a solid 460 yards from the most forward tees, and demanding a pair of massive wood shots to set up an approach that might present a birdie opportunity.

The inward side opens with a trio of par fours. The first is gentle, but hold onto your hat. Number 11 is tight with one of the toughest greens to approach on the Champions Course. Architect Jones has built an elevated green with a wedge of bunkers right and left, all but eliminating a bump-and-run approach. A high, soft, accurate approach is required to have any hope of a birdie here. The 12th is visually unique. Players tee off through a chute of trees with marshy wetland on the right. Your drive must avoid a treacherous, long, thin bunker on the left side of the fairway. Three nasty bunkers protect the elevated green, including one lurking directly in front of the putting surface.

A truly demanding test for everybody is the long par-five 13th. There's water in play off the tee. A long straight drive, down the Rees Jones signature alley of mounds and bunkers, will be rewarded. Keep your second shot left of center or your approach to the plateaued green may require a forced carry over sand. "It plays our hardest hole," said Golf Director Nancy Henderson. She noted with pride that she had eleven holes-in-one during her competitive playing career. "You've got to hit a couple of really long shots. And if you miss the elevated green it's a really hard up-and-down."

A solid par three and a long par four take you to #16, a short par five, dogleg left. There's a lake on the left and the hole has an elevated green. Lay-up second shots need to avoid bunkers right and left. The green is saddle-shaped with an elevated middle and drop-offs to the right and left. Three-putting this thing is a snap.

Wrap up your round with a fine par three and a long, tight par four. The one-shot hole has water guarding the left and

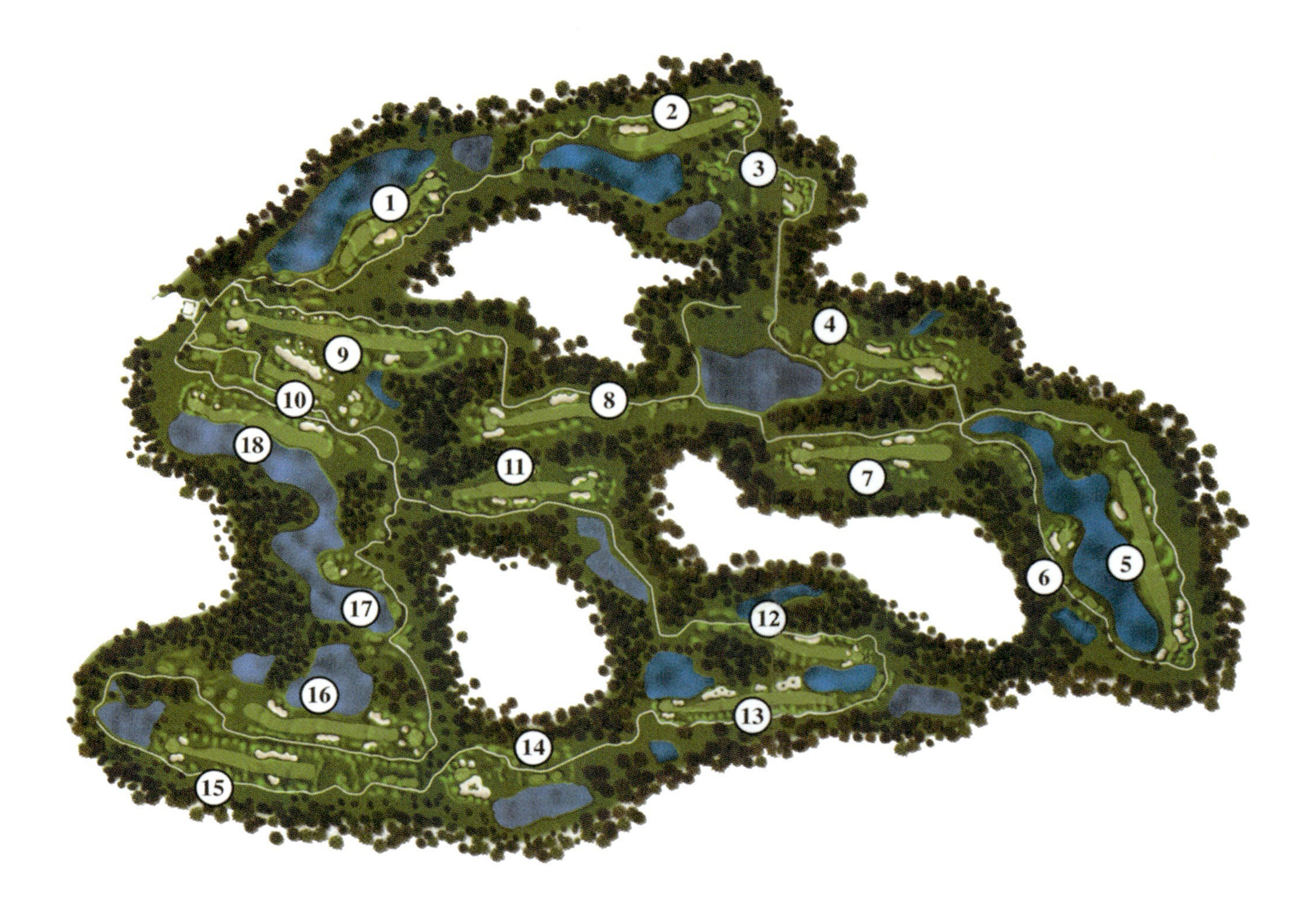

The Champions Course

HOLE	Ra	Sl	1	2	3	4	5	6	7	8	9	OUT	10	11	12	13	14	15	16	17	18	IN	TOT
BLACK	74.0	134	401	457	197	363	545	162	444	383	569	3521	338	411	403	576	191	468	525	203	452	3567	7088
BLUE	72.0	130	383	428	174	355	518	141	413	369	549	3330	332	378	363	548	159	429	513	168	444	3334	6664
WHITE	70.1(m)/75.6(w)	124(m)/146(w)	358	402	167	328	469	137	372	360	522	3115	312	356	356	533	151	391	475	148	388	3110	6225
GOLD	67.1(m)/72.4(w)	118(m)/131(w)	348	364	145	321	448	120	338	325	464	2873	305	346	348	482	143	338	424	140	345	2871	5744
MEN'S HCP			12	4	18	16	2	14	6	8	10		17	11	13	1	15	5	7	9	3		
PAR			4	4	3	4	5	3	4	4	5	36	4	4	4	5	3	4	5	3	4	36	72
RED	68.9	122	296	316	94	244	401	91	333	275	460	2510	231	320	284	478	108	334	419	107	340	2621	5131

wrapping around behind the elevated green. A bunker to the right front leaves precious little bail-out room.

The Champions Course is kept in splendid condition with fast, true greens that hold well and are generally receptive. The sand is particularly well maintained. The fairways are lush.

It's not everybody's cup of tea. Some good players—more men than women—say it's a little too easy. Golf Director Nancy Henderson conceded that it's open and forgiving. "The average golfer tends to prefer the Champions [Course] because you can hit it a little off line and still find your golf ball. On the Legends Course, if you hit it a little off line, you're not going to find your golf ball."

Don't be misled by the comparative openness of the Champions Course. It's a tournament-level track, tough enough to be the LPGA Tour's final qualifying course. It is deceptive, in that it's harder than it looks. There's good reason that very few of those world-class women hoping for the chance to make their living on the LPGA Tour walk away bemoaning how easy it is.

LEGENDS COURSE

Arthur Hills is a brilliant golf course designer. He manages to marry the technical and mechanical elements of modern golf course architecture with classic, traditional considerations that preserve the characteristics that contribute to the game's greatest courses designed by such masters as Dr. Alister MacKenzie and Donald Ross. It is his ability to meld the old and the new so successfully that define his greatness. The Legends Course at LPGA International is among his best.

The course is long, but not marathon length; it's difficult, but not unfair; it's undulating, serpentine, and contoured with abundant hazards, but it's not contrived or tricky for the mere sake of making players jump through hoops. Essentially, it's an amalgam of what nature put there and what man can enhance with modern machinery and tools, not an exercise in how much earth can be bulldozed.

There's no handshake or introduction. The opening hole is a precursor of what you're headed for. It's a medium par four with a green hidden behind hills. You can see the flag blowing in the breeze but not the putting surface. Natural terrain abuts the hole—to the right there are palmettos and scrub-brush, to the left a forest of pines through which the entire course is cut.

The 2nd is a long, tough par-five dogleg left, with a long thin fairway sand trap guarding the left length. That bunker fans out to brush the front and left of the green. All but women playing the most forward tees have a forced carry over a hazard to get into play. Your lay-up second must stay to the right for a clear look at the flag.

The best scoring opportunity on the Legends Course may well be the attractive little par-three 3rd. A least it gives you a breather before you tackle #4, a short but difficult par four. Your tee shot has to avoid water to the right and forest to the left and find an island of landing area. The hole favors a right-to-left drive; players like me, whose normal shot is left-to-right must take great pains to keep the ball in play. From the landing zone, your second shot must clear a marsh that intersects the fairway.

The dogleg left par-four 6th is a classic risk-reward hole with a lake in front of the tees. Each player must decide how much of the lake to carry, and thus how short to make the approach to the green. The putting surface is guarded by the lake on the left and a gaping hillside sand hazard on the right.

Number 7 is as beautiful as it is tough, uphill all the way. The long one-shot hole presents a chute of pines and oaks, over an expanse of man-eating vegetation, to the long, thin green. "It's very demanding, one that you'll remember after you've played it," said Golf Director Nancy Henderson, noting the "very narrow opening over marsh and an elevated green." She added proudly, "It's one of the best par threes in the state."

Number 8 is a par-five dogleg left

Your tee shot plays between towering trees on the long, uphill par-three 7th on the Legends Course at LPGA International.

around a lake. It's a three-shot hole for almost everybody. Two bunkers in front of the tees create a split fairway. The best drive stays just to the right of the bunkers. The small green is button-hooked around a corner of the lake, down in a little valley. Water to the left and a trio of strategically placed bunkers to the right lie in wait to catch stray golf balls.

The side finishes with a medium-length par four that can yield pars and birdies if you avoid the water hazard along the left. If you don't land on the slightly depressed green, miss it long; all of the serious trouble is in the front. The inward side opens with a fantastic par-four dogleg right, a visual feast from the tees. A marsh intersects the fairway in front of the green and requires a high, precise approach to the putting surface. Keep your tee shot left; anything that goes too far right will be blocked out by a stand of oaks.

A tight par four, a deceptive uphill par three, and a moderately long par four lead you to the par-five 14th. It's a dogleg right with a green that is down in a basin sunk behind pines and palmettos. Your lay-up second must be kept far enough left to open up the hole.

Number 15 is a semi-blind par three. A hill in front of the green obscures much of the putting surface from view, although the flag is visible from the tee boxes. The bunkers visible from the tees appear to be greenside, but they're not. They are a good twenty yards from the putting surface.

The 16th is the number one handicap hole, an enormous, long par five that plays to a lakeside green. Number 17 is a nice, straight hole that presents a fine scoring opportunity before you head to the brutally hard, but lovely, finisher. The 18th is a solid par four with a severe dogleg left. Trees guard the left side of the hole and your tee shot must be long enough to have a glimpse of the flag. The green sits behind a marsh and is framed by trees that guard the narrow opening to the putting surface like sentries. "It's another one of those holes that you'll remember for a long time," said Golf Director Nancy Henderson. No kidding! The smart money says if you can't see the flag on your second shot, lay the ball in front of the marsh and play for an up-and-down, rather than being heroic. This hole yields at least as many double- and triple-bogeys as it does pars and birdies.

Overall, architect Arthur Hills has created a brilliant golf course at LPGA International. Both courses—Champions Course and Legends Course—are great fun to play, but the Legends Course is worth a long detour for a wonderful golfing experience.

In addition to the world class golf, LPGA International has a lovely new clubhouse that's scheduled to open just about the time this book is released, along with a golf academy, and an award-winning pro shop.

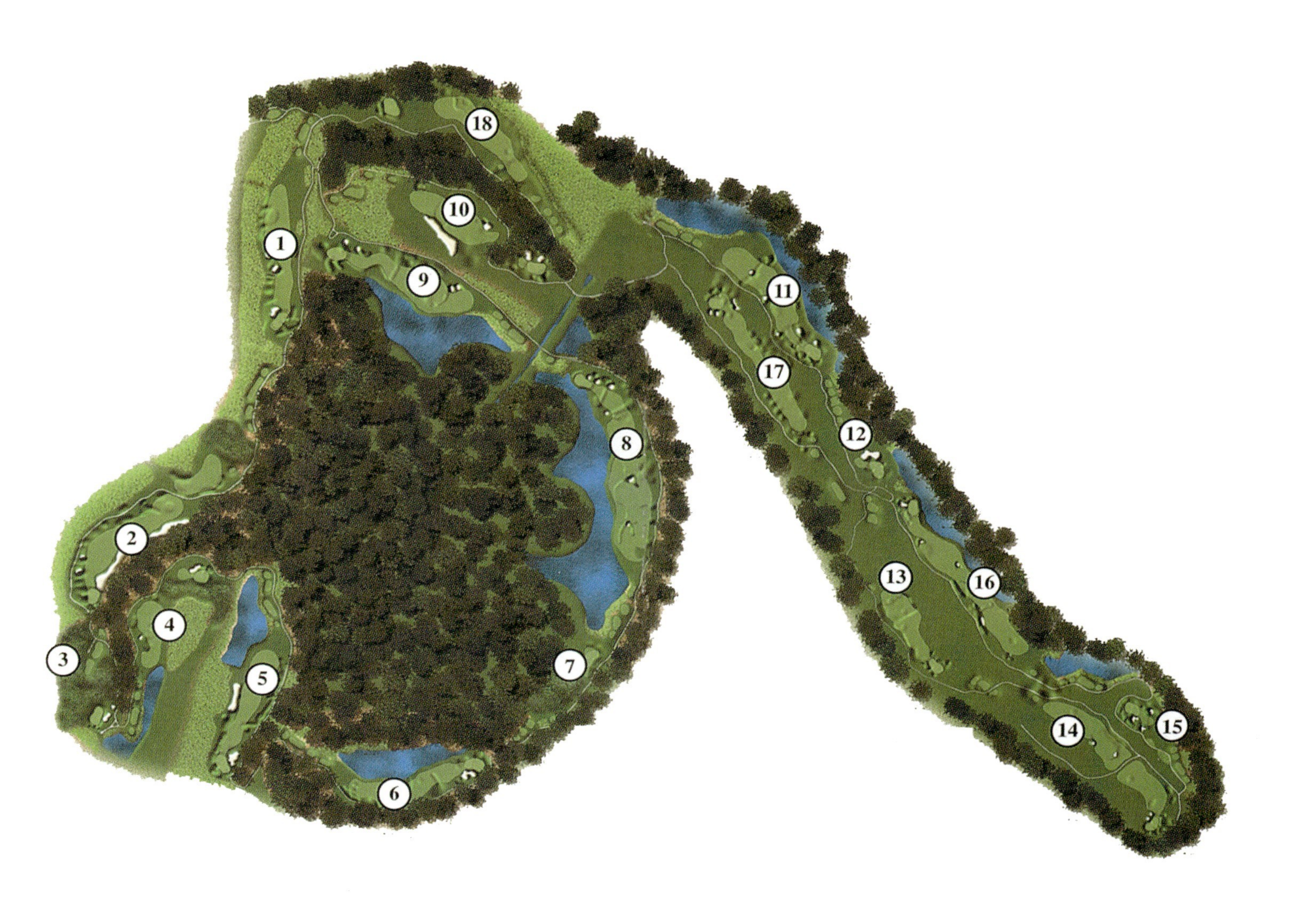

The Legends Course

HOLE	Ra	Sl	1	2	3	4	5	6	7	8	9	OUT	10	11	12	13	14	15	16	17	18	IN	TOT
BLACK	74.5	138	386	561	165	371	380	406	207	532	441	3449	406	410	185	393	531	195	567	434	414	3535	6984
BLUE	72.6	134	374	548	140	340	366	393	195	518	374	3248	371	381	168	378	516	177	539	419	397	3346	6594
WHITE	71.3(m)/77.3(w)	128(m)/144(w)	362	527	130	325	353	382	185	509	366	3139	356	370	149	368	502	164	510	407	374	3200	6339
GOLD	69.1(m)/73.8(w)	122(m)/132(w)	352	485	118	302	323	346	168	479	338	2911	314	329	130	350	482	140	496	335	340	2916	5827
MEN'S HCP		16	6	18	8	14	4	10	2	12			9	7	17	11	3	15	1	13	5		
PAR			4	5	3	4	4	4	3	5	4	36	4	4	3	4	5	3	5	4	4	36	72
RED	70.2	123	324	464	101	280	294	317	136	443	318	2677	262	311	113	224	397	125	441	313	292	2478	5155

MISSION INN GOLF & TENNIS RESORT

10400 County Road 48, Howey-in-the-Hills, Florida (From Florida Turnpike north, take exit 285; from Florida Turnpike south, take exit 289; follow state road 27 to state road 19 north, about 7 miles; entrance is on the left.)
Phone: (352) 324-3885

El Campion Architect: Charles Clarke   Year opened: 1926
Las Colinas Architect: Gary Koch   Year opened: 1992

El Campion course rating/Slope rating for men:
Blue—74.2/135   White—71.2/132
Gold—67.9/122

El Campion course rating/Slope rating for Women
Gold—73.3/136   Red—67.9/119

Las Colinas course rating/Slope rating for men:
Blue—73.3/132   White—70.1/125
Gold—66.1/113

Las Colinas course rating/Slope rating for women:
Gold—71.6/122   Red—67.5/110

Back in the early 20th century—before air conditioning, before interstate highways, before theme parks, or jet airplanes—there simply wasn't very much in central Florida except 'skeeters, gators, and snakes. That was to change with the vision of a wheeler-dealer from Illinois named William J. Howey. William J. Howey was determined to build an empire based on a new industry—oranges.

So in 1916, the Illinois entrepreneur bought some 60,000 acres in Florida's Lake County, prime citrus land with sandy soil and an ideal climate. Howey figured he would sell the land in small parcels at a big profit and then get the buyers to hire Howey's company to clear the land and plant, tend, and harvest the oranges. Howey dispatched a sales force of about 200 to peddle his notion to mostly northern investors. Those Yankees, in turn, they were invited to Howey's tent city for a first-hand look at this new agricultural bonanza.

Not surprisingly, many of the up-scale investors found tent living in rural and isolated central Florida a little too rustic. Howey had an answer. In 1924, he built the 75-room Hotel Floridan to pamper his prospective investors. Two years later Charles Clarke of Scotland's renowned Royal Troon Golf Course was hired to build a golf course on the property to provide some recreation.

The economic boom of the roaring '20s, however, was on a collision course with disaster. In 1929, the stock market crashed, the Great Depression hit, and to add insult to injury, central Florida suffered one of the most prolonged and severe freezes in history, killing thousands of citrus trees. It also killed William Howey's dreams of an empire.

But the hotel and golf course remained, albeit not treated kindly by weather or time. The fortunes of the old place were reversed in 1969 when it was bought by business executive Nick Beucher, who undertook a multi-million dollar project of restoration and expansion. The result was the resurrection of one of Florida's oldest resorts and a modern, full-service facility that offers fine accommodations, good food, and top-notch amenities—most notably the golf.

EL CAMPION

Golf course construction back in the 1920s was a far cry from what it is today. Golf course architects were limited in how much earth they could move and how much of what Mother Nature put there could be recreated, reworked, or redesigned. Men with saws and axes cut the dense Florida trees and brush; the land was leveled by tractors or horses pulling crude timber contraptions. If the flow of a stream or the banks of a lake were to be revised, it had to be done by hand.

As it turned out, the tract of land on which Scottish designer Charles Clarke was hired to work was highly unusual for Florida in that it sits in one of the only hilly areas of the state. Most of Florida is fairly flat, requiring modern golf course architects to impose elevation changes on the terrain, a feat not possible in the 1920s. But Clarke had a rich topographical expanse on which to construct the golf course that became known as El Campion—"The Champion."

The course is old-fashioned in the very best sense of the word. The tees and greens are close together—convenient for the golfer of the 1920s who had never heard of a golf cart. The feel of the place is very much like a British or Irish parkland golf course, although you are reminded that you are in a very different part of the world by the moss-laden trees, the palms, and the humidity. The outgoing nine is a par 35 (36 for women); the back side features three par fives and is a whopping par 37.

The opening three holes provide a good appetizer for the banquet that awaits. The opener is a short, but extremely tight par five. Your tee shot must be to the right-center or your second will be blocked by a pair of towering ancient pines that occupy the left side of the fairway about 225 yards from the green. The hole constricts to ribbon-thinness as you approach the putting surface with water on both sides of the smallish green. Number 2 is a medium length par three tightly guarded by water right and a pair of bunkers in front of the slightly elevated green. The 3rd is a long dogleg left par four. Men drive through a chute of leafy old trees and a huge fairway bunker sits about driving distance on the right.

It is the long par-four 4th that gives you your first real taste of the elevation changes on El Campion. The hole plays straight uphill. If it's not mountain golf, it's as close as you'll get in the Sunshine State. Number 4 is reminiscent of several holes at Cascades in Hot Springs, Virginia, or Banff in Alberta, Canada. Your drive must carry a lake to start the uphill climb. In the style of many early 1900s golf courses, all the trouble is taken

Your drive on the par-four 5th at Mission Inn's El Campeon is from hillside tees, into a valley, and back uphill to the green.

out of play for women. The forward markers simply start the uphill trek on the drive, *sans* lake. The neck of the green is narrowed with bunkers on both sides. The locals advise at least one club and often two more than you might normally use on the approach because of the severity of the uphill angle. The small green is pitched back toward the fairway and back down the hill.

The walk to the next tees reveals a lovely panorama laid out against the backdrop of elevation changes. Terraced tees play into a valley; your second shot is back uphill to an elevated, extremely undulating green with the resort complex behind it. Number 6 tees off from hillside tees into a valley with fairway bunkers narrowing the landing area precipitously. It's parallel to the previous hole and almost a mirror image of it.

The 7th is a long, difficult par four. You drive from hilltop tees down toward a canal that intersects the fairway about 165 yards from the green. The long thin two tiered hillside green is guarded by sand hazards right and left. It completes a quartet of visually stunning par fours.

Number 8 is a lovely one-shot hole that demands a forced carry over water to a green that has been wedged into a pond. A gigantic bunker caresses the left. On this hole it's easier to hit the small green from the elevated tees than try to find a place to bail out. A short par four then presents a marvelous scoring opportunity from which to make the turn.

The back nine on El Campion opens with a long, tight par five with water down the right. Your second shot here is critical, as an enormous old oak stands guard where the dogleg bends to the right, about 145 yards from the green. Your shot must be far enough left to avoid being blocked by the oak, but not so far left that you find a large fairway bunker. The well-protected green is a Donald Ross-style turtleback, a slightly elevated green with an embankment around it that will reject any approach shot that doesn't find the putting surface.

Number 11 is a solid par-four dogleg left with a blind tee shot and a downhill approach. The green has no bunkers around it, but it is a classic Scottish-style parkland green. The front is fairly level, inviting a run-up or bump-and-run approach, but the sides of the long thin green are sloped and will cascade a shot that misses right or left into deep rough. The green is pitched away from the fairway, the back half substantially lower than the front.

An uphill par three takes you to the par-four 13th. It's a short hole in terms of yardage, but the force of gravity makes it longer. You tee off from the base of a hill—and across a pond for men, not for women—to the green high above. It is among the most dramatic elevation changes on a single hole in the state of Florida, some 85 feet. To make matters even more arduous, the fairway is constricted by a trio of bunkers left and one big sandy monster right, about 130 yards from the green. If you don't hit your tee shot far enough up the hill, your approach will be blind. All you'll see from the fairway is the flag fluttering in the breeze. The long, thin British parkland-style green—with no bunkers around it—is pitched sharply back down the hill. Take enough club. I opted for three clubs more than I would normally hit and just barely made it into a slight breeze.

Number 14 is a short par five dogleg right that a big hitter can consider going for in two. Your tee shot is downhill. A pond guards the right side and defines the bend in the dogleg. Trees hug the left and are replaced by a series of bunkers from about 175 yards to the green. The green is slightly elevated and offset to the right behind a giant old oak tree and a bunker. If you are playing a lay-up second, keep it far enough left to open up the green for your approach. If you're going for it in two, a big left-to-right shot is needed to avoid the tree.

Two short holes follow: A par three to a green peninsulaed into a lake and a par four on which many players opt for something other than a driver off the tee. Catch your breath before you tackle the magnificent 17th. It is the signature hole on El Campion, rated the most difficult on the course for men and women. They call it "the Devil's Delight." It's a double dogleg that is perilously tight and demanding from tee to green. The margin for error on any shot is zero. The key here is to put your second shot to the right of the towering old oak, ominously named "Devil's Grasp," that stands at the left side of the fairway about 100 yards from the green. Your approach is an exercise in how well you can control your nerves and how much fear you can tolerate. The shot is to a wide, elevated, highly contoured green, across a gaping bunker and a lake. Walk away with a par here and you can be well satisfied.

Number 18 is a risk-reward finisher with a lake down the right length of the dogleg right. The long, thin green is guarded by trees on the left and bunkers right. It's a brilliant finish to an exhilarating golf course.

El Campion is a marvelous classical layout. It has a feel and texture unlike any other course in Florida. It is the kind of course that you remember long after you've played it, the kind of course that when you think about it you simply can't wait to go back and play it again. "It never goes out of style," said long-time head pro John Viera. If you're anywhere in central Florida, El Campion is a must.

El Campeon

HOLE	Ra	Sl	1	2	3	4	5	6	7	8	9	OUT	10	11	12	13	14	15	16	17	18	IN	TOT
BLUE	74.2	135	503	176	460	405	450	398	448	190	349	3379	569	431	240	340	514	142	347	538	423	3544	6923
WHITE	71.2	132	467	168	367	374	382	364	421	155	334	3032	495	374	164	332	477	138	317	518	388	3300	6292
GOLD	67.9(m)/73.3(w)	122(m)/136(w)	422	163	308	335	360	308	367	140	318	2721	414	359	152	237	432	125	301	498	369	2887	5608
MEN'S HCP		8	16	12	6	4	14	2	10	18			5	17	9	13	7	15	11	1	3		
MEN'S PAR		5	3	4	4	4	4	4	3	4	35	5	4	3	4	5	3	4	5	4	37	72	
RED	67.9	119	353	115	247	241	293	257	367	100	283	2256	409	343	123	237	386	140	236	436	281	2555	4811
WOMEN'S HCP	14	18	12	4	2	10	6	8	16			3	15	17	11	5	13	9	1	7			
WOMEN'S PAR	5	3	4	4	4	4	5	3	4	36		5	4	3	4	5	3	4	5	4	37	73	

On Las Colinas at Mission Inn, the toughest hole on the course is the par-five 12th. The fairway is tightened by trees on both sides.

LAS COLINAS

In Spanish Las Colinas means "the hills" and is an apt name for this lovely golf course designed in 1992 by PGA Tour star Gary Koch. It's a different style of golf course than its older neighbor, a more open and user-friendly course. "We already had a difficult course," said head pro John Viera who tenure had begun at Mission Inn before 1992 and who oversaw the construction of the new course. He said it's almost impossible to compare Las Colinas and El Campion. "They're so different, you wouldn't even know they were on the same piece of real estate," he said. That is not to suggest that Las Colinas is a pushover by any stretch of the imagination. It is a very solid, challenging, interesting par 72 golf course that will require all of your course management skills and shot-making prowess.

Unlike El Campion, this is a modern golf course with long distances between greens and tees, lots of man-made mounding and contours, and an abundance of strategically placed sand and water. Architect Koch leads you into Las Colinas gently with a straight par four without much trouble and a medium length par three. It starts to get more challenging the deeper you go. The par five 3rd is a dogleg right with a wetland running the entire right length of the hole. And the long par-four 4th with a generous fairway and a difficult approach shot, is a real test. The long, thin green is two-tiered, guarded by bunkers left and a steep drop-off to the right.

But it is not until you get to the par-five, dogleg right 5th that you sample the full flavor of Las Colinas. It is a visually lovely hole, with dense forest down the right. While it's not grotesquely long, it is a difficult hole to attempt to go for in two shots. A pond with a rocky embankment sits in front of an enormous long, thin, three tiered green. It is just shy of 50 yards from front to back. Trees stand at both sides of the pond, creating a window through which you must hit your approach. As if that's not enough, bunkers guard the right and left of the green.

Number 6 is a beautiful one-shot hole over water and rocks to a small well-bunkered green. The next, a par four, requires men to drive through a chute of oaks and pines to a narrow fairway. The hole plays more easily for women who do not have to negotiate the trees on their tee shots.

Two more par fours finish the side. Number 8 is a long and fairly straight. The green, however, is hooked to the left behind a big bunker and a lake, which guards the left side of the hole from about 150 yards out. The green is divided by a ridge. The 9th is a perilous short hole, one of the tightest in Gary Koch's design. Your tee shot—men and women—must thread its way between stands of trees and across a marsh to a fairway the width of a country lane. There's a wetland to the left and pines to the right. The shallow green, which is angled to the left, is protected by bunkers at the left and a marsh to the right rear. Don't be too long here.

The back nine opens with a pair of par fours. Number 11 is a short par four that presents an excellent scoring opportunity for women. It plays only 263 yards from the Red Tees.

They call the par-five 12th "Alligator Alley." It is not as long as it is tight and dangerous. Any shot that strays will find dreadful trouble, mostly in the form of trees that line the fairway. In addition, architect Koch left several tall pines in the fairway, itself. Pines to the left and oaks to the right join forces to narrow the entrance to the green.

Number 13 is a severe dogleg left with a blind tee shot. It's a risk-reward hole that favors a right-to-left tee shot. About 100 yards from the green, a creek intersects the fairway. Long hitting women playing the forward markers must be careful not to drive into the creek, and something other than a driver may be the best club selection.

Two par threes are interrupted by a par four. Number 14 plays uphill to a green that is a shelf, sculpted out of the side of the hill. This is a slight dogleg left intersected by a marshy creek about 100 yards from the elevated green. And Number 16 is a long par threewith the smallest greenonLas Colinas.

The course wraps up with solid par four dogleg right followed by the longest hole on the golf course. Only such players as Tiger Woods or Ernie Els will contemplate going for this one in two. Your second shot plays across a marshy wetland that is tightened by ranks of trees on both sides. Your approach is to a green in the shape of an inverted pear that is offset to the right behind a gaping bunker to the right and two more to the left and rear. Par this one and you can leave the hills of central Florida well pleased.

In all, Las Colinas is fine, fair, and fun, an excellent challenge for men and women. While it is not as difficult as El Campion, it is certainly worth your time to play it while your at Mission Inn.

Las Colinas

HOLE	Ra	Sl	1	2	3	4	5	6	7	8	9	OUT	10	11	12	13	14	15	16	17	18	IN	TOT
BLUE	73.3	132	396	208	511	432	500	175	420	416	380	3438	415	368	493	441	174	421	194	389	561	3438	6894
WHITE	70.1	125	376	150	481	386	463	142	327	381	362	3068	383	342	452	363	144	389	182	372	510	3137	6205
GOLD	66.1(m)/71.6(w)	113(m)/122(w)	356	140	431	361	437	118	307	368	340	2858	291	314	425	330	125	368	151	318	426	2748	5606
MEN'S HCP		16	10	8	2	6	18	12	4	14			11	15	1	5	17	7	13	9	3		
PAR			4	3	5	4	5	3	4	4	4	36	4	4	5	4	3	4	3	4	5	36	72
RED	67.5	110	280	124	352	307	337	94	259	299	283	2335	284	263	301	283	106	271	107	294	408	2317	4652
WOMEN'S HCP		14	18	12	6	4	8	16	2	10			13	17	3	7	15	9	11	5	1		

ORANGE COUNTY NATIONAL GOLF CENTER AND LODGE

16301 Phil Ritson Way, Winter Garden, Florida (From Florida Turnpike take exit 272, go east one mile on route 50, turn right onto County Road 545 and go south for about 9 1/2 miles to entrance on the left.)
Phone: (407) 656-2626 or (888) PAR-3672

Panther Lake Architects: Phil Ritson, Isao Aoki, Dave Harman Year opened: 1997
Crooked Cat Architects: Phil Ritson, Isao Aoki, Dave Harman Year opened: 1999

Panther Lake course rating/Slope rating:
White—75.7/137 Blue—73.2/132
Green—70.7/128 Red—71.5/125

Crooked Cat course rating/Slope rating:
White—75.4/140 Blue—72.9/134
Green—69.3/121 Red—70.3/120

If you're looking for a full service resort—four-star restaurants, Olympic pool, spa, wall to wall servants—you're in the wrong place. There's only one reason to come out to Orange County National Golf Center and Lodge: golf, golf, and more golf. The drive out to the facility looks as if you're headed into the middle of rural central Florida. The reality is that it's only a short drive and a chip-shot from Orlando and all of its attractions. Leave the non-golfers behind to do other things, but golfers—from beginners to pros—shouldn't miss this place.

In addition to a pair of world class championship golf courses, there's a nine hole executive length course (called "The Tooth"), a 36 hole putting course (called "Whiskers"), a 42 acre practice facility (which hasn't been given a feline moniker yet), the Phil Ritson Golf Institute, a comfortable 50 room lodge, and a pleasant new clubhouse. The pro shop is well stocked. The staff is among the most knowledgeable and friendly in the state. The grounds crews treat each player's shots with the respect and courtesy usually reserved for a major championship, and they keep the golf courses in superb condition.

Not to diminish the importance of the supporting cast, the stars of the show at Orange County National are the two beautiful golf courses. They are long and challenging for players of every ability. They feature enough topographical variation to create an interesting and appealing texture and feel—Panther Lake has 60 feet of elevation changes and Crooked Cat has 50 feet. While hazards abound, there is nothing artificial or contrived about either course. They are exceptionally well designed. Both play to a par 72.

For the pros and wannabes, they're both more than 7,200 yards from the back tees. For average players, they are not so difficult that you'll feel like you've served a prison sentence or been beaten up when you've finished, but you'll know you've been tested. Short-iron accuracy will be rewarded; stray shots will often result in penalty strokes.

For women, both courses are fair and demanding, with careful placement of the women's tees and enough variation in yardage on each hole to require a battery of shots with your full arsenal of clubs. Panther Lake is the more difficult for women because of forced carries and difficult approach shots; Crooked Cat is the longer of the two.

PANTHER LAKE

For a relatively new golf course, Panther Lake has amassed an impressive list of awards and honors, and deservedly so. But the public accolades don't tell the full story of just how good this golf course is. This is a course you will remember fondly long after you've played it. It's long and tight, with abundant sand, marsh, and water. The greens are big and highly contoured and they are fast.

From the terraced hilltop opening tees the golf course—with all of its hills and valleys—lays before you. You drive down a substantial hill and then back up to the green. Three long, highly contoured bunkers are angled across the fairway and you must place your tee shot either short of them or over them. The elevated green is multi-level. Welcome to Panther Lake.

The short par-five 2nd hole is visually delightful and offers a generous landing area. Big hitters thinking about going for it in two would be well advised to bring their shot in from left-to-right. Average players laying up should play just short of the lake in front of the green to set up a high, soft approach. The hillside green above the lake is surrounded by bunkers.

The toughest hole on Panther Lake for men is the long, long par four #3. It's a straight hole until you get to the green which is hooked to the left behind a creek that intersects the fairway. The embankment on both sides of the hazard is extremely steep, making the area from about 50 yards out to the collar a no-man's-land.

A solid par three with an extremely long, thin green follows and leads you to a par four with a difficult approach. The green is pinched by a marshy wetland to the right and a stand of ancient oaks to the left, whose canopies almost overhang the putting surface. The green is only about 12 yards wide at its waist, but it is just shy of 50 yards from front to back. Number 6 is a short but dangerous par three.

The 7th is an obstacle course that sets up as a three shot hole for almost everybody. It's rated the toughest hole on the course for women. A live oak grows in the left-center of the fairway. Keep your tee shot right of the tree. A marshy area comes into play about 175 yards from the green. The ideal second is aimed at a fan of bunkers on the hillside at the point where the fairway turns left toward the green. That area provides a comfortable look at the flag, otherwise you'll have some of the marsh to carry.

They call the 8th hole "Pot Bunkers" because there's a field of them in front of the elevated green. This is not a hole on which you want to come up short.

Your shot to the green on the long par-three 6th at Orange County National's Panther Lake must clear an expanse of marsh and sand.

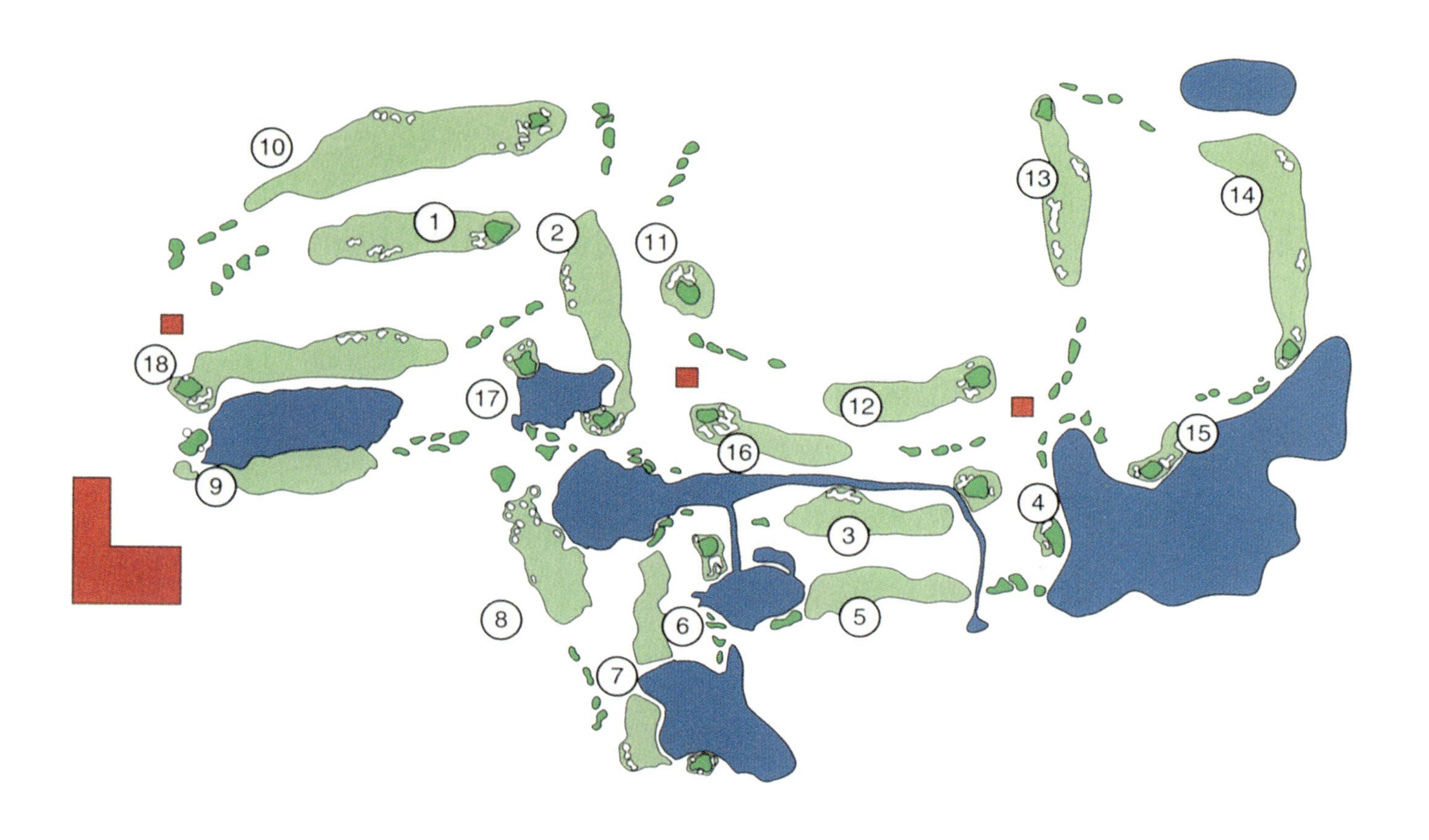

Panther Lake

HOLE	Ra	Sl	1	2	3	4	5	6	7	8	9	OUT	10	11	12	13	14	15	16	17	18	IN	TOT
WHITE	75.7	137	459	515	470	200	405	186	562	428	430	3655	520	228	439	441	622	227	426	167	570	3640	7295
BLUE	73.2	132	431	496	450	185	377	159	550	398	400	3446	485	206	416	419	573	193	389	160	529	3370	6816
GREEN	70.7	128	409	472	414	170	355	130	536	359	368	3213	440	181	385	390	539	162	369	135	484	3085	6298
MEN'S HCP		7	11	1	13	9	17	5	15	3			16	2	12	4	6	8	14	18	10		
PAR			4	5	4	3	4	3	5	4	4	36	5	3	4	4	5	3	4	3	5	36	72
RED	71.5	125	349	397	317	127	316	104	388	287	313	2598	381	141	283	294	438	127	296	104	432	2496	5094
WOMEN'S HCP		11	3	9	15	5	17	1	13	7			6	12	14	10	2	18	8	16	4		

Number 9 is a dogleg right par four with a lake along the right length of the hole. A bit of the hazard must be cleared in order to reach the two-tiered green. The left tier is higher than the right and feeds almost all shots from left-to-right.

The back side on Panther Lake features three par threes, three par fours, and three par fives. The 10th is an uphill par five with a well-protected green. Add a club on your approach because of the elevation change. What follows is the longest one-shot hole on Panther Lake. It plays across a little valley to an elevated green guarded in front by a huge, serpentine bunker. Two long par fours, both of them uphill, lead you to the lovely 14th. Your tee shot on this very long hole—622 yards from the back tees and 438 for women—is from a terraced set of tee boxes, into a valley. The hole arcs to the right around a high hill. The green is squeezed by a bunker with a trio of palm trees growing in it on the left and a steep hill on the right. Don't be too bold here as the steep embankment at the back of the green leads down to a lake.

The 15th is another solid par three with a lake and marsh along the left and intruding enough between tee and green that a forced carry may be required depending on pin placement. Number 16 is a par four with a blind tee shot uphill approach a well-bunkered green.

The short par three 17th is a good scoring hole and can put you in a very positive frame of mind for the home stretch. You drive on the par five finishing hole to a narrow plateau of fairway. The green sits above a lake with hillside bunkers above the putting surface to the right.

Panther Lake is a golf course that makes you feel good, makes you glad that you play the game. It is difficult but fair. But most of all it is fun.

CROOKED CAT

There is hardly anything to dislike about Crooked Cat. It's scenic. It's demanding. The greens are true and fast, ranging in size from merely large to gigantic. Good shots are rewarded. Bad shots will cause you anguish and cost you strokes. From the opener to the long par four 18th, it is a memorable golf experience.

Your round starts with a short, straight par five. The fairway splits about 120 yards in front of the green; a hillside of rough gives you the option of playing the high plateau or the valley. The left option is the more favorable. The two-tiered green is smallish—by Crooked Cat standards—and offset to the left. You then climb to an elevated series of tees. The fairway is ample on your first shot; the trouble is all in front of the hilltop green. Nine bunkers lie between the landing zone and a successful approach to the triple-tiered putting surface.

A short par four with a huge elevated green sets the stage for the toughest hole on the course for both men and women. Number 4 is a three-shot hole for all but the biggest boomers. It gets progressively narrower as you approach the two-tiered green. A ridge runs from the front of the putting surface to back, the left side is substantially higher than the right.

The next three holes are both pleasant to look at and challenging to play. Number 5 is a short par four dogleg right. The green is divided by a swail that runs from front to back—take note of where the pin is placed. Then comes a tough, uphill par three that requires a forced carry over a sandy wilderness between the tee boxes and the green. The par-four 7th demands accuracy from the tee. The fairway is a plateau with drop-offs on both sides. An elevation change, a giant step with an area of rough in the middle, splits the fairway about 100 yards from the green. The putting surface is protected by a gigantic long bunker, a unique design that looks like a pitch fork designed by Salvador Dali, with a thin runway of grass separating the sandy tines.

Heading to the turn, the 8th is a long par three that's called "The Pit." Elevated tees play to an elevated, hillside green. Take enough club—you don't want to have to hit a second shot from down in the valley. The 9th hole is a medium-length par four dogleg left around a lake. The green is hooked onto a hillside above a pair of bunkers that separate the putting surface from the water. It's a demanding hole in that the landing area is compressed by a cluster of hillside bunkers to the right and a long lakeside bunker down an embankment to the left.

The back side opens with a trio of moderate-length par fours. On the 10th, an oak tree, that looks innocuous enough from the tees, stands about 150 yards from the green along the left side of the fairway and can cause problems if you drift over that way. The next hole plays to a mesa and then over a hill. From the tees, you can just barely see the flag off in the distance. Your tee shot needs to remain short of the 150-yard marker, as the fairway drops off and gives way to rough and a field of mounds leading to the green. The 12th is a tough test. A lake with a marshy bank plays along the right length of the hole and a wedge of the wetland intrudes dangerously into the fairway. The two-tiered green is angled to the right behind a sweep of the marsh and water.

On Crooked Cat at Orange County National, the 2nd green is guarded by a minefield of bunkers.

Number 13 is a lovely par three that requires all players to play across a lake to an elevated green. The 14th is rated the easiest hole on the golf course, unusual for a par five. Two difficulties: the green is uphill, and a little marshy area extends almost across the fairway about 175 yards from the green. A fine one-shot hole that plays from elevated, terraced tees down to a well-bunkered green follows, leading to the par-four 16th. It's uphill all the way to an elevated, hilltop green.

Number 17 is a dogleg right par five that's short enough that a lot of players will think about going for it in two. But it's longer than it appears, playing uphill to the green. Gravity will prevent most shots from running up to the plateaued putting surface. If you're hitting a lay-up, beware of the waste bunker that intrudes into the fairway about 175 yards from the flag.

On the final hole, you drive across an expanse of waste area to a generous fairway. In front of the green, grassy indentations and pot bunkers await any shot that comes up short. It is, nonetheless, a good scoring hole on which to finish and head to the inviting clubhouse for refreshment.

When I finished playing both courses, one of the guys who wiped down my clubs asked which one I preferred. My honest answer was that I liked them both. Both are simply lovely, challenging golf courses. I thought Panther Lake was the tougher of the two, but Crooked Cat is hardly a pussycat.

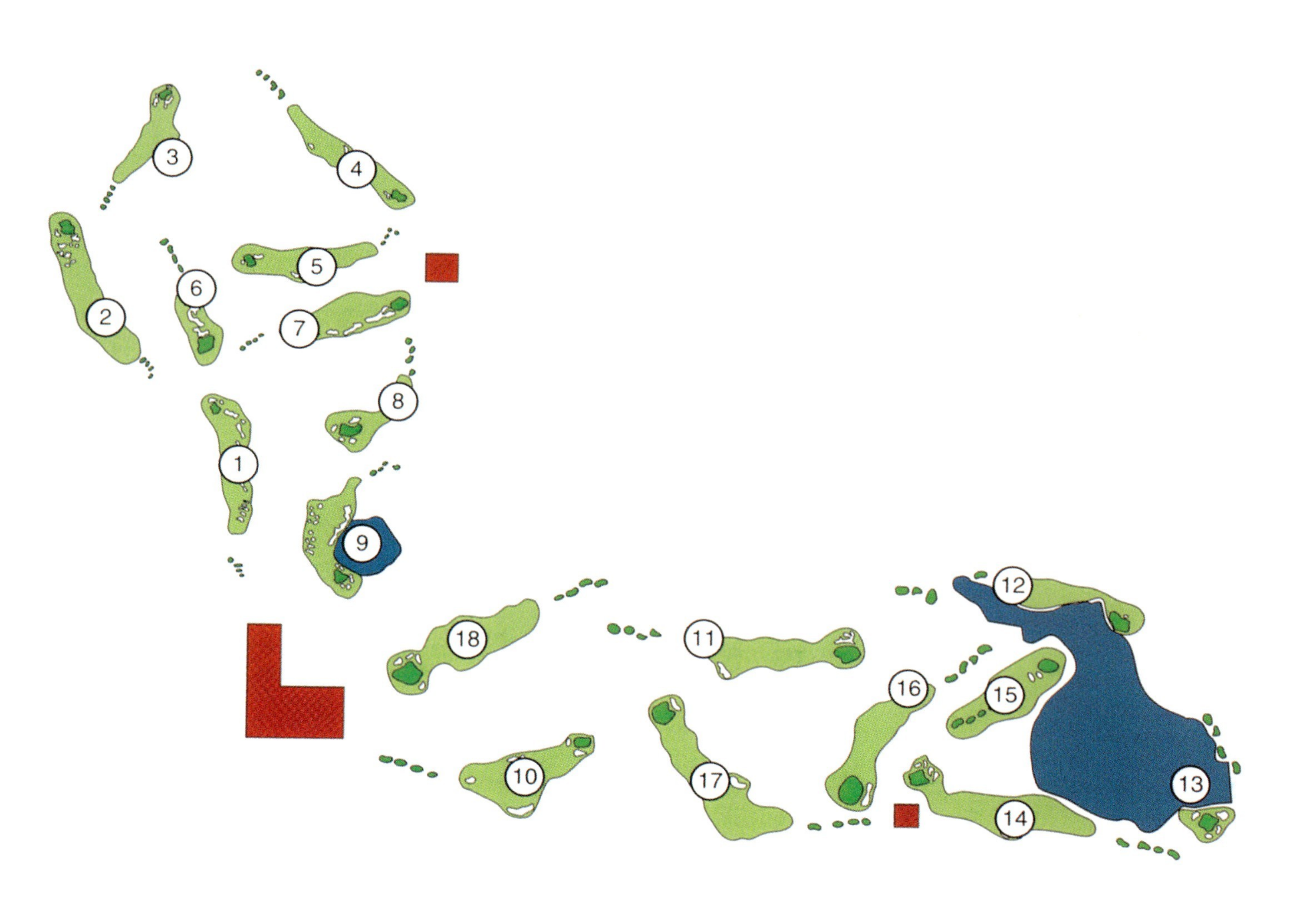

Crooked Cat

HOLE	Ra	SL	1	2	3	4	5	6	7	8	9	OUT	10	11	12	13	14	15	16	17	18	IN	TOT
WHITE	75.4	140	503	439	396	544	403	204	414	217	400	3520	459	446	461	210	528	235	454	506	458	3757	7277
BLUE	72.9	134	481	400	369	506	374	180	389	199	375	3273	426	415	417	185	480	210	432	480	430	3475	6748
GREEN	69.3	121	438	357	344	447	334	145	367	171	324	2927	375	370	373	163	423	179	400	423	402	3108	6035
MEN'S HCP		17	3	13	1	11	15	7	5	9			10	12	2	4	18	14	6	16	8		
PAR			5	4	4	5	4	3	4	3	4	36	4	4	4	3	5	3	4	5	4	36	72
RED	70.3	120	413	330	293	413	296	129	329	121	279	2603	327	318	279	90	372	153	375	372	347	2633	5236
WOMEN'S HCP		3	15	17	1	13	11	9	7	5			12	10	2	4	18	8	6	16	14		

Architect Tom Fazio uses natural and man-made hazards to enhance the visual impact and the shot-making challenges on the South Course at PGA Golf Club. This is the par-five 6th hole.

PGA GOLF CLUB

1916 Perfect Dr., Port St. Lucie, Florida (From I-95 take exit 63C and go west about a half mile; follow signs to the clubhouse.)
Phone: (800) 800-4653

South Course Architect: Tom Fazio Year opened: 1996
North Course Architect: Tom Fazio Year opened: 1996
Dye Course Architect: Pete Dye Year opened: 1999

South Course rating/Slope rating for men:
Black—74.3/141 Gold—72.3/137
Gray—70.1/129 Blue—67.5/123
Green—67.6/123

South Course rating/Slope rating for women:
Blue—72.5/129 Green—68.7/119

North Course rating/Slope rating for men:
Black—73.8/133 Gold—72.1/129
Gray—70.1/124 Blue—67.5/118
Green—67.5/118

North Course rating/Slope rating for women:
Blue—72.8/125 Green—68.8/114

Dye Course rating/Slope rating for men:
Black—74.7/133 Gold—72.4/128
Gray—69.3/123 Blue—67.8/121
Green—64.6/113

Dye Course rating/Slope rating for women:
Blue—71.7/122 Green—67.8/109

There's just not much about the PGA Golf Club that a serious golfer won't like. It's modern. It's high-tech. It's efficient, friendly, accommodating, and reasonably priced. From the moment you're told that you can't tip the folks who unload your clubs onto the golf cart to the moment they tell you again that they don't take tips for cleaning your clubs and putting them back in your trunk after your round, the place is first class.

That is not to suggest that the three courses that make up the PGA Golf Club don't get a lot of play. They do. But the facility is managed in such a way that it doesn't seem like a golf factory or assembly line. In fact, one of the best policies of the PGA Golf Club is the constant reminders from the starters and rangers that pace of play is a high priority.

In addition to top-notch player management, the golf courses themselves are kept in superb condition, with good, fast greens and manicured fairways. From the pro shop to the grounds keepers, the staff is unfailingly courteous and knowledgeable.

SOUTH COURSE

There are better-known golf courses in Florida than this Tom Fazio gem, but few are better tests of the game. The South Course at the PGA Golf Club requires good game management to score. It rewards good shots, and punishes those that stray. It is difficult and demanding, while remaining fair to players of most skill levels. This is simply not a course for the rankest beginners.

There isn't much in the way of hidden hazards or unexpected trouble. What you see is what you get, although what you see is occasionally enough to make you weak in the knees. The fairways are narrow. There's lots of water and wetland. The greens vary in size and are uniformly receptive, fast and true.

Fazio does not provide much of a handshake on the South Course. It's right to business from the 1st tee. The opening hole is a long par five dogleg left with a blind tee shot. The green is hidden among the palms and pines. It's 40 yards long, perilously thin, highly contoured, and canted steeply from back to front. Your second shot needs to stay right of center to prevent your approach from being blocked.

Number 2 is a long par four, slight dogleg right with a generous landing area from the tees. The fairway then constricts the closer to the green you get. The small, oval green is itself a hillside shelf with mounds above the putting surface to the right and a sheer drop into a cavernous bunker to the left. There's a basin in front of the green that makes a run-up shot all but impossible. It's rated the toughest hole on the course.

A par four and par three respectively lead you into the heart of the course. Number 3 is moderately long with a pair of strategically placed fairway bunkers right and left about driving distance. A ridge splits the fairway about 75 yards in front of the green. The one-shot 4th is long. For women the forward markers measure 145 yards from tee to green, but there's a bail-out room in front.

The par-four 5th is the only hole on the South Course without a single sand trap. That does not mean there aren't enough opportunities for trouble. The mounded fairway offers precious few flat lies. Close to the long, thin two-tiered green the left side of the fairway is guarded by water.

Play the watery par three and get ready for the par-five 7th. While long hitters can make it in two, the locals tell you that it generally rewards accuracy more than brute strength. The entire left length of the hole is a mosaic of sand, water and mounds. The right features three huge and well-positioned fairway bunkers and dense forest. The lake arcs around the left and back of the undulating kidney-shaped green, and five deep bunkers lie in wait to catch approach shots that fail to find the putting surface.

The 8th hole is a unique little par four with two greens and sand, marsh, and water everywhere. Long hitters should consider something other than a driver on this hole. But the key to success is to determine which of two tiny greens is in play. The left green—the tougher of the two to approach—sits behind a long waste bunker and a small swamp. The entrance to the right green is protected by that same waste bunker and another greenside sand hazard to the right. The ideal approach to the left green is down the left-center of the fairway. The ideal approach to the right green is over the big fairway bunker on the right.

Number 9 gives you a little break off the tee, but the wide, shallow green is at the base of a hill, tucked behind a deep bunker and a lake. It's is a beautiful hole on which to finish the outgoing nine and takes you to a short gentle par four with which to start the back side. The green is elevated above two steep-faced bunkers right and left, and the green itself is domed, making it hard to hold with precision.

The next hole is a solid par three playing to a wide, shallow green, protected on the right by sand and water and by deep grass bunkers and collection basins to the left. That leads to the par-four 12th, which is extremely tight. A dense forest waits to snare any shot that drifts off the fairway to the right. A giant fairway sand trap looms menacingly about driving distance down the left.

The long, dogleg left par-five 13th demands an accurate tee shot to avoid the sand and the water. Your lay-up second is a risk-reward shot depending on how close to the green you try to get. The closer you go the more trouble there is. The green itself is nestled between hills.

Two interesting par fours follow. Number 14 is brutal—long and dangerous. The long, thin green lies behind a valley, with marsh to the right. It's the second hardest hole on the course. "I treat it like a short par five," said my playing partner from Detroit, who plays the course several times a year. "I think I've only parred it once." The 15th is a severe dogleg right around a lake. It's a short hole on which many players use something other than a driver. Approach shots that fail to find the hilltop green, risk sliding off into the huge bunker or the lake to the right.

Number 16 is the shortest of the four par fives, but architect Tom Fazio has employed an array of difficulties to make it a challenge. It's a dogleg left with a small green. The only place to put your tee shot—to avoid the trees right, water left, and fairway bunkers on both sides—is down the middle. The fairway, itself, is a mesa on the top of a ridge, with both sides beveled steeply toward trouble. The small green is button-hooked behind a vast lakeside waste bunker.

Number 17 is a long par three for men, but plays only 101 yards from the forward tees and provides a good scoring opportunity for women. That sets the stage for a beautiful, but tough finisher. It's a sharp dogleg right par four with a narrow landing area from the tees and a long thin green sitting amid bunkers at the side of a lake. Your drive must land precisely between the huge waste bunker on the right and the forest on the left. Ideal placement is just about adjacent to the fairway bunker that architect Fazio has placed at just about driving distance for everybody.

There are a lot of good Tom Fazio golf courses in Florida, but the South Course at the PGA Golf Club is simply spectacular. Fazio is utterly brilliant in his use of water, marsh, sand, and topographical contours to merge nature and the handiwork of man into a marvelous golf experience. It's a delight to the eye. It's fair from every set of tees. Yet it will test the skills of even the very best touring pros. This course is worth a special detour and deserves to be high on your "must play" list in the Sunshine State.

NORTH COURSE

Tom Fazio's North Course at the PGA Golf Club is not quite as demanding as his South, but it is still top-notch work by one of the best golf course architects in the business. The North Course is lovely and tranquil, but difficult. Typical of Fazio's best courses, it is extremely fair. Together, the two courses could serve as a model for aspiring modern golf course designers. An in depth analysis of how Fazio combined what nature put there with what man and his machines could add could make up a text for a post-graduate seminar.

The North Course opens with a trio of visually appealing par fours. The lead-off hole is generous off the tee. It's long, but with an ample green. It's a good chance for a par or birdie to start. A nice long dogleg right follows. There's a fairway bunker about driving distance on the right and a tight out-of-bounds along the left. Number 3 is a tight driving hole and plays to an elevated, multi-tiered green.

Now the heavy lifting begins. The 4th is a risk-reward par five with a lake along its right length. The hole is a crescent-shaped dogleg right and the golfer must decide on the tee how much of the corner to cut. It's rated the toughest hole on the course. And while precise shot-making will yield birdies and pars, the number of balls that end up in a watery grave paints a picture of how easily the hole will punish you with bogeys, double-bogeys, and worse.

The par-five 6th is a long dogleg right that plays uphill to a wide but shallow heart-shaped green. The fairway near the green is constricted by tall trees and big bunkers on both sides, making the entrance to the putting surface look as scrawny as a chicken's neck from, say, 140 yards out.

The par three 7th is long—nearly 240 yards from the championship tees. The following par four is a slight dogleg left. It is an absolutely lovely golf hole, with strategically placed fairway bunkers right and left, and a marsh area to the right. The green is intersected by a ridge, exacerbating the breaks.

Head back to the clubhouse on the long, tight par-four 9th. The hole is lined by trees and an out-of-bounds along the left side, and a huge bunker at driving distance on the right. The big oval-shaped green sits atop a hill and is canted severely back toward the fairway. Stray shots may find a gaping greenside bunker well below the putting surface or come to rest in a gnarly, grassy collection area.

Two par fours lead you into the back nine. The 11th is a fascinating dogleg right. Big hitters will consider trying to carry the series of fairway sand traps along the right at the bend of the dogleg, which leaves an approach of less than 150 yards. Shorter hitters will want to avoid the risk of having to play out of one of those bunkers and will keep their drives in the center of the fairway.

Two bunkers to the left front of the par-three 12th create an optical illusion that the flag is closer than it is. The huge green has at least four separate levels, as well as more subtle contours and breaks. The next hole is a good straight three-shot par five. That takes you to the par-four 14th. It is a severe dogleg left with a blind tee shot. Again, big hitters can think about cutting across the fairway bunker to the

Deep bunkers and high hills surround the green on the par-four 3rd hole at PGA Golf Club's North Course.

left to straighten the dogleg, but a towering, ancient pine tree at the side of the bunker lies in wait to slap down a shot that goes too far to the left. If your shot doesn't clear the bunker completely, you won't be able to see the pin.

Number 15 is a long par four. The green is tucked behind a hill, and while you can see the flag fluttering in the distance, you cannot see the putting surface from the tees.

A par three and a par five provide the run-up to the finishing hole. The par-four 18th, a dogleg right, is a magnificent way to end your round. Pin placement on the long, thin green—measuring 45 yards from front to back—can have a profound effect on club selection. Finish with a par or birdie and your pleasure is guaranteed.

If Tom Fazio's South Course is a three-star gourmet feast, the North Course is mom's home cooking. It is immensely satisfying and it is something you want to return to again and again.

DYE COURSE

Architect Pete Dye is both revered and reviled in the golf world. Some critics say his courses are contrived, verging on hokey, too difficult and too punitive for the average player to enjoy. His legion of fans, however, say the man is inspired, a genius, raising golf course design to the level of fine art. If there is an absolute certainty, it is that you will not walk away from the Dye Course at PGA Golf Club neutral. There is nothing ho-hum about this layout.

In fact, the first time I played it—only about six months after it opened—the architect himself was out playing it to see what needed tweaking or adjusting. Pete Dye and his dog, Sixty, rode in the same golf cart, as they always do, the dog sitting dutifully in the passenger's seat with the wind blowing his black fur, Dye taking notes as he played.

You will come away from the Dye Course with vivid memories of the unique and sometimes diabolical bunkers, many sculpted out of mounds or dug deeply into the ground like the pot bunkers of such links courses as St. Andrews or Lahinch. If water is a critical design element on the two Tom Fazio courses at the PGA Golf Club, sand and waste bunkers are the hallmark of the Dye Course. If it weren't a golf course they could use it for a remake of *Lawrence of Arabia.* Flat lies anywhere are all but impossible. Dye likes big, undulating greens with lots of humps and bumps to make putting a challenge.

The opening hole, for example, tees off across a waste bunker to a well-mounded and contoured landing area. Along the right length of the hole is a waste area that looks like it could be the site of the Dubai open complete with guys on camels wearing caftans riding by in the distance. The short par four is a dogleg right that plays to a long, thin, highly contoured green.

Number 2 is a long par four that requires accuracy off the tee to avoid sand traps to the left and a waste area along the right. The neck of the green is choked in front by another waste area on the left and another sand trap scooped out of a substantial hill on the right.

The next hole, the first of Dye's par threes is nothing but carry over waste area. The par-four 4th provides an ample fairway landing area from the tees, although the hole is virtually surrounded by waste area. The green is hooked to the right, out into the waste bunker. On the

The intimidating view from the back tees on the par-three 6th at the Dye Course on PGA Golf Club.

fairway, there is almost no flat place to stand with all the hills and mounds. The lake to the extreme right comes into play only on the most errant shots.

The par-five 5th plays long and hard, again surrounded by waste area and with a strategically placed trio of sand traps along the left side and intruding into the left center of the fairway about driving distance. This dogleg left plays to a long, thin green angled left and tucked behind a nasty corner of the waste area.

Number 6 is a daunting par three. From the back markers both a lake and a waste area are in play almost up to the green. Women playing the forward markers get a bit of a break, looking straight at the hole. But the huge green, with at least three separate tiers, is bulldozed—or perhaps blasted—out of a hilltop with steep inclines on all sides. If you have any doubt about club selection, be long and right. All of the trouble here is short and left.

Number 7 is a long par five that requires all players to drive over an expanse of waste area. The landing area is fairly generous off the tees, but the hole constricts the closer you get to the green. Placement of your lay-up second shot is critical. Architect Dye has constructed a minefield of bunkers—ten sand hazards and a plot of waste area big enough to contain a Bedouin encampment—inside 100 yards.

The side wraps up with a pair of par fours. The first is short, the second is quite long. The giant 9th green is hooked to the left behind a waste bunker. Long hitters need to avoid a deep sand trap in the middle of the fairway just short of where most average players will aim.

The back nine opens with a long par five—a landscape of waste areas to the right, steep mounds along the left length, scrub brush everywhere, and sand hazards galore. Number 10 is a slight dogleg right, although sometimes that's not obvious given the brutal topography that must be navigated between tee and green.

Two par fours—a long dogleg right and a short straight hole—take you to the lovely little par-three 13th. It's an island hole, a verdant oasis in a sea of waste area and sand. Number 14 is a solid par four, the only hole on the course on which there is no sand or waste area in the proximity of the green. But beware the hills and contours.

Number 15 is a long par-four dogleg left on which only the most skilled, bravest, or most foolhardy of players will try to cut off much of the dogleg. The smart play is left of the 150-yard marker, which leaves a fairly unimpeded approach to the pin. The 16th is a belligerent par three. Miss the putting surface and you can pick your peril—waste area, scrubby hills, severe contours, or grassy bowls.

As if the long, tight par-five 17th wasn't tough enough, architect Dye decided that the front of the green should be blocked by a high hill with a sand trap scooped out of it. From the fairway, it appears to be almost at greenside. In reality, it's about 40 yards away. Your approach shot must carry far enough over the impediment to find the putting surface.

To finish the Dye Course you face a long, daunting par four with no less than fourteen sand traps strategically placed between the tee boxes and the green. Two waste areas and dense marsh stretch along the left length of the hole. To the right is the same Dubai-sized desert that met you on the opening hole. All but the most forward tees must drive across an expanse of marsh. Walking away with a par or birdie here is most satisfying.

Pete Dye has taken pains to present a fair challenge for women, with two sets of tees. The PGA Golf Club recommends the second set for women with single digit or low teen handicaps. A woman with her husband visiting from Massachusetts was bubbling with enthusiasm after her round, even on a very windy day. "It's marvelous!" she said. "I've never played anything like it and I can't wait to play it again." She said she had an eighteen handicap and shot the course in 92, two over her target.

Do not harbor any illusions; the Dye Course is one of the toughest courses in the state, especially if the wind is up. You cannot afford to let your concentration slip for even a moment. The mounds, hills, and humps that play such an integral role in the design of the Dye Course can wreak havoc with your golf game. A shot—even a well-played shot—that lands atop or on the side of one of the elevations can be redirected many degrees and many yards from the intended line. In some cases landing on the side of a greenside mound can careen your ball into the wasteland. On the other hand, the occasional stray shot can be directed back toward the flag by a fortuitous bounce off one or several of Pete Dye's hills. In general, the greens on the Dye Course are a bit faster and a bit less receptive than the greens on the North and South Courses.

While you're at the PGA Golf Club you shouldn't miss the chance to test your skill and your golfing wits against this design challenge.

South Course

HOLE	Ra	Sl	1	2	3	4	5	6	7	8	9	OUT	10	11	12	13	14	15	16	17	18	IN	TOT
MEDAL	74.5	141	548	461	414	222	404	178	535	370	449	3581	365	199	401	545	463	345	507	228	442	3945	7076
TOURNAMENT	72.3	137	520	428	383	198	356	164	505	341	400	3295	353	186	375	511	439	336	491	217	403	3311	6606
STANDARD	70.1	129	509	401	347	189	309	141	492	326	384	3098	338	165	337	483	390	308	472	191	365	3049	6147
MIDDLE	67.8(m)/72.5(w)	123(m)/129(w)	483	369	287	166	292	109	430	301	362	2799	320	143	293	449	359	287	436	159	345	2791	5590
HCP			7	1	9	15	13	17	5	11	3		10	18	8	6	2	14	12	16	4		
PAR			5	4	4	3	4	3	5	4	4	36	4	3	4	5	4	4	5	3	4	36	72
FORWARD	68.7	119	374	340	266	145	281	98	416	259	319	2498	263	112	270	438	311	234	416	101	290	2435	4933

North Course

HOLE	Ra	Sl	1	2	3	4	5	6	7	8	9	OUT	10	11	12	13	14	15	16	17	18	IN	TOT
MEDAL	73.8	133	430	413	400	522	169	544	239	368	450	3535	346	395	184	523	389	451	216	549	438	3491	7026
TOURNAMENT	72.1	129	413	396	379	484	154	527	206	342	423	3324	337	379	173	502	372	425	194	527	416	3325	6649
STANDARD	70.1	124	379	372	362	456	141	506	195	326	406	3143	311	334	155	488	354	390	178	506	395	3111	6254
MIDDLE	67.5(m)/72.8(w)	118(m)/125(w)	369	354	323	416	127	469	154	308	365	2885	291	317	139	417	293	359	146	463	364	2789	5674
HCP			5	11	7	1	17	9	15	13	3		12	10	14	8	18	2	16	4	6		
PAR			4	4	4	5	3	5	3	4	4	36	4	4	3	5	4	4	3	5	4	36	72
FORWARD	68.8	114	316	317	299	348	109	416	123	276	320	2524	259	289	114	365	265	310	108	432	327	2469	4993

Dye Course

HOLE	Ra	Sl	1	2	3	4	5	6	7	8	9	OUT	10	11	12	13	14	15	16	17	18	IN	TOT
MEDAL	74.7	133	375	455	190	365	520	165	575	395	450	3490	540	430	340	200	405	480	225	565	475	3660	7150
TOURNAMENT	72.4	128	340	415	160	350	495	155	535	370	410	3230	510	385	330	175	390	440	195	530	440	3395	6625
STANDARD	69.3	123	315	380	145	340	470	140	500	350	340	2980	490	335	320	150	350	380	160	505	360	3050	6030
MIDDLE	67.89(m)/71.7(w)	121(m)/122(w)	310	375	135	310	420	120	475	320	330	2795	475	325	310	140	340	360	135	485	350	2920	5715
HCP			13	3	17	7	1	15	5	9	11		2	6	16	18	12	4	14	8	10		
PAR			4	4	3	4	5	3	5	4	4	36	5	4	4	3	4	4	3	5	4	36	72
FORWARD	67.8	109	280	330	120	285	415	105	425	280	265	2505	410	270	290	115	275	325	120	430	275	2510	5015

Looking across the lagoon, the moss-draped oaks back up the par-four 11th hole at Radisson Ponce de Leon Golf & Conference Resort.

RADISSON PONCE DE LEON GOLF & CONFERENCE RESORT

4000 U.S. Highway 1 North, St. Augustine, Florida (From I-95 take exit 95 and go east about 7 miles on SR16; turn left at U.S. Highway 1 and go north about 1 mile; the entrance is on the right.)
Phone: (904) 829-5314 or (888) 829-5314

Architect: Donald Ross Year opened: 1916

Course rating/Slope rating for men:
Blue—72.9/131 Gold—71.1/127
White—68.6/123

Course rating/Slope rating for women:
White—73.2/133 Red—70.6/121

Dornoch, Scotland, is about as far north as you'd ever want to go to play golf. It's a continent, five time zones, and a culture away from sunny Florida. The town of Dornoch lies at the mouth of Dornoch Firth, looking out at the blustery and baleful North Sea. It is so close to the Arctic Circle that, during the short summer, daylight extends to twenty or more hours and, during the long wet winter, there's hardly any daylight at all. It was in the late-1800s that a young man from this often gloomy place, named Donald Ross, started to hone his golfing and agronomy skills and became the head pro and groundskeeper at a fabled links golf course known as Royal Dornoch.

It was just before the dawn of the 20th century that this young man, son of a Scottish craftsman, set out for the New World, where he forged a career as a golf course architect, something largely unheard of at that time. A few commissions dribbled his way. Then there were more. Then young Donald Ross won the commission to design the North Carolina masterpiece that would be known as Pinehurst #2. With it, Donald Ross established himself as the premier golf course designer of his day, a giant in the field who has earned a place in the pantheon of great traditional golf course architects.

What Donald Ross did was quite simple. He put a little bit of Royal Dornoch, the course on which he grew up, the course on which he got his start, into virtually every golf course he designed. It doesn't matter which Donald Ross course you play—Pinehurst #2, the Old Course at the Homestead, or Ponce de Leon—there is something distinctive about it. The relationship of man's work and nature's, the turtleback greens (those elevated greens with shaved banks all around to reject imprecise approaches), and the adroit use of hazards, all have their genesis in that damp, dour town on the Scottish coast.

The Donald Ross golf course known locally as Ponce de Leon or just "the Ponce" graces the shores of what is the Atlantic Intracoastal Waterway. It's named after the Spanish explorer who, according to legend, came to this part of Florida looking for the Fountain of Youth. It was opened for play in 1916. While it has been reworked and redesigned several times since, it still bears the unique earmarks of Donald Ross.

Save for a few wind-bent palm trees and stately old oaks, the front nine (which, over the years, has been both the back and the front) is about as close to real links golf as you'll get in Florida. Traditional linksland is the buffer zone between arable land and the sea. Linksland is hilly, sometimes rocky, sandy, hard, with few trees and shrubs, where the wind blows almost constantly. Tight lies and greens that don't hold particularly well are the rule. What you get on the front nine at Ponce de Leon bears the look of traditional links, but unlike those American courses that have adopted only the look, the course has firm, links-like turf that drains extremely well and the wind is almost always a factor. It is less sandy than Scottish links, but if you want an idea of what it's like to play Royal Dornoch (or the Old Course at St. Andrews or Royal Troon) this will provide it.

The back nine at Ponce de Leon is something else entirely. It is carved through a dense forest of pines and oaks with inky lakes and ominous swamps brooding at every turn. The back nine is quintessential Florida golf, a la Donald Ross tight, troubled, and treacherous. The wind is muted by the forest. The humid, often tropical intensity is alive with the sounds of birds and insects the like of which nobody has ever seen in Dornoch, Scotland.

The first three holes—a moderate par four, a long par three, and a demanding par five—introduce you to the old Scot's handiwork. If the wind is from the north, the 3rd is easily reachable in two, but the other two can be almost impossible to hit in regulation. Conversely, if the wind is from the south, the par five plays more like a par six.

The 4th is a long par four. The right length of the hole is brushed by the marsh that separates dry land from the Intracoastal Waterway. The green is small, elevated, and two tiered. That takes you to the daunting 5th. It's a par three with a forced carry over marsh to a tiny green that looks like a hatbox stuck out into the wetland. Women playing the Red Tees have only an 85-yard straight run at the flag.

Number 6 is a fine par-four dogleg right around the Intracoastal marsh. Two lakes on the left squeeze the fairway. The highly contoured green is tucked among mossy old trees and deep bunkers. The 7th is one of the toughest holes on the outgoing side. It's a par five with a lake in play between the landing zone for your drives and the landing zone for your lay-up. The side finishes with a pair of par fours.

You leave the links-like nine and head into the Floridian nine with a transitional par five that's reachable in two for even moderately long hitters. The short par four eleventh is one of the prettiest holes on the course. You drive through a chute of trees to a narrow fairway. Your approach is downhill to a green that juts back into a lagoon. It's protected by bunkers and water.

The 12th is an extremely tight, straight par four. Your tee shot must find the tightrope of fairway. There's an enormous bunker on the left and the fairway drops off to the right into a no-man's-land of nasty plant life and water. The long, thin green is multi-tiered. Go along a little wooded path to the 13th tees and face a long par three, before you tackle the toughest hole on the back nine. It's a narrow par five with a lake directly in front of the hilltop green. A lot of players use something other than a driver to keep their tee shots in play between the forest that lines both sides of the hole.

The lane to the next tee takes you under a canopy of mossy oaks and pines and around a lagoon. The dogleg right 15th can be a good scoring hole. But be aware that the bunker in front of the green looks closer to the putting surface than it is. A great number of first time players believe their eyes instead of the yardage markers and find themselves in the swail between the bunker and the green.

A fine par three with a forced carry over a pond and a solid par four take you to the finishing hole. Number 18 features a dangerous forest along the left and an elevated green that is compressed between a marsh on the left and a bunker on the right.

Ponce de Leon is the kind of golf course people like to play again and again. It's an interesting and challenging layout that gives you a fine feel for the work of one of the greatest golf course architects of all time. "It's long and hard for women," said my wife, Barbara, who plays it regularly. "Some of the par fours make you hit two good woods if you want to get on in regulation."

In addition to the championship golf course, there are good practice facilities including a putting green and a chipping green, a pitch-and-putt course, tennis courts, and a full service resort and conference center.

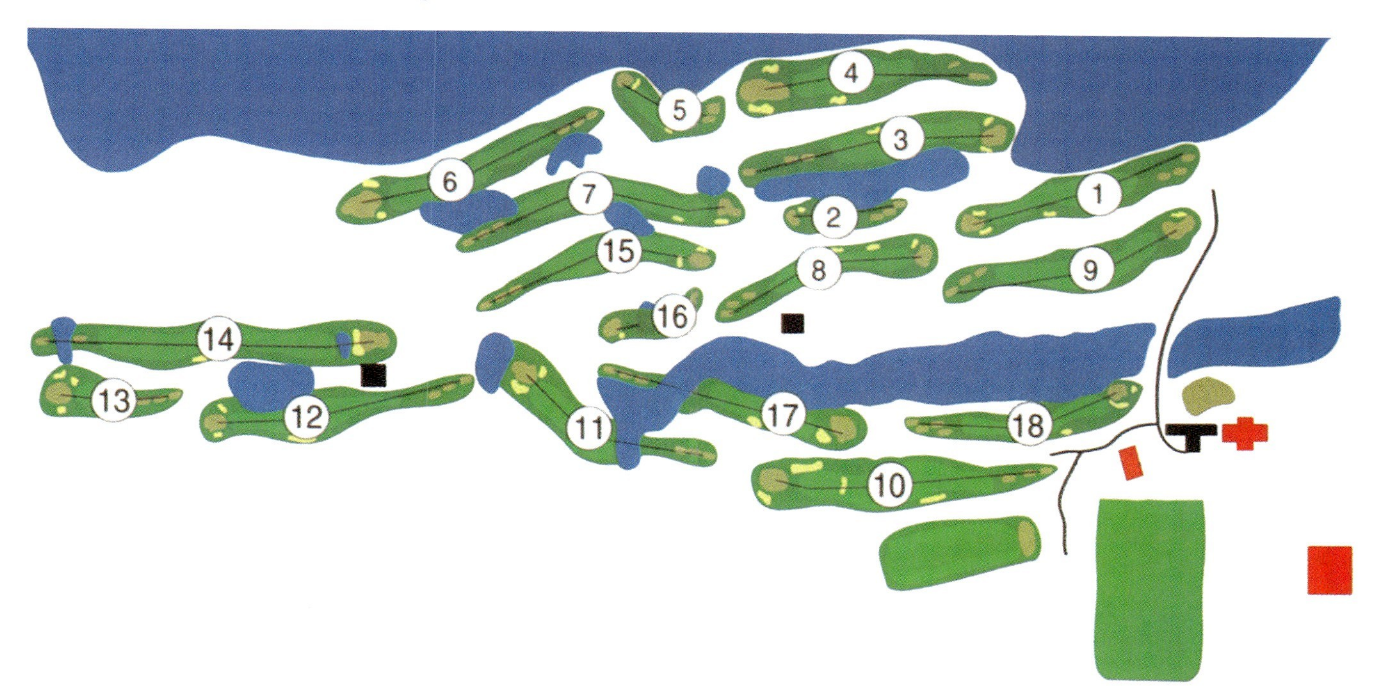

Radisson Ponce de Leon Golf & Conference Resort

HOLE	Ra	Sl	1	2	3	4	5	6	7	8	9	OUT	10	11	12	13	14	15	16	17	18	IN	TOT
BLUE	72.9	131	380	204	544	439	158	416	509	383	399	3432	509	405	416	212	498	387	177	391	396	3391	6823
GOLD	71.1	127	360	189	501	379	149	385	493	373	373	3202	481	358	396	203	484	374	153	367	381	3197	6399
WHITE	68.6(m)/73.2(w)	123(m)/133(w)	350	167	428	296	138	371	474	346	348	2918	464	302	354	189	476	355	132	330	346	2948	5866
MEN'S HCP		17	15	3	1	13	5	7	11	9			14	4	6	12	2	10	18	16	8		
PAR			4	3	5	4	3	4	5	4	4	36	5	4	4	3	5	4	3	4	4	36	72
RED	70.6	121	320	153	416	287	85	340	422	330	329	2682	410	279	344	145	401	325	113	283	326	2626	5308
WOMEN'S HCP		11	15	5	13	17	3	1	7	9			12	10	4	14	2	6	16	18	8		

Your drive, on the beautiful par-five 9th hole at Ravines Inn & Golf Club, is into a valley. The green is perched on the side of a second steep hill.

RAVINES INN & GOLF CLUB

2932 Ravines Road, Middleburg, Florida (From I-95 take exit 95 and go west on S.R.16 for about 25 miles; turn right onto C.R.218 north for about 7 miles to the Ravines entrance on the right.)
Phone: (904) 282-2701

Ravines Course Architects: Ron Garl and Mark McCumber   Year opened: 1979

Course rating/Slope rating:
Black—72.4/133   White—70.0/128
Gray—68.0/123   Red—67.4/120

Ravines Inn & Golf Club—all the locals just call it Ravines—is one of the most unusual golf courses in northeastern Florida. There's a hilly and highly contoured part of the state near Orlando, but in the Jacksonville area hilly natural terrain is rare. Unlike some flat Florida real estate where golf course designers brought in the bulldozers to make hills, nature did the work here. Over the centuries, Black Creek and the runs that drain into it formed deep ravines into which lush north Florida vegetation has grown with abandon. Using the creek—a tributary of the nearby St. Johns River as a boundary and the ravines associated with it as natural hazards, architects Garl and McCumber fashioned this extraordinary piece of land into a golf course.

Ravines plays uphill, downhill, sidehill, from valleys to hilltops, and from hilltops into valleys. There are only a handful of Florida golf courses that approach the level of elevation change that you get here. El Campion at Mission Inn, Diamondback, Diamond Players Club, and El Diablo are among the few that are in a league with Ravines when it comes to natural topographical contours.

Black Creek, lakes, ponds, and ravines are in play on eleven holes. Elevation changes are in evidence on all but two or three holes. The greens tend to be on the small side. The fairways are narrow. When ravines or water are not in play, mature old trees generally are. It's a par 72 for men, par 70 for women. Architects Garl and McCumber have shortened the course from the forward markers, requiring fewer forced carries from the tees.

The bunkers on the course are an interesting mix. In addition to traditional bunkering, a significant number of the greenside sand hazards have been constructed with wooden bulkheads shaping their face. While the look is pleasing, the result of landing too close to one of those wooden embankments is anything but.

You charge into the golf course with a pair of par fours, the first a dogleg right, the second a dogleg left. The opening hole plays to an uphill green. The 2nd requires a force carry, through a chute of trees, over a ravine. The green is downhill from the landing area and hooked behind a corner of forest. For women, the 2nd is a par three with a downhill shot to the green. Catch your breath on the par three third and then get ready for a trio of seriously difficult holes.

The 4th, a dogleg right par four, is the hardest hole on the course. You hit your drive onto a shelf of fairway that comes to an abrupt end about 120 yards in front of the green. It drops away into an abyss of nasty plant life. The green is nestled in a basin at the base of the hill. Next comes a long, tight par five that's a three shot hole for almost everybody. Trees in front of the green compress the entrance to the putting surface. The 6th is a gentle dogleg right with a pair of huge bunkers squeezing the entrance to the green.

The one-shot 7th plays downhill to a kidney-shaped green that's about as small as a real kidney. That's followed by the lovely short par four that plays over a hill. The canopy of a giant old oak shades the left front entrance to the green, waiting for stray shots to see if the tree really is 90 percent air. It isn't.

The side finishes with an absolutely spectacular golf hole, one of the best golf holes in the Sunshine State. Your drive on the par five is from the top of a hill, into a valley. Black Creek flows along the right length of the hole. A pond is in play on the left on your second shot. Your approach is to a small elevated green.

Go around the hilltop clubhouse to the 10th tees, which are terraced on a hillside with a ravine in front of them. The bank of Black Creek, which bends to the right, forms the definition of the dogleg. The green is not visible on your drive, which is down onto a long runway of grass. Women get a substantial break here, with the Red Tees at the base of the hill, across the ravine. The green is guarded by bunkers and a pond on the right.

Number 11 is a precariously narrow hole, playing from elevated tees, into a valley and then back uphill to a green that's a shelf on the hillside. Water is in play on the right. Climb the hill behind the green and find the next series of elevated tees that take you down a thin valley path. Long hitters will consider going for this par five in two even though you can't see the hilltop green from the fairway. A good par four through the trees takes you to the beautiful par three 14th. It's a downhill shot to a small green squeezed between a bunker on the left and Black Creek on the right.

The 15th is a par five for men, a par four for women. Men tee off over a hill; women play from the top of it. A rocky stream intersects the fairway at the base of the hill. Women must avoid finding the stream from the tee. The green is a mesa on top of the hill with a cluster of bunkers shielding it from most bump-and-run approaches. Even moderate hitters will think about going for this in two.

The last three holes on Ravines are

delightful to the eye and a superb golfing challenge. The 16th is a downhill par three with a menacing creek bed in front of the small putting surface. The long par four 17th requires a forced carry over a lake to the fairway, where you start your climb to the green. The flag is visible all the way; the putting surface is not. The finishing hole plays across a ravine and then downhill. The fairway on this long par four drops off almost vertically into a nasty little basin about 130 yards from the hillside green.

The uniqueness of the tract of land on which it is built, the beauty that adorns almost every hole, and the skill of the design contribute to the overall fine golfing experience that is Ravines. In addition to the wonderful, championship golf course, Ravines offers a par three golf course, a putting course they call the Himalayas, fine practice facilities, tennis, an Olympic sized pool, fitness center, spa, and a recently refurbished Inn. The place is an all-around winner.

Ravines Inn & Golf Club

HOLE	Ra	Sl	1	2	3	4	5	6	7	8	9	OUT	10	11	12	13	14	15	16	17	18	IN	TOTAL
BLACK	72.4	133	348	360	220	422	539	406	173	372	529	3369	407	383	504	397	157	501	186	399	430	3364	6733
WHITE	70.0	128	334	330	181	377	513	354	150	345	475	3059	365	363	484	374	144	471	173	366	415	3155	6214
GRAY	68.0	123	292	290	148	347	426	340	142	332	445	2762	356	355	477	347	137	448	162	354	381	3017	5779
MEN'S HCP		13	5	15	1	7	3	17	9	11			6	4	12	10	18	16	14	8	2		
MEN'S PAR		4	4	3	4	5	4	3	4	5	36	4	4	5	4	3	5	3	4	4	36		72
RED	67.4	120	282	150	116	309	405	273	125	305	401	2366	280	321	452	263	126	331	119	278	281	2451	4817
WOMEN'S HCP		7	17	15	1	5	11	13	9	3			6	2	4	18	16	8	12	14	10		
WOMEN'S PAR		4	3	3	4	5	4	3	4	5	35	4	4	5	4	3	4	3	4	4	35		70

Approaching the wide, shallow 6th green at Riverwood is made even more challenging by a deep bunker and a towering old pine that sit directly in front of the putting surface.

RIVERWOOD

4100 Riverwood Dr., Port Charlotte, Florida (From U.S. Highway 41 take State Route 776 south for about 5 miles; turn right into the Riverwood entrance and follow the signs to the clubhouse.)
Phone: (941) 764-6661

Architect: Gene Bates   Year opened: 1992

Course rating/Slope rating for men:
Black—73.8/133   Blue—71.9/128
White—69.6/122   Gold—66.3/112

Course rating/Slope rating for women:
White—75.1/135   Gold—71.5/122
Red—68.0/114

If Riverwood isn't your home course, you'll wish it was. It is a wonderful layout—tight, watery, sandy, and woodsy—but without the hoopla attendant to some of the big-name, big-ego courses. It is not a fancy golf resort. The clubhouse has a nice pro shop, bar and grill, and locker rooms. But if you mention Riverwood to golfers who live in southwest Florida, their eyes light up and you'll be regaled with tales of the pleasure of the place.

Paul and Pat Stenberg make at least one trip a year to the Florida Gulf Coast from their home in Escondido, California. "We really like this course," said Paul. "We've been playing it for years and always look forward to coming back."

"It's a very good course for women," added Pat. "It's tight. I'm playing the Reds today, but if you drop back and play the Golds it's real long." She noted that with a few exceptions, architect Gene Bates took pains to give women and men a similar view of each hole.

The character of the golf course is evident from the start. Riverwood demands accuracy. Architect Bates favors big greens with lots of very subtle breaks and contours. There is very little that's hidden here, nothing much that will sneak up on you and cause problems. How well you execute your shots and how well your putter is working will determine your score.

The first hole offers a good introduction and presages things to come. It's a fairly straight par four that's tightened with pine trees and palmettos lining the left and mounding to the right. The wide, shallow green—pitched sharply back toward the fairway—is protected by a gaping bunker to the front right. If the pin's behind the sand, it's a very difficult approach.

Number 2 is a pretty hole, a short par four with a pair of gnarled, bare trees haunting the right side of the fairway like specters keeping watch over the inky lake adjacent to them. Keep your tee shot left to avoid the trouble. A short par five follows with water down the right and a dense thatch of Florida scrub-brush and pines to the left. To go for it in two, your tee shot must avoid a yawning fairway bunker that's been bulldozed out of the side of a hill about driving distance down the right side of the fairway.

The 4th hole is a solid par four dogleg left. That leads to a visually intimidating one-shot hole with water in front of all but the most forward tees. The lake guards the front and right side of the green along with a pair of long thin sand traps that caress the putting surface. If you need it, there's a little room to bail-out to the left, short of the green.

The par-four 6th is protected down the left by water and marsh. The first water hazard is in play off the tees to the left. There's water and marsh in play on both sides of the fairway as you near the green, which is angled to the left, toward the weeds. This is a hole that requires a well-placed tee shot. To score, you need a delicate approach that holds the green and avoids the hazards and the towering old pine that protect it.

Number 7 is a lovely long par three with a forced carry over water. In fact there's only about two feet of collar between the planked bulkhead and the putting surface. It's a tough green to hold, only 34 yards long and only about 17 yards wide. The 8th is a solid par four that's intersected by water about 100 yards from the green. Be aware that for women playing the forward markers, it's only 160 yards to the water.

The only place to be on the par five 9th is down the middle of the fairway. Opportunities to take penalty strokes abound here. There's trouble right, trouble left, and trouble in front of the green. The hazards include, but are not limited to, out-of-bounds, water, marsh, pines, palms, palmettos, and scrub brush. Select whatever club it takes to keep the ball in play. The elevated green is hooked behind a bunker and a corner of the lake, and is pitched from the back to the front. Par is a good way to make the turn.

A pair of par fours takes you into the back nine. The first is straight, the second a dogleg left with trouble everywhere but on the fairway. Keep your tee shot far enough to the right that the approach to the green will be open. Number 12 is a risk-reward par-five dogleg right with water in play down most of its right length. Each player is burdened with the decision of how much of the lake to try to cut.

That takes you to a very tough par three for men. There's a forced carry over water and you must clear the menacing bunker that sits in front of the green. The water is largely taken out of play for women, although the bunker still must be negotiated.

Two par fours follow. The lovely, long 14th is a dogleg left with a blind tee shot and a two-tiered green. Number 15 is short, but tricky. The elevated green is hooked behind a bunker that contains palm trees and tufts of Pampas grass. A wedge of water intrudes in front of the green. The driving area is generous. The approach is hard.

1
2
3
4
5
6
7
8
9
10
11
12
13
14
15
16
17
18

Riverwood's three finishing holes are simply wonderful—pleasant to look at and challenging to play. The one-shot 16th requires everybody to clear an expanse of environmentally protected wetland in order to find the putting surface.

That sets up one of the most interesting par five holes in Florida. It's a double-dogleg. Long hitters may think about going for it in two, but it's a blind shot to the flag if you do. A marshy hazard intersects the fairway about 100 yards in front of the putting surface and the hazard surrounds the green. There's only a tiny opening in the foliage through which the flag is visible. "It is really picturesque," said head pro Rich Meadows. "It's an island green with palmettos growing around it."

Number 18 is a par-four dogleg right with an extremely skimpy landing area for your tee shot. But from there the hole opens up and offers a fine scoring opportunity with which to finish the side.

My playing partners, the Stenbergs, are from California, a state that has no shortage of good golf courses. They pronounced their return to Riverwood immensely satisfying and were already discussing their next cross-country trip. I left with a touch of envy for the local members who get to play it all the time. If you're in the area, Riverwood is not to be missed.

Riverwood

HOLE	Ra	Sl	1	2	3	4	5	6	7	8	9	OUT	10	11	12	13	14	15	16	17	18	IN	TOT
BLACK	73.8	133	396	375	500	400	171	424	197	435	539	3437	405	400	549	179	416	334	212	551	455	3501	6938
BLUE	71.9	128	380	343	472	380	141	393	188	412	503	3212	387	382	490	167	402	307	156	514	427	3232	6444
WHITE	69.6(m)/75.1(w)	122(m)/135(w)	369	335	433	358	128	360	172	401	485	3014	352	345	485	135	358	296	149	413	2982		6023
GOLD	66.3(m)/71.5(w)	112(m)/122(w)	316	290	396	319	122	329	163	342	432	2709	335	310	417	123	320	278	108	439	337	2667	5376
MEN'S HCP		7	13	11	9	17	3	15	1	5			10	4	12	18	8	14	16	6	2		
PAR			4	4	5	4	3	4	3	4	5	36	4	4	5	3	4	4	3	5	4	36	72
RED	68.0	114	280	245	367	264	100	276	122	278	381	2313	296	270	374	97	292	253	103	396	301	2382	4695
WOMEN'S HCP			9	13	7	11	17	3	15	1	5		12	10	14	18	6	8	16	2	4		

SADDLEBROOK RESORT

5700 Saddlebrook Way, Wesley Chapel, Florida (From I-75 take the exit for State Route 54 and go east for about 1 1/2 miles to the entrance on the right.)
Phone: (813) 973-1111 or (800) 729-8383

Saddlebrook Course Architect: Dean Refram   Year opened: 1976
Palmer Course Architects: Arnold Palmer and Ed Seay   Year opened: 1986

Saddlebrook Course rating/Slope rating:
Blue—72.0/127   White—69.7/122
Red—70.6/126

Palmer Course rating/Slope rating:
Blue—71.9/134   White—69.6/129
Red—71.0/127

From the moment you take the winding drive through the community of Saddlebrook up to the resort complex, the feel is of understated elegance. Once under the canopy at the entrance, your first feelings are confirmed. The service is efficient, but not overbearing; the attitude is of genuine friendliness, not in any way pretentious or smothering. The resort is simply first rate. There's something for everybody from the comfortable, well-appointed guest rooms to the outstanding, gourmet restaurants, the spa, the gigantic pool, the fitness center, the meeting and conference facilities, and the 45 tennis courts.

But the soul of Saddlebrook is golf. The patron saint of the place is Arnold Palmer. In addition to the championship par 71 golf course designed by Palmer and his long-time partner Ed Seay, there's the Arnold Palmer Golf Academy, Arnold Palmer golf camps for teenagers, and the Saddlebrook Prep School that educates young minds and produces world class golfers. The golf shop is well stocked and the staff is knowledgeable and helpful.

Golf came to Saddlebrook in 1976 when Dean Refram's par 70 golf course was opened. The Florida golf boom was in its infancy then. But the reputation of the Saddlebrook course spread quickly. What had once been a local secret in the Tampa area soon developed a national reputation.

SADDLEBROOK COURSE

They built golf courses differently back in the '60s and '70s than they do these days. They didn't move as much earth. The holes were closer together. The hand of man was less evident than the touch of Mother Nature. The par 70 Saddlebrook Course is a splendid example of that kind of golf course architecture. It was hewn through forests of cypress and pine, a tight but walkable course, with the greens and tees fairly close together. The greens are on the small side. There is abundant water and sand, along with dense forests. It is tight. Accuracy is essential or the wooded preserves and water will wreak havoc on your score.

In the 1970s, three sets of tees were the standard—blue mostly for tournament

The view from the green back down the long, narrow par-four finishing hole on the Saddlebrook Course.

play, white for men, and red for women. That's the way it is at Saddlebrook today. And it seems perfectly in keeping with the nature of the golf course.

Architect Dean Refram doesn't waste much time on introductory holes. You enter the primordial forest that surrounds the 1st tees and drive across a small canal to an irregularly shaped landing area. Your approach shot on this par four must clear the water hazard that intersects the fairway about 50 yard in front of the small, elevated green. The green, itself, is well bunkered, including one dangerous little sand trap right in front. Another par four, this one long and straight, follows. It plays to an elevated green. Moss-draped old cypress trees hug the right length of the hole.

Exit the green and move to the tees of a very solid par three with the green tucked behind a lake. The planked bulkhead comes right up to the collar. The long thin green is angled to the left and sandwiched between the lake and a bunker. Number 4 is a long, very narrow dogleg left par five, the only one on the outgoing side. It's a three shot hole for virtually everybody, the toughest hole on the course for women.

Three par fours are next in line. The 5th is long. You drive down a tree-lined alley and must avoid the bunker down the left side of the fairway. The two-tiered green is fairly open and receptive to a run-up approach. Number 6 is a short par four that plays to a long thin green. The 7th is long with an elevated green. The fairway is bordered by dense forest to the right and bunkers about driving distance down the left.

Number 8 is a long par three. The green is a stage, set against a backdrop of dense cypress and pine forest. It's a tough hole for women, 145 yards from the forward markers. The green is open in front and will accept a run-up approach. "Hit it crisp and straight and you'll be fine," said my wife, Barbara.

You head to the turn with a truly superior golf hole. It's a slight dogleg right par four. Your tee shot is over an arm of the lake that plays down the right length of the hole. A second arm of the lake intersects the fairway in front of the smallish elevated, multi-tiered green.

Two interesting par fours open the inward nine. Number 10 is a dogleg right that's so short some huge hitters may think about trying for it in one. If you do that, you must carry the water hazard that borders the right side of the hole—a 250 yard carry from the championship markers, about 235 yards from the White Tees, and around 200 yards from the forward markers. Most local members play a fairway-wood or long-iron just inside the 100 yard mark and have an easy approach.

Number 11 is long and straight, with a large, elevated, two-tiered green that's boxed in by four bunkers. It's an easier hole for women—playing only 255 yards from the forward tees—than for men. My wife, Barbara, who birdied it, was ecstatic. "When you get the chance to play driver and short-iron, you have a lot better scoring chance than when you're playing a couple of woods to get to the green."

A short par three takes you to the long, par-four 13th. The long thin, multi-level green is only 13 yards from side to side at the front and poses one of the tougher targets on the Saddlebrook Course. Number 14 is a short, but tight par five. Trees and hazard run down the right and left sides of the fairway and a strategically placed fairway bunker on the left is just about driving distance for everybody. The elevated green is angled to the left between a

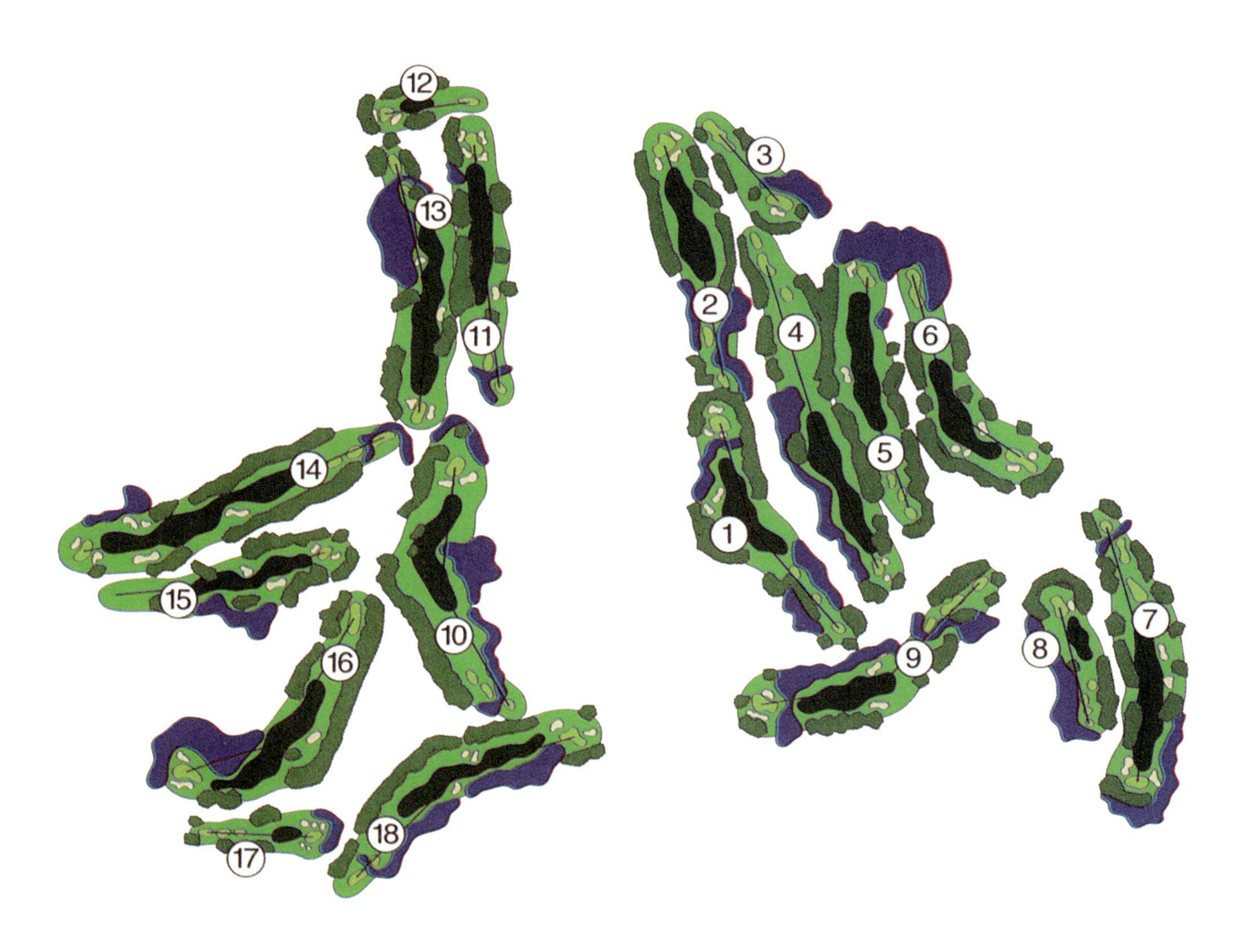

Saddlebrook Course

HOLE	Ra	Sl	1	2	3	4	5	6	7	8	9	OUT	10	11	12	13	14	15	16	17	18	IN	TOTAL
BLUE	72.0	127	390	393	170	555	414	340	448	211	406	3327	360	421	145	418	511	345	407	205	425	3237	6564
WHITE	69.7	122	361	385	155	513	390	321	405	194	376	3100	346	383	135	374	482	331	384	176	416	3027	6127
MEN'S HCP		10	14	12	2	6	18	8	16	4			11	7	17	5	9	13	3	15	1		
PAR			4	4	3	5	4	4	4	3	4	35	4	4	3	4	5	4	4	3	4	35	70
RED	70.6	126	301	270	125	425	316	283	335	145	317	2517	295	255	120	337	420	297	255	140	305	2424	4941
WOMEN'S HCP			5	11	15	1	7	13	9	17	3		10	14	16	8	2	12	6	18	4		

pair of bunkers. Number 15 is a short par four that's tougher for women than men. The 16th is a ***J***-shaped par four with the green hooked to the right behind a lake on a hillside shelf. Your tee shot is through a chute of cypress trees, but even a medium-long drive that veers right will find the water hazard.

A par three leads you to one of my favorite finishing holes in Florida. It's a beautiful hole with water down the right and a wooded wilderness to the left, creating a very narrow runway of short grass. Your approach shot is over a lobe of lake (with a lovely fountain in it) that wedges in front of the huge, elevated, multi-level green. The ideal placement of your tee shot is left-center to take the clump of trees on the right side out of play and to give yourself as much green to work with as possible.

The Saddlebrook Course leaves you with a smile of satisfaction after you've finished. It's an aesthetically pleasing golf course that requires your best shot-making to score. The tight, old-fashioned nature of the course favors course management and finesse over brute strength. It's short, only a par 70, but so is Turnberry, where they have played the British Open. It's quaint, woodsy, and absolutely charming.

PALMER COURSE

I have been a fan of Arnold Palmer, the golfer, since I was a kid. I first became acquainted with Arnold Palmer, the golf course architect, in 1984 at a brand new golf course in Tralee, Ireland. I thought it was one of the best examples of golf course design I had ever experienced, and it elevated Palmer to an even loftier level of respect in my mind. I still feel that way. Over the years, I have had the opportunity to play other courses by "the king" and have drawn some conclusions. His experience as a champion, as a player of golf courses, has given him a remarkable feel for what a golf course ought to be. His design skill has been tested on all kinds of terrain. Arguably, Tralee remains Palmer's best, but there are others that could vie for the crown.

With his design partner Ed Seay, Palmer's course at Saddlebrook is a simply superb test of the game. It has many of the features you might expect from a Palmer course, but one in particular stands out here. As you play it, pay careful attention to the greens. They vary in size, shape, undulation, and elevation. They are tough, treacherous, and sometimes terrifying. They are brilliantly conceived and masterfully placed within the design framework. They are, in fact, the heart and soul of the Palmer Course at Saddlebrook. Add to them the artful use of bunkers and water and you have the colors and hues that go into making the track so memorable.

Like its older neighbor on the property, the Palmer Course is not breathtakingly long. It's only a par 71. But length alone does not necessarily determine the level of excellence achieved by the designer of a golf course.

The course opens with a solid par four that plays from elevated tees into a valley that leads to a huge, multi-tiered green. Water is in play on the left as you approach the green. Number 2 is a fine par three with a marshy waste area to the right and intruding in front of the long, thin green.

Those openers take you to the toughest hole on the course for men. A lake is in play on the left from the tees, with a second lake on the left mid-way down the hole. The wide, shallow green is a

Saddlebrook Resort's Palmer Course opens with a demanding par-four that plays to a large, well-bunkered green.

mogul-field of mounds, bumps, and humps. Safely on is no guarantee of an easy two-putt. Number 4 is the number one handicap hole for women. It's a long, demanding dogleg left par five, with water on both sides of the fairway compressing the landing zone for your drive. The tree-lined approach to the long thin green is about as wide as a country lane and uphill all the way.

A pair of excellent par fours are next. You drive through a chute of pine trees that line the tees on the picturesque 5th. A lake angles in front of the large green. Number 6 is a ribbon-thin hole with trees lining both sides of the fairway. The undulating, elevated, hourglass-shaped green is angled to the left between a pair of bunkers.

A par three and a short par five that most players can try for in two take you to the short par-four 9th. There's a lake to the right that is well within driving distance for most players. Something other than a driver is a wise club selection here. The women's tee is under the canopy of an oak tree which adds an interesting aesthetic to the drive. The uphill approach to the plateaued green is longer than it looks.

A short par four and a par five take you into the back nine and lead to the challenging 12th. It's a straight par four that opens with a blind, uphill tee shot. The forward markers are so far to the left that for woman it's almost a dogleg left. The hole narrows severely from the landing area to the hillside green perched above a lake.

Number 13 is a par three with a forced carry over water to a kidney-shaped green that's angled to the right behind a bulkhead. There's a little bail-out room to the left if you need it. "It's all carry, but it's a reasonable distance," said my wife, Barbara. "It's just under a hundred yards from the reds and that gives you a chance to score. But the look is intimidating."

Architect Palmer has constructed a lovely quartet of par fours to follow. Steep mounds and hills line the left side of the 14th hole; trees, bunkers, and a close out-of-bounds line guard the right. The last 150 yards of the hole play uphill to the only green on the course that features no greenside bunkers. Number 15 is a hillside hole, pitched from left to right. The tiny, elevated green is two-tiered and sloped severely back toward the fairway.

You tee off across water on the diabolical 16th. Palmer, the architect, has created the kind of hole that Palmer the champion player loved—a precarious landing area and a difficult green that rewards precise approaches and superior putting. He gave no break to women. "It's very challenging from the tee," said Barbara. "You're required to clear both water and a small bridge and then you're angled left looking right at a fairway bunker." The long green is thin, measuring only 13 yards at its widest points and less than a first down across at its narrowest. It's not rated the toughest hole on the course, but it should be a contender for the honor. The fourth of the par fours is straight and hilly with water in play on both sides of the fairway and a tiny, oval, highly contoured, uphill green guarded by a pair of bunkers.

The finisher is a short par three that plays to one of the toughest greens in Florida. It's an elevated, two tiered saddle-shaped green that's 32 yards from front to back and only 8 yards wide at the waist. Water laps at the bulkhead that edges the front. Bunkers squeeze the sides. One day, after missing the saddle and finding the sand, I stood and watched four other groups play the hole—a twosome, two threesomes, and a foursome. Two players hit the green, scooted off the back, three players found the water, two ended in the sand, and the rest ended up in another zip code.

Arnold Palmer, the player, was once quoted as saying that neither the golf ball nor the golf course know you're a hotshot, so you have to prove yourself every time you pick up a club. Palmer, the golf course architect, designs golf courses that make even the best players prove themselves repeatedly. From the first drive to the final putt, Palmer demands both physical skill and mental adroitness. He also believes in relaxation, but not on the golf course. The Palmer Course at Saddlebrook will test you. Walk off with a score that matches your handicap and you will have earned a bit of relaxation.

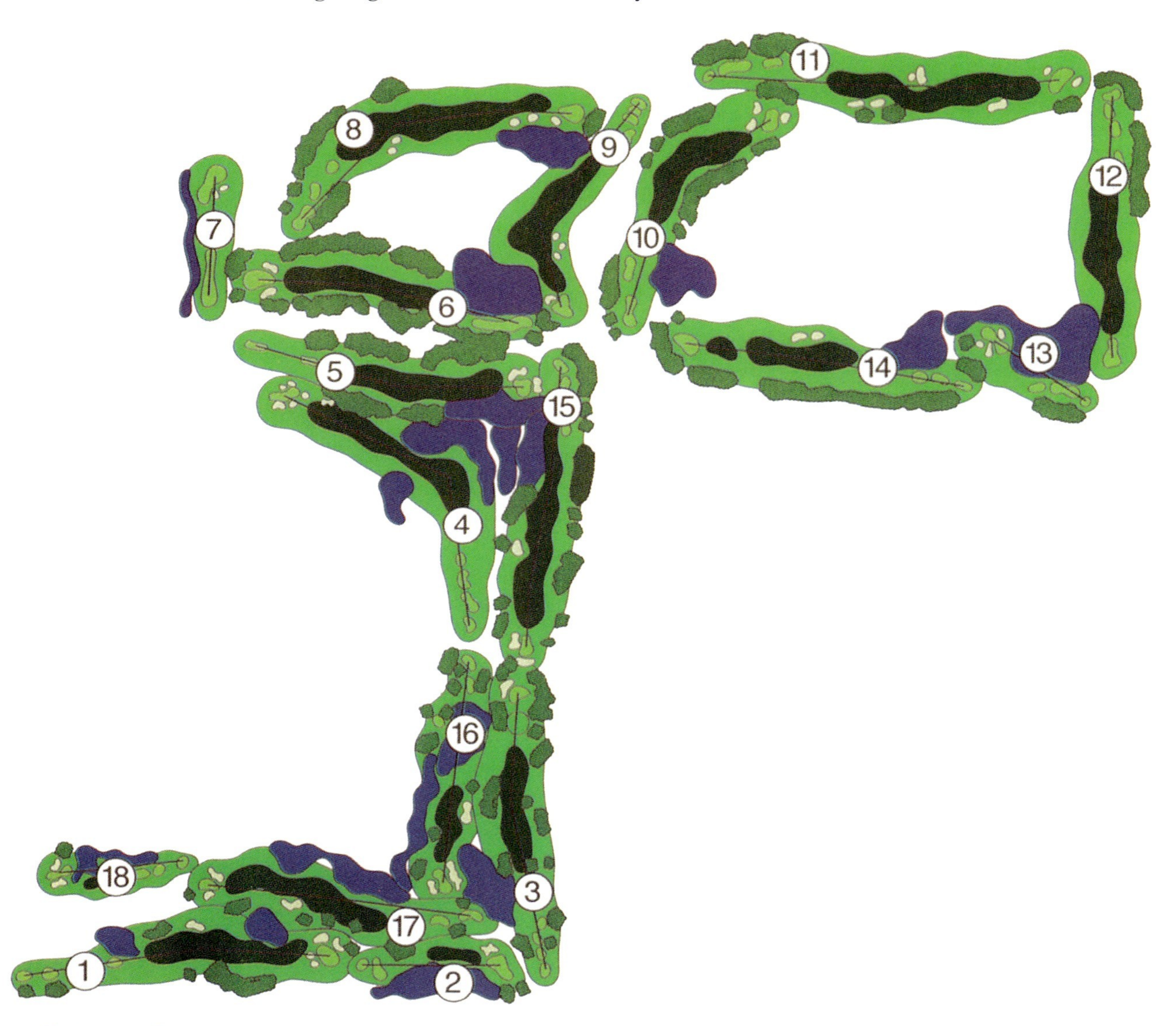

Palmer Course

HOLE	Ra	Sl	1	2	3	4	5	6	7	8	9	OUT	10	11	12	13	14	15	16	17	18	IN	TOTAL
BLUE	71.9	134	423	191	445	560	383	355	156	495	360	3368	368	510	391	161	411	397	347	373	143	3101	6469
WHITE	69.6	129	390	168	418	530	365	334	128	475	349	3157	348	480	372	143	377	366	316	357	128	2887	6044
MEN'S HCP		2	9	1	3	5	16	18	17	12			12	14	11	15	8	6	7	4	13		
PAR			4	3	4	5	4	4	3	5	4	36	4	5	4	3	4	4	4	4	3	35	71
RED	71.0	127	323	110	373	458	300	306	95	415	301	2681	305	414	339	90	344	307	283	315	109	2506	5187

SANDESTIN GOLF AND BEACH RESORT

9300 Highway 98, Destin, Florida (From I-10 take exit 14 and go south on US Highway 331 for about 15 miles; turn right onto State Route 20 and go about 15 miles; turn left and cross the Mid-Bay Toll Bridge; turn left and go east on U.S. Highway 98 about 6 miles to resort entrance on left.)
Phone: (850) 267-8144
Baytowne Golf Club and Raven Golf Club phone: (850) 267-8155
Burnt Pine Golf Club phone: (850) 267-4199

Links Course Architect: Tom Jackson Year opened: 1973
Baytowne Golf Club Architect: Tom Jackson Year opened: 1985
Burnt Pine Golf Club Architect: Rees Jones Year opened: 1994
Raven Golf Club Architect: Robert Trent Jones Jr. Year opened: 2000

Links Course rating/Slope rating:
Gold—72.8/124 Blue—70.8/120
White—68.7/116 Red—69.2/115

Baytowne course rating/Slope rating:
Gold—73.4/127 Blue—71.1/121
White—68.1/116 Red—68.5/114

Burnt Pine course rating/Slope rating for men:
Tee 1—74.1/135 Tee 2—71.5/130
Tee 3—68.7/124

Burnt Pine course rating/Slope rating for women:
Tee 3—71.4/131 Tee 4—69.4/122

Raven course rating/Slope rating:
Raven—73.8/137 Silver—71.5/135
White—68.4/128 Gold—70.6/126

For more than two decades, the Sandestin Golf and Beach Resort has been one of the most popular vacation destinations in Florida, yet it has been largely unknown outside the deep south. It has long been the first choice for holidays, conferences, and major events for people from Louisiana, Mississippi, Alabama, Georgia, and Tennessee. But that's rapidly changing as the rest of the country discovers the attraction of Florida's panhandle. Sandestin is a full service, family resort with a wide spectrum of accommodations, restaurants, health clubs, and spas. There are beach, boating, and water sports both on magnificent Choctawatchee Bay and the Gulf of Mexico.

All that aside, Sandestin is one of

Florida's premier golf resorts, with four courses from which to choose. The courses themselves fit the skill level of virtually every player. The Links Course and Baytowne Golf Club are superb resort tracks that will provide both a challenge and a good time for all levels of players—from low handicappers to those who only play occasionally or whose golf is limited to vacations. That is not to suggest that either is a pushover. If you're prone to hit the ball other than in the fairway, bring lots of golf balls because the water and wetlands will gobble up stray shots like moviegoers and popcorn. For those average to championship-level players, Burnt Pine and Raven will give you all that you can handle, and then some. If you think you're really hot, try Raven from the tips or if you're a woman with a low handicap, give Burnt Pine a shot from the teeing ground marked number 3—5,950 yards worth of demanding golf.

All of the courses at Sandestin are superbly maintained by knowledgeable and impeccably polite grounds crews. The greens and bunkers are kept in tournament condition. The pro shop people are as friendly and accommodating as anyplace in the country. In short, from the moment you enter the gate at Sandestin you are treated like somebody special, more often than not, like an old friend dropping by for a visit—even if you've never been there before.

LINKS COURSE

Linksland in the British Isles is traditionally the strip of hard-packed coastal sand and lofty dunes that form a buffer between the sea and the land. About the only foliage you see is tall grass, gorse, heather, and buckthorn. Purists insist that only land never used for grazing or agriculture qualifies as true linksland. The Links Course at Sandestin is "links" in name only. In reality it is a beautiful, albeit short, golf course that is carved from an ancient pine forest. Water comes into play on a dozen holes. Sand is strategically placed to force golfers to make precise shots. Unlike true links on which the ground is so hard that playing for the pin is perilous business, the greens are lush and hold approach shots extremely well.

To enhance the natural beauty of the Links Course at Sandestin, a half dozen holes present unparalleled views of Choctawatchee Bay, the enormous body of water that separates the barrier island on which the resort is located from the mainland. On holes #9 and #15 it is to possible to plunk a stray shot right into the waters of the bay that plays along the length of both. Golfers must guard against letting the views and vistas distract them too much from their game.

Architect Tom Jackson takes you into the course with a short par five. The dogleg left is a strip of fairway and rough between lakes. The entrance to the green is very narrow, compressed by sand on the left and water on the right.

If there is a generality that holds true for this track, it is that straight shots (regardless of length) will reap greater rewards than shots that stray from the short grass. Number 2, a short straight par four, is a perfect example. About 80 yards from the green a pair of towering pines stand like sentries. Anything other than a straight shot will have to go over or around those trees to find the well-bunkered green.

Two par threes embrace a long par four to take you to the 6th hole, the toughest on the course. It's a long risk-reward par-

The home hole on Sandestin's Links Course is an exercise in staying out of the water if you want to finish your round with a birdie or par.

four dogleg right around a lake which runs along the right from tee to green. The hole narrows severely the closer you get to the green. The green, itself, is a peninsula jutting into a lake, surrounded by water in front, on the right and to the rear. Number 7 is another risk-reward par four, this time a dogleg left. The water intersects the fairway about 75 yards in front of the two-tiered elevated green.

Number 8 is one of the tighter holes on the outward side. Your drive is across water. The ideal placement for your tee shot is to the left of the fairway bunkers that guard the right side of the hole. Water on the left and sand on the right are far enough away from the putting surface that you'll have a fairly easy approach to the long, thin green that measures some 50 yards from front to back.

You finish the side with a visually spectacular hole. Choctawatchee Bay plashes along its left length of this short par five. Despite it's diminutive length, most players opt to treat it as a three-shot hole. Your tee shot must come up short of an expanse of marsh that extends almost all the way across the fairway. From the edge of the marsh you've got about 250 yards to the green. A strip of beach guards the left front of the green and water laps right up to the collar enhancing the risks associated with going for it in two. A trio of bunkers guards the right.

You start the back side with a long par four that funnels down to a tricky green. A lake comes into play down the right, toward the green. The putting surface is extremely thin (less than 15 yards across in some places) and is shared with the 17th hole.

Two of the next three holes are par fives, separated by a pleasant par three. Number 11 is long and uphill, one of the narrowest holes on the Links Course. The entrance to the green is an alley between bunkers. The 13th is a short but difficult par five. A lake is in play down the entire left length of the hole and intrudes into the fairway about 150 yards from the undulating hourglass-shaped green. A marsh guards the right length of the hole. The fairway is a long mesa, with drop-offs into the water or marsh if you stray more than a few yards from the short grass. The bunker at the left of the green has wooden planking along one side in a style often associated with architect Pete Dye.

Danger and beauty join forces on the next two holes. The bay caresses the back of the wide shallow green on the short par-four 14th. The fairway ends at a marsh about 50 yards from the green. The hole is short enough that a big drive can go straight into the hazard. Some of the local power hitters occasionally try to drive the green, but it's a perilous shot in that there is almost no margin for error on any side. The dogleg left, par-four 15th is another treacherous hole, with the bay to the right and a lake to the left on your tee shot. The bay is replaced by another lake on your approach. The extremely contoured and irregularly shaped green is more than 50 yards from front to back.

Number 16 is the shortest par three on the Links Course, but it provides the most trouble. A forced carry is required on your tee shot to find the wide, shallow green. From there, it's a short ride to the sporting little par-four 17th. A little wedge of water sits at the right front of the well-bunkered green—the same green that's shared with hole #10.

The home hole presents an exercise in staying out of trouble. The tendency is to hit your drive to the right, because your eye sees the lake to the left. In reality, across the lake there is a lot of room to play safely to the left and then have a straight approach across the second water hazard onto the serpentine green.

Architect Tom Jackson was ahead of his time in the mid-1970s in both his bunker and green designs. He favored generous but irregular shapes for his greens and provided them with abundant humps, bumps, rolls, and swails. The copious bunkers are large, often with steep faces, and full of grassy lobes and runways. The back is tougher and tighter than the front, though there are only a few yards difference between them.

In general, the Links Course is a superior resort course and is the kind of course you can play again and again with pleasure—as is evidenced by the large number of local members who happily call the Links their home course.

The Links Course

HOLE	Ra	Sl	1	2	3	4	5	6	7	8	9	OUT	10	11	12	13	14	15	16	17	18	IN	TOT
GOLD	72.8	124	514	359	193	415	193	414	371	355	536	3350	425	529	172	504	338	412	164	391	425	3360	6710
BLUE	70.8	120	458	340	175	401	174	392	343	334	496	3113	399	502	165	483	316	390	139	347	411	3152	6265
WHITE	68.7	116	432	322	157	367	156	352	320	310	456	2872	373	475	138	462	286	359	114	323	375	2905	5777
HCP			5	13	17	3	15	1	9	11	7		4	8	18	2	12	10	16	14	6		
PAR			5	4	3	4	3	4	4	4	5	36	4	5	3	5	4	4	3	4	4	36	72
RED	69.2	115	334	301	133	312	142	279	287	279	416	2483	299	435	124	371	260	300	95	302	300	2486	4969

BAYTOWNE GOLF CLUB

Tom Jackson—the same architect who designed the Links Course—is also responsible for the Baytowne Golf Club at Sandestin. The tract of land on which the course is laid out offers the greatest changes in elevation of any of the four Sandestin courses, and it provides spectacular views of both Choctawatchee Bay and the Gulf of Mexico. It is an example of resort golf at its best. Baytowne is difficult and challenging enough to demand shot-making and course management from players of all skill levels, but it is not so difficult that the average or vacation player will exhaust his or her supply of golf balls by the 3rd or 4th hole.

As with architect Jackson's other Sandestin design, the Baytowne track plays through a pine forest, among lakes and bunkers. The undulating greens are fast, but not blistering, and they are receptive. The bunkers are well maintained. The fairways tend to offer a lot of room off the tee and get narrower as you approach the greens. The course offers a nice mix of par fours, from the tiny #8—which some big hitters think about driving—to the mammoth #13 which will test the shot-making prowess of even low handicappers.

The course is especially fair to women, who will face only a few of the hazards from the tees as men. For the average woman player it enhances the enjoyment of the course; for the good player it's a great ego booster in that it yields pars and birdies fairly easily.

A pair of par fours sends you into the woods and offers a preview of what lies ahead. An uphill one-shot hole that plays to an elevated green follows. The 4th is a medium length par four with water down the right length. The hole narrows as you

The par-four 14th at Baytowne Golf Club plays from a terraced set of hillside tees into a valley. The hole narrows precipitously the closer to the green you get.

near the elevated, irregularly-shaped green. A wedge of the lake intrudes into the fairway about 60 yards from the putting surface and compresses the entrance to the green against a stand of trees.

Number 5 is a short par-five dogleg right, rated the toughest hole on the course. Your tee shot must avoid the fairway bunker on the right. Going for it in two is tricky as the big, elevated green is tucked behind a part of the forest to the right and a huge bunker to the left. The sand hazard is one of architect Jackson's odd-shaped creations with lobes and jetties of grass forming patterns that make the sand look like the globs in a lava lamp floating in a sea of green.

The 6th is one of the tightest driving holes on the course. It's a treacherous, long, dogleg right with sand in play down the right side from about 160 yards away from the green. Bunkers all but surround the putting surface, making a par four here a good score.

A little, watery one-shot hole takes you to the two holes that finish the outgoing side. The 8th is a spectacular short par four. Many players use something other than a driver here, as accuracy reaps greater rewards than raw power. A lake to the left offers visual intimidation from the tees; water down the right length offers a real threat on every shot. A wooden bulkhead defines the limits of the green's collar and water tightens the noose at the neck of the putting surface against a bunker on the left. For those who would rather be long than risk the hazards in front, there's a gaping bunker at the back of the green as well. The 9th is a long par five. The approach to the green is tight and sandy.

The back nine opens with a short par four, an uphill par three with a two-tiered green, and a long par five. The marvelous, if daunting, 13th hole tees from the base of a hill and plays uphill, through a trough all the way to the hilltop green. There's a steep, nasty incline to the right that's full of unpleasant foliage; to the left is forest, sand, and unforgiving terrain. A tee shot that drifts to the right will be blocked out by the hillside and the Florida scrub, leaving a blind approach to the green. The fairway itself narrows to less than 15 yards in width about 150 yards from the green.

Number 14 is a breathtaking but dangerous hole. From the elevated, terraced tees, the panorama of the Gulf of Mexico stretches out before you. (This is a world class photo op, if you're into that sort of thing.) The hole features a generous landing area, but the approach to the green is tough. The water that plays down the left side of the hole balloons out in front of the two-tiered green requiring a forced carry on most approach shots. Six bunkers form an inverted *J* around the green.

The short par-five 15th plays uphill all the way. It's a dogleg left with the hilltop green hooked behind a cluster of bunkers and a stand of trees. From 150 yards out, the fairway is squeezed by a series of bunkers on the left and a steep hill on the right.

Number 16 is a medium-length par four. You drive from an elevated set of tees. The ideal shot splits the fairway between the right and left bunkers. A long bulkhead holds back the lake to the left of the hole.

A short par three leads you to the closer, a very solid par four. Baytowne is not the most difficult golf course in Florida, or even in the panhandle, but you've got to go a long way to find a more picturesque and aesthetically pleasing golf course.

Baytowne Golf Club

HOLE	Ra	Sl	1	2	3	4	5	6	7	8	9	OUT	10	11	12	13	14	15	16	17	18	IN	TOT
GOLD	73.4	127	371	414	167	415	491	409	172	330	529	3298	411	172	548	464	366	586	433	186	426	3592	6890
BLUE	71.1	121	341	376	135	393	479	389	154	312	496	3075	363	149	511	401	337	485	393	165	391	3195	6270
WHITE	68.1	116	276	353	123	359	409	361	136	286	467	2770	337	117	485	359	311	467	373	146	364	2959	5729
HCP			13	11	17	3	1	5	15	9	7		12	18	8	2	14	4	6	16	10		
PAR			4	4	3	4	5	4	3	4	5	36	4	3	5	4	4	5	4	3	4	36	72
RED	68.5	114	238	290	73	253	375	294	101	234	436	2294	294	79	419	343	278	439	293	105	318	2568	486

BURNT PINE GOLF CLUB

The name of the golf course is right out of the folklore of the Florida panhandle. The yarn is spun of a Scottish sea captain in the 1860s who sailed into Choctawatchee Bay while trying to dodge a civil war naval blockade. The captain put to shore with a chest full of treasure around what is now the 14th hole at Burnt Pine Golf Club, and he buried it at the base of a pine tree that had been scorched, presumably by lightening. But as time passed, a devastating forest fire destroyed much of the pine forest in that area. One burnt pine looked very much like all the others and the treasure was lost to time. The fact remains that hundreds of treasure hunters—including the old Scot's ghost, according to the folklorists—have searched in vain for the treasure chest.

That coastal landscape may not have yielded the loot, but it has certainly become the home for a fabulous championship golf course, the work of golf course architect Rees Jones. Rees Jones golf courses have a number of signature characteristics, all of which are present at Burnt Pine, including fairways lined with mounds and manmade hills, copious amounts of water, large and undulating greens, and the adventurous use of bunkers. Jones likes to create long par fours and an interesting mix of par threes.

The course plays just short of 7,000 yards from the back tees. Most women will be content to play from the forward markers. My wife, Barbara, who is a low handicap player, noted that even from the forward tees, three of the par four holes are in excess of 340 yards. "That means unless you're Kari Webb you're hitting two woods and probably a chip," she said. The tees are not color-coded. They are simply numbered 1 through 4, longest to shortest.

An introductory par four and a long, three-shot par five take you to the first of Rees Jones's interesting and memorable par threes, a medium length hole with an enormous sand trap that runs down the left side from tee to green. The bunker is highly contoured with mounds and ribs of grass creating runways into the sand. Your tee shot is to a small, highly contoured green.

The first thing you see from the 4th tee boxes is marshy hazard separating you from the fairway. The multi-level green is protected by a trio of bunkers on the right and a lone sand trap sculpted out of a mound on the left. Number 5 is a tight, demanding par five with water down the left side from tee to green and with mounding along the right. It's rated the toughest hole on the course. The elevated green is angled to the left behind a bunker and part of the lake. A huge bunker arcs around the back of the putting surface.

Architect Jones' second fine par three on the outgoing side is long and difficult. To get to the green your shot must carry across the edge of a pond. The green is guarded by water to the right and a bunker to the left-front.

Three par fours finish the side. A swail in front of the large 7th green is a double whammy—it creates the optical illusion that the green is closer than it is and it imprisons any approach shot that does not fly to the putting surface. Number 8 is short but very tight. The bumpy green is protected by two pot bunkers in front and one on each side. Head to the turn with a watery, risk-reward par four. The lake laps up to the left side of the irregularly shaped green.

The potpourri of par fours continues on the back nine. Number 10 is a gentle dogleg left with water down the left length and

The last par three on Burnt Pine Golf Club at Sandestin—#14—requires players to carry over a marsh to a highly contoured green. Choctawatchee Bay shimmers through the pines at the right.

Rees Jones' signature mounding and forest to the right. The 11th is an intriguing short hole that plays to one of the smallest greens on Burnt Pine. The bunkering on this hole is what makes it tough. Three fairway bunkers to the right and one to the left must be avoided on your tee shot. Not only does architect Jones protect the green with bunkers right and left, but he's got a long one in the shape of an apostrophe right in front of the putting surface, as well. There are no run-up approaches to this hole.

Pick your poison on the short par-three 12th. A straight or right-to-left shot must carry the lake that's in play down the right side from tee to green. A left-to-right shot must carry an enormous bunker. With another gaping sand hazard behind the green, there is no room to bail out.

Number 13 is a long dogleg right par four with a lake in play down the right side off the tee. At about the point where the dogleg bends, a stand of trees hugs the right fairway. A second lake then comes into play from about 150 yards out to the green. Keep your tee shot far enough left so that you can see the flag. The wide, shallow two-tiered green is angled to the right behind a long, thin sand hazard.

The best of architect Jones' par threes is the last you encounter. It is a treacherous hole, with a forced carry over marsh to a multi-level green. The panorama of the bay to the right is spectacular, with sails billowing in the distance and pleasure boats plying the water near shore. But keep your mind on business here. It's an easy par or birdie if your tee shot is precise; it can be a depressing bogey or worse if you fail to find the green from the tee.

Your drive on #15 from the edge of the bay is across a stretch of marsh. It's one of the only holes on which the forward markers are places ahead of all the trouble, which makes it a considerably less difficult hole for women than for men.

The par-five 16th is not a terribly long hole, but it is tight and demanding with one lake down the entire right length of the hole, and a second in play on the left for part of it. Number 17 is a short par four dogleg right around a lake.

Rees Jones decided to deliver one last test on the finisher, a long dogleg right par five that's a three shot hole for all but the longest hitters. The fairway is a shelf with high mounds down the right side and a drop-off into the woods on the left. Keep your drive to the left of the cluster of bunkers. Put your second about 100 yards from the green. The green is guarded by five bunkers—three pot bunkers scooped out of the mounds behind it and two wide, thin sand hazards in front that look as if they are underscoring the putting surface.

Burnt Pine is a beautiful and challenging championship golf course. It's not for beginners. And with all the water and woods on it, even good players should stick an extra sleeve of golf balls in their bag.

Burnt Pine Golf Club

HOLE	Ra	Sl	1	2	3	4	5	6	7	8	9	OUT	10	11	12	13	14	15	16	17	18	IN	TOT
TEE 1	74.1	135	404	569	183	444	531	202	425	356	403	3517	408	371	149	433	212	439	515	375	577	3479	6996
TEE 2	71.5	130	355	548	161	420	491	188	404	334	364	3265	371	342	139	408	193	363	489	357	547	3209	6474
TEE 3	68.7(m)/71.4(w)	124(m)/131(w)	307	524	131	389	456	167	373	308	333	2988	342	313	124	380	165	331	460	339	508	2962	5950
HCP			11	5	17	3	1	15	7	13	9		12	16	18	6	8	14	2	10	4		
PAR			4	5	3	4	5	3	4	4	4	36	4	4	3	4	3	4	5	4	5	36	72
TEE 4	69.4	122	274	448	93	344	416	137	342	258	293	2605	263	291	97	343	118	244	403	289	443	2491	5096

RAVEN GOLF CLUB

Robert Trent Jones Jr. has created a masterpiece at Sandestin. His design is original and contemporary, yet influenced by the great classical designers of the past, not the least of whom is his father, Robert Trent Jones Sr. The subtle amalgamation of old and new creates a wonderful golfing experience. Jones offers golfers a variety of options for playing almost every hole.

His par 71 track is far from short—nearly 7,000 yards from the back tees and more than 5,000 for women playing the forward markers. The mix of holes, including five par threes, is satisfying and memorable. His par fives are all three-shot holes for everybody but people who hit the ball like Tiger Woods or John Daly. The course is actually made up of nineteen holes. Jones created a pair of par threes that are #16A and #16B. They are played alternately, every other day.

Jones has constructed greens that require a variety of approach shots, from forced carries over water to bump-and-run shots. The greens, themselves, are a joy to play—fast, true, and receptive. Jones favors extremes in green length and width, and he likes irregular shapes with lots of breaks and bends. His bunkers are well placed and reflect the thoughtful and deliberate character of the architect. Water is in play on thirteen of the holes.

My wife was especially impressed with the design and placement of the forward tees. "It's obvious that women were not an afterthought here," she said. "If men have to clear a hazard from the tee, women have to clear a hazard from the tee. If it's a dogleg for men, it's not gratuitously straightened for women."

Two good par fours get you right into the challenge that is the Raven. The opener plays over a slight hill and then down to a long, multi-tiered green. The 2nd is a long dogleg left. Your tee shot has to stay clear of the left fairway bunkers that define the bend in the dogleg. The green is guarded by a hill on the left and a pair of large bunkers on the right.

Number 3 is a crescent shaped dogleg right. It is a long par five. Your drive is to a plateaued fairway with drop-offs on both sides. The green is nestled behind a wedge of lake that intrudes in front of the putting surface. The irregularly shaped green has a bowl in front into which tentative shots will feed.

A short, watery par three leads you to the solid par-four 5th. Again Jones has designed an elevated fairway that drops off into a lake on the right and into a forest on the left. The long, thin green—protected by a bunker to the left and an embankment that leads to the lake on the right—is not quite 50 yards from front to back and depending on pin placement, it can vary club selection by two or three. The green comes almost to a point at its furthest end, and it is less than 15 yards wide across the dome.

The next hole may be my favorite on the Raven. It's a gorgeous par three that plays to an island green. The big, multi-level green is pitched from back to front, but architect Robert Trent Jones Jr. has provided a buffer between the putting surface and the water. If you miss the green, you may avoid a penalty stroke, but there's no guarantee you'll avoid a bogey or worse.

Number 7 is a huge double-dogleg par five. The hole plays more than 600 yards from the back tees, a monstrous 487 yards for women from the forward markers. There is water along the left and hillside bunkers on the right. The bunkers that appear to be in front of the green are not at

The par-three 6th at Sandestin's Raven Golf Club—designed by Robert Trent Jones, Jr.—features a multi-tiered island green.

greenside, but rather 25 or so yards away, creating the optical illusion that the green is closer than it is.

A short par three takes you to the toughest hole on the course with which to finish the side. It's a long, gentle dogleg left with water along the left side and hills, trees, and a waste area to the right. The wide, shallow green is elevated slightly and angled to the left with the majority of it behind the lake. A par four here is most satisfying.

The back nine opens with a short par four that's fairly straight with an uphill tee shot and a long, multi-tiered green at the end of a mesa. Clusters of bunkers create a chute of fairway that leads to the putting surface. Anybody daring a bump-and-run approach needs the accuracy of a professional bowler. Number 11 is a long, straight par five with a lake down the left. The 12th is a cute par three with an elevated green that's extremely wide and shallow, and guarded by water on the left and sand on the right. The putting surface is less than 15 yards deep and more than 45 yards from side to side.

Three fine par fours follow. Number 13 is long with most of the trouble along the right. The green is pitched left to right. Number 14 is a sharp dogleg left around a lake. It's a risk- reward hole. The long thin green is pitched steeply from back to front. To my eye the back of the green is 4½ or 5 feet higher than the front. The 15th features a fairway that's split by a cluster of bunkers. Players are faced with four possible options: lay-up short of the bunkers, play to the low side on the left and shoot up to the green, play to the high side on the right and have a downhill approach, or boom it over the bunkers and have a short-iron to the flag.

The following two holes are played on alternate days. Number 16A is long, with a big elevated green. Number 16B is a shorter hole, but the more visually stimulating of the two and the hole that requires the more precise shot-making. The elevated green is surrounded by bunkers.

Number 17 is a tight, long par five with water down the right side about half of its length. A second lake comes into play on the other side of the fairway. The lake starts just beyond the halfway point, plays up to the green, and intrudes in front of the putting surface. Hillside bunkers on the right and left make the approach shot difficult.

There's no letup as you head to the clubhouse. The 18th is a par four dogleg right with water about halfway down the right, and a second lake in play on the left up near the green. Your risk-reward tee shot must come to rest between the bunkers on the left and the lake. The green is guarded by a stand of oaks that shadow the putting surface to the right, and a bunker and water to the left.

In addition to all of the other delights at the Raven, there are people riding around in golf carts called "player assistants" and among the things that they have to offer are mango-scented ice-cold towels that will help fend off the ravages of the Florida panhandle heat and humidity.

The Raven is a course you'll savor, like fine wine or great art. It is well designed, impeccably maintained, and superbly managed. Players feel like members of an exclusive country club during their visit.

Raven Golf Club

HOLE	Ra	Sl	1	2	3	4	5	6	7	8	OUT	10	11	12	13	14	15	16A	16B	17	18	IN A	IN B	TOTAL A	TOTAL B	
RAVEN	73.8	137	389	460	587	193	400	203	604	158	460	3454	379	562	130	438	421	321	228	172	546	431	3456	3400	6910	6854
SILVER	71.5	135	346	415	565	148	367	174	558	131	432	3136	337	522	113	398	388	298	207	146	522	424	3209	3148	6345	6284
WHITE	68.4	128	325	396	545	104	356	162	522	104	365	2879	312	480	95	369	370	282	185	117	481	414	2988	2920	5867	5799
HCP			13	5	7	15	11	9	3	17	1	12	2	18	6	10	14	16	16	8	4					
PAR			4	4	5	3	4	3	5	3	4	35	4	5	3	4	4	4	3	3	5	4	36	71		
GOLD	70.6	126	281	324	471	88	340	64	487	86	343	2484	286	450	72	340	308	250	118	90	438	319	2581			

Fourteen separate bunkers surround the green on the par-three 14th at Southern Dunes Golf and Country Club.

SOUTHERN DUNES GOLF AND COUNTRY CLUB

2888 Southern Dunes Blvd., Haines City, Florida (From I-4 take exit 23 and follow U.S. 27 south for 7 miles; entrance is on the left.)
Phone: (941) 421-4653 or (800) 632-6400

Architect: Steve Smyers   Year opened: 1993

Course rating/Slope rating for men:
Black—74.7/135   Blue—72.6/129
White—70.2/123

Course rating/Slope rating for women:
Yellow—72.4/126   Red—68.8/118

Southern Dunes is a long, picturesque golf course designed to emulate certain aspects of the coastal links of Scotland and Ireland. The mounding and hills are reminiscent of linksland dunes. Likewise, a paucity of trees adds to the links-like flavor. In general, the course is firm and fast. The sandy base on which it is built drains well. It is extremely well bunkered. Architect Smyers uses enormous traditional sand hazards and Florida waste bunkers, studded with tufts of wild grass bunkers—in the style of designers such as Rees Jones, Dick Wilson, and the Fazio brothers, Tom and Jim. What water there is comes into play at strategic points. The greens are large and well contoured, fast, and true. There's nothing tricky here. This is not a design that is fraught with hidden hazards or contrived difficulties.

Keep your shots in play and you will score well. Shot making that finds the sand, hills, or water will drive your numbers into the stratosphere. "It's a course that will give you a lot of shot-making opportunities," said head pro Eddie Frye. He noted that with the overall length of the course, when the central Florida wind kicks up it can be extremely demanding.

The par 72 course features five sets of tees—three for men and two for women. At 5,633 yards from the longer set of women's tees, women are advised to bring their *A* game and get ready for a marathon. Three of the four par fives are in excess of 450 yards and all of the par three holes are longer than 120 yards.

Long hitting men who want a real test should try the back tees. Seven of the par fours are longer than 400 yards; all of the par fives average around 550 yards; and two of the one-shot holes measure well over 200 yards. This is a big golf course from the tips.

The par-four 1st introduces you to the kind of bunkering you're going to see all day. The effect is to create a chute between lengthy clusters of fairway sand traps. Architect Smyers likes to separate his bunkers with strips of grass or let grassy tongues lap into the sand creating little peninsulas. The visual effect is pleasing, and the effect on your score can be disastrous. On most holes here, if you hit an errant shot, it is easier to find sand than grass.

The 2nd—which is shorter than the

opener—gives you an ample landing area but a cluster of big, deep bunkers hugs the right side of the fairway to the front of the green. A demanding one-shot hole, with the elevated green guarded by six separate sand traps, leads you to the long par-five 4th. It's fairly straight until you approach the green, which is offset to the right behind a cluster of bunkers. Seven hillside bunkers split the fairway on the short par-four 5th. The most generous landing area is on the downhill side of the sand, on the right. But that requires you to avoid a lake into which the green is peninsulaed. The more difficult tee shot is to the left, but that gives you an open, downhill shot to the green.

Number 6 is a lovely par three that features an elevated set of tees and a multi-level green, sitting in a basin with a steep hill to the left and a trio of hillside bunkers to the right. The putting surface slopes sharply from back to front. On the next hole, a dogleg left par four, you can either try to carry the bunkers on the left and cut across the bend in the dogleg or you can play out to the right, giving yourself a longer but safer look at the hole. Six enormous bunkers line the right side of the fairway from about 165 yards out to the uphill green.

Number 8 is a short uphill par four with your drive across an expanse of waste bunker. Once you've cleared the waste area, the landing zone is substantial, but the entrance to the elevated and undulating green is choked by sand right and left. The side concludes with a risk-reward par five. It's a dogleg right around a waste area. How much of the sand you dare to challenge will determine the length of your second shot. The hole plays up a small incline from the tees and back down to the green that sits at the far end of a highly mounded and contoured valley. Placing your lay-up about 100 yards from the flag will set up a good scoring opportunity.

After the turn you face an extremely long, tight par four dogleg left, that can play like a par five if the wind is in your face. An accurate tee shot down a slight incline is required here. For long hitters it's a snap; for shorter hitters it can be driver, three- wood, and hope you're in the vicinity of the green. If you can't make it in two, make sure you avoid the enormous bunkers that line the right side of the hole. That takes you to a lovely par three that requires your tee shot—from a terraced set of tee boxes—to carry a field of sand traps to a green that's at the base of the hill.

Number 12 is a long par five with nothing but trouble down both sides, including sand, trees, and water. Two accurate shots will set up a fairly easy approach to the green for average players. Big hitters who want to go for it in two will likely need a right-to-left approach to find the open front of the putting surface. This is a very tough hole for women, requiring two long accurate shots to set up a medium approach.

Two par fours sandwich a par three in the middle of the incoming nine. The 13th fairway is a shelf. There's a drop-off along the right side. In front of the green, about 75 yards out, that shelf goes between four hillside bunkers and slopes so severely to the right that few shots will fail to roll off the short grass, through the rough, and into the sand or the trees. The next hole, the short par three called "Bunkers by the Dozen" is an understatement. There are actually fourteen separate bunkers all around this wide, shallow green. The 15th is a slight dogleg right that will entice some power-hitters to think about going for in a single shot. If you can clear the right-side bunkers that define the bend in the dogleg, the hill will work your ball toward the hole. Mere mortals will want to put their tee shots probably using something less than a driver in front of the bunkers or to the left of them, and play a medium- to short-iron in to the flag.

Number 16 is a long straight par five that can play tougher than it looks. The hole plays downhill from the tees then up and over a hill directly in front of the green. The green, itself, is a brute with a back tier and a front tier divided by a trough that intersects the putting surface.

Southern Dunes finishes with a pair of long par fours. Number 17 is a straight hole that plays over a small hill to a long thin green. The green is on a hillside ledge with the hill above to the left and a steep drop-off into a bunker or grassy collection area to the right. The name of the dogleg right finishing hole—"Choke Alley"—says it all. A pair of long straight shots will be rewarded; errant shots will render a disappointing finish.

In all, Southern Dunes is a fine, fair test of the game. It is a seriously long golf course. If you can hit it solidly and keep it in play, you'll love this place. If you are prone to spraying your tee shots you may want to reconsider your itinerary. It's a friendly golf course that makes you feel like a long-time member from the moment you enter the parking lot.

Southern Dunes

HOLE	Ra	Sl	1	2	3	4	5	6	7	8	9	OUT	10	11	12	13	14	15	16	17	18	IN	TOT
BLACK	74.7	135	426	374	233	555	378	187	454	413	542	3562	471	216	551	461	167	369	548	421	461	3665	7227
BLUE	72.6	129	390	359	221	520	361	179	440	395	524	3389	451	197	517	429	149	347	507	397	420	3414	6803
WHITE	70.2	123	350	333	197	474	314	167	409	364	498	3106	420	166	481	401	134	326	499	384	381	3192	6298
HCP			9	13	15	1	7	17	5	11	3		8	16	2	6	18	14	4	12	10		
YELLOW	72.4	126	291	286	127	438	280	138	375	327	485	2747	383	140	455	345	122	303	473	342	323	2886	5633
RED	68.8	118	249	252	95	384	239	103	345	304	450	2421	363	113	418	298	91	257	439	303	284	2566	4987

The Golf Club at South Hampton's yardage book says two charred and leafless oaks that stand guard on either side of the 6th fairway were "frozen in time by lightening."

THE GOLF CLUB AT SOUTH HAMPTON

315 South Hampton Club Way, St. Augustine, Florida (From I-95 take exit 96 and go west about three miles to the entrance on the left)
Phone: (904) 287-7529

Architect: Mark McCumber   Year opened: 2000

Course rating/Slope rating for men:
Gold—73.2/133   Black—70.9/129
Blue—68.7/119   White—65.7/113

Course rating/Slope rating for women:
White—71.8/121   Green—68.2/113

I generally like the golf courses designed by PGA Tour star Mark McCumber. They are tougher than average, but beyond sheer difficulty, they are very cleverly and skillfully designed. McCumber combines what nature put there with his own skill at massaging the landscape into a unique golfing test. There's nothing cookie-cutter about one of his designs. Each one is unique.

In the case of South Hampton (everybody simply calls it South Hampton, rather than "The Golf Club at South Hampton"), McCumber has created a lovely, challenging track that will test the shot-making skills of every player. Five sets of regular tees provide a wonderful look at each hole for golfers of every skill level. "There's a premium on some tee shots," said head pro Chris Rocha. "And if you get away from the fairway and into some of the trouble areas, some of the fairway bunkers, you can find yourself looking for a one putt par."

And there's a brilliant and unique touch as well. M. G. Orender, Secretary of the PGA of America, has taken the PGA mission "to grow the game" to a new level. To encourage beginners and family play, the course features an entire set of short tees—just shy of 3,000 yards—to make the course user friendly for junior golfers and beginners. These aren't just plunked down in the fairway. The Burgundy Tees at South Hampton are regular, mowed tee boxes with yardage marked on the scorecard. Members play it as a par-three course and even have par-three tournaments. Juniors use it for competition. The pros use it as part of a teaching program for beginning players.

It's an added plus at a facility that already has a lot going for it. The general attitude of the place—friendly, efficient, and knowledgeable from the pro shop to the people who load your bag on the golf cart—is simply outstanding. The goal is to provide a great golfing experience, country club amenities, and reasonable prices. South Hampton succeeds on all levels.

The golfing experience is excellent. It starts with two par fours, the opener playing uphill to a green fronted by a huge bunker. On the next hole, architect McCumber gives you a very tight landing area for your tee shot, with two big fairway bunkers sandwiching a narrow strip of fairway. The approach to the well-protected green is over a slight rise, rendering the lake and two bunkers to the right front of the putting surface all but invisible.

Number 3 is a nice par three that plays to an elevated green. That's followed by a short, par four dogleg left that's rated the easiest hole on the course. I like it. It's not as easy as it's rated. While it can be a good scoring hole, it will clobber you if you find any of the four strategically placed hillside bunkers or the one giant greenside sand hazard. The 5th is a long par four with a pine forest down the left length of the hole. A lake is in play on the right.

South Hampton's signature hole is #6, a three-shot par five dogleg right. Your tee shot must come to rest between a pair of ancient lightening-charred oak trees that stand like ghostly sentries on both sides of the fairway. A cluster of pot bunkers, largely hidden from view, lies in wait to devour a lay-up shot that is too aggressive. The long, thin green is squeezed by a series of mounds, a bunker, and a lake.

Number 7 is a fine par three that presents players with a marshy wetland and a deep greenside bunker between the tee boxes and the putting surface. The green is elevated and contoured. There's bail-out room to the right front. The 8th is a long, tough par four dogleg left that plays to an elevated green. The big fairway bunker at the left side of the hole is within driving distance for most players. A horseshoe-shaped greenside bunker sits menacingly to the right front of the green.

My favorite hole on the course is the last one on the outward side. It's a long par-five dogleg right. Sand and trees are problems off the tee and a lake and marsh to the right squeeze the entrance to the green against a trio of bunkers. "Number 9 has a great green complex," said head pro Chris Rocha. But he notes that careful shot making can yield pars and birdies. "It can give you momentum going into the back side." My wife, Barbara, who played the course from the White Tees, noted that at 460 yards it took her three good woods to get to the green in regulation.

Your tee shot is critical on the uphill, par-four 10th. Make sure you keep your drive between the fairway bunkers. But don't be so cautious you come up short. Failure to get up the hill can leave a blind approach to the plateaued putting surface. A bunker arcs around the left side of the green and another deep sand hazard resides at the right. The green itself is sloped sharply from back to front.

Number 11 is a par four with a sharp dogleg left. On the left side is a large waste area, and a fairway bunker defines the bend in the dogleg. The green is elevated. The 12th is a moderate par three with a slightly elevated green surrounded by three sand traps. The yardage booklet suggests that one should, "take danger out of play by hitting to the right front of the green." Give me a break! If I could hit it that precisely I wouldn't be writing about golf, I be out on the Senior PGA Tour.

The next hole is the shortest par five on South Hampton. It's a gentle dogleg left with architect McCumber exercising exuberance in his placement of bunkers. Bunkers are in play on your drive; a pair of bunkers about 135 yards from the green obscure the putting surface from view; a cluster of greenside bunkers lurk to snare an imprecise approach to the small green. That's followed by a par four called "Lone Cypress" for one towering old cypress tree about 140 yards from the green.

A long par three and a short par four take you to the two finishing holes. Number 17 is called "Armageddon." It's a wonderful, long par-five risk-reward hole that immediately bends to the right around a lake providing the opening risk. The fairway then narrows dangerously the closer you get to the green, a funnel with pine forest on the left and elevated, hillside bunkers to the right. The green sits behind a wedge of forest on the left with a giant bunker right front. "The definition [of Armageddon] is where good meets evil," said pro Chris Rocha. "If you hit good shots you'll score well. But you can really make a big number there as well."

The final hole at South Hampton is a lovely dogleg left par four. "You come out of a chute and then face the dogleg," said Rocha. "It's a neat finishing hole." It's a lot neater if you avoid the water, the bunkers and the trees and find the putting surface in two.

The course is well maintained and managed. "It's a tough, but a fair test for women," said my wife, Barbara, noting that it's substantially easier from the Green Tees (a mere 4,784 yards) as opposed to the women's championship White Tees (an exhilarating 5,462 yards). This is a golf course that's destined to get better and better as it matures.

The Golf Club at South Hampton

HOLE	Ra	Sl	1	2	3	4	5	6	7	8	9	OUT	10	11	12	13	14	15	16	17	18	IN	TOT
GOLD	73.2	133	408	409	179	355	417	545	205	434	533	3505	379	402	178	493	425	215	374	571	410	3447	6952
BLACK	7.9	129	394	360	168	325	382	506	193	393	513	3234	365	376	169	470	394	199	345	533	394	3245	6479
BLUE	68.7	119	372	346	144	312	370	486	159	373	475	3037	308	364	133	458	377	173	285	493	377	2968	6005
WHITE	65.7(m)/71.8(w)	113(m)/121(w)	343	304	122	266	338	447	145	316	460	2741	296	335	122	427	343	163	270	463	302	2721	5462
HCP			14	10	16	18	4	12	6	2	8		15	7	17	9	5	3	13	1	11		
PAR			4	4	3	4	4	5	3	4	5	36	4	4	3	5	4	3	4	5	4	36	72
GREEN	68.2	113	298	234	89	253	298	403	116	275	401	2367	266	294	108	367	299	138	235	419	291	2417	4784
BURGUNDY	NA	NA	171	156	67	161	183	196	93	149	192	1368	183	152	63	206	161	109	194	234	176	1478	2846

There's little margin for error on the par-three 16th at Timacuan Golf and Country Club.

TIMACUAN GOLF AND COUNTRY CLUB

550 Timacuan Blvd., Lake Mary, Florida (Take exit 50 off I-4 northeast of Orlando and turn toward Lake Mary; drive about one mile and turn left onto Rinehart Rd.; drive about one mile to Timacuan Blvd. and turn right; follow signs to the clubhouse.)
Phone: (407) 321-0010

Architect: Ron Garl and Bobby Weed Jr. Year opened: 1987

Course rating/Slope rating for men:
Gold—73.2/133 Blue—70.7/126
White—68.4/117 Green—64.8/109

Course rating/Slope rating for women:
White—73.9/134 Green—70.5/125
Red—66.8/118

This fine, challenging golf course is named for some of Florida's earliest settlers, a tribe of Indians known as the Timacua. The Timacua were water people, living along the Atlantic coast and on the banks of rivers and streams in northeast Florida. Archaeologists studying the Timacua and their culture tell us that they were a physically imposing people with men and women often standing more than 6 feet tall and bearing elaborate full-body tattoos. They hunted the deer, bear and wild boars of the region; they fished both fresh and saltwater species; they grew crops that included squash, beans, and yams. A Timacuan dietary staple was alligator, which they introduced to the Spanish explorers who came exploring Florida in the mid-1500s.

A Timacuan canoe is the symbol of the golf course that bears the name of the tribe. Fittingly the course is a watery test with lakes coming into play on nine of the eighteen holes. The majority of the water is on the back nine, which is also more tightly treed. The front is somewhat more open but more hilly. Assistant pro, Adam Brackett, observed, "The front side is pretty typical of Florida courses. It's fairly open. The back side is more like what you find in South Carolina and North Carolina, with lots of trees lining the fairways."

The greens vary in size, and while the contours are not highly exaggerated, they are very difficult to read and are kept fast. The breaks and bends are subtle, especially for the first-time player. A little local knowledge is useful on the putting surfaces. Overall, Timacuan is a fine and satisfying test, nearly 7,000 yards from the back markers.

A gentle, uphill par four is your introduction. Cross the street and you come to the signature hole. The tee boxes are fanned out along the shore of a pretty little lake. "It's a risk-reward hole," said assistant pro Adam Brackett. "You have a pretty good forced carry off the tee and then another forced carry to the green." To the right, you can see the water off the tee, but there's water in front of the green that you can't see. The fairway is a peninsula that juts out into the lake. It is entirely possible to put your tee shot through the fairway and into the water beyond the landing zone. The large, kidney-shaped green is tucked behind a tongue of water. It's rated the most difficult hole on the course for men, the number three handicap hole for women.

The 3rd is a tight par four, with the lake that engulfs the 2nd hole in play down the left and a marshy wetland down the right. That's followed by a long, uphill par three with a pair of enormous, gaping bunkers on the right. The undulating green atop a plateau is tucked behind another steep-lipped sand trap. The 5th is a short par five that will tempt even moderate male hitters to go for in two, especially if the wind is helping. For women it's a long hole—418 yards from the green markers (which most woman at Timacuan play) and 398 from the red or forward tees. It's appropriately rated the toughest hole on the course for women.

Number 6 is a long, tough par four that plays downhill into a valley and then back uphill to an elevated green. Steep mounds on both sides create a trough of fairway. The green is angled steeply back toward the fairway creating something of a false front, in that if your shot does not travel far enough onto the putting surface it will roll back down the hill, as often as not right off the short grass. The short par-three 7th green is an oasis in the middle of the desert. An enormous waste-bunker—so large that the cart path is constructed right through it—extends from tee to green and surrounds most of the putting surface.

The side concludes with two par fours. The dogleg left 8th features a blind tee shot over a hill. The short 9th hole is a pretty way to finish the side. The key here, with a forest of pines guarding the left and water to the right, is not length from the tees as much as shot placement.

Go around the clubhouse to the first of two solid par fours to begin the back nine. The 10th is a dogleg right with water on both sides. Your tee shot is through a chute of trees. The green is tucked behind a tongue of marsh and water that extends more than half way across the fairway. Number 11 is short, with a huge waste-bunker in front of the tees to about 135 yards from the putting surface. The big par-five 12th is a long three shot hole. Assistant pro Adam Brackett said, "It's a par five dogleg left with a bunch of water running around the outside of the dogleg. Most courses have the water on the inside of the dogleg, especially on a par five. It makes it quite a challenging hole." The water then snakes down the right side of the fairway with trees protecting the left. The tee shot is blind. The green sits at the bottom of a hill cradled in a basin.

Two short holes team up next. Number 13 is short a par three with a crescent-shaped bunker arching around the right side of the green; this is followed by a diminutive par four. You drive across a bit of water that then hugs the right side of the fairway. There are trees to the left, but their proximity is an optical illusion. There is ample room to play to the left-center of the fairway, but a couple of local members remarked that you see a lot more players finding the water than you might expect. My wife Barbara noted, "The Green Tees are positioned to make the hole a dogleg right. That creates a much more difficult driving hole for women than for men."

A long watery par five with a lake on both sides leads you to the three splendid finishers at Timacuan. One of my favorite holes there is the long par-three 16th. Everybody has a forced carry over water to a green. A wooden bulkhead delineates the front of the putting surface. The hole has the feel of many Robert Trent Jones Sr. par threes, in that there is precious little bail out room anywhere. For women this is a very difficult hole. From the Green

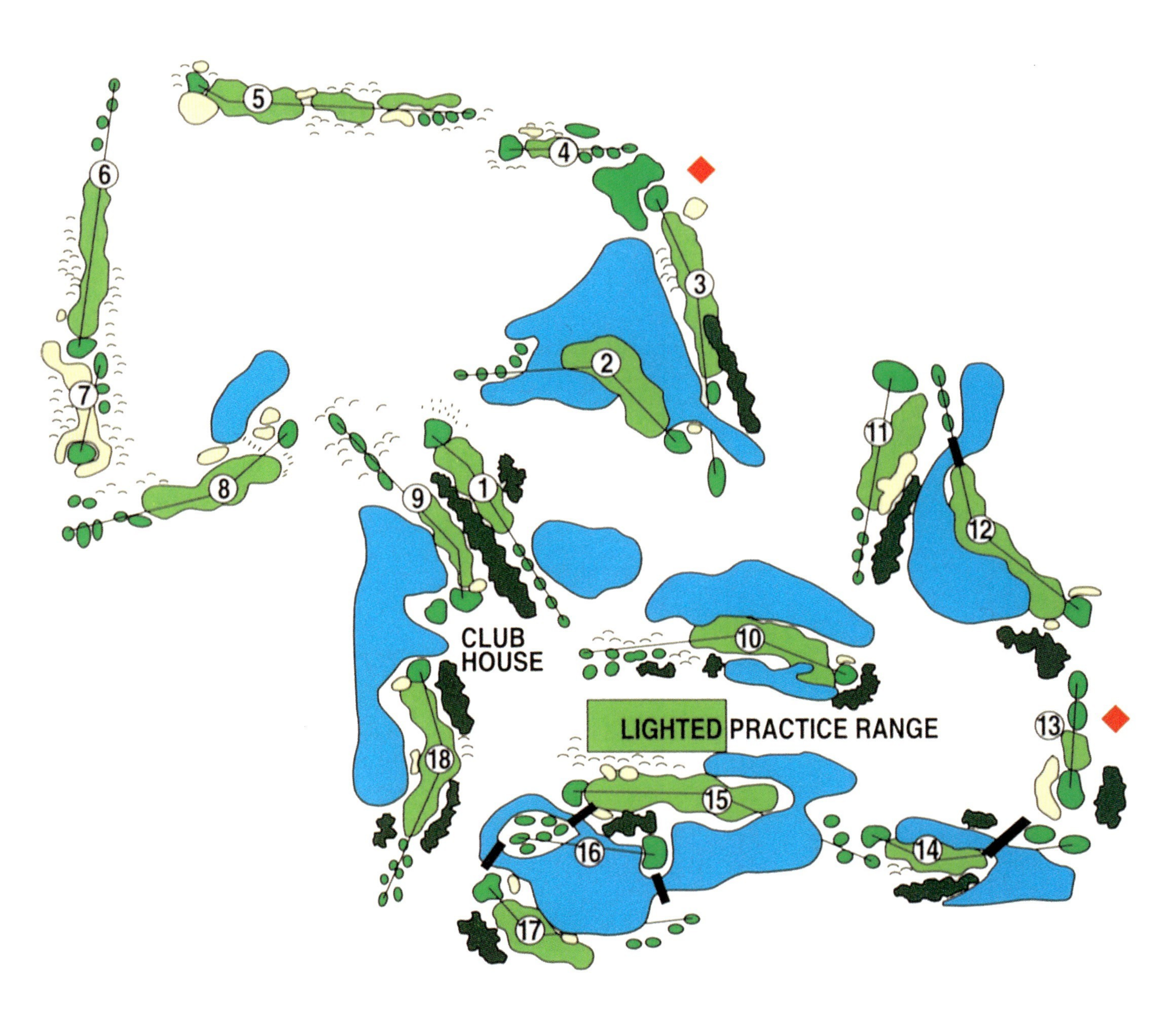

Timacuan Golf and Country Club

HOLE	Ra	Sl	1	2	3	4	5	6	7	8	9	OUT	10	11	12	13	14	15	16	17	18	IN	TOT
GOLD	73.2	133	397	421	400	214	526	457	171	464	391	3441	444	364	508	166	395	532	203	412	450	3474	6915
BLUE	70.7	126	368	389	388	184	489	417	158	434	365	3192	408	337	488	156	379	489	168	368	418	3211	6403
WHITE	68.4(m)/73.9(w)	117(m)/134(w)	331	340	374	175	456	387	129	371	339	2902	383	331	444	145	346	451	159	339	392	2990	5892
GREEN	64.89(M)/70.5(W)	109(M)/125(W)	294	290	338	134	418	312	122	341	301	2550	315	397	400	125	335	409	148	306	348	2693	5243
MEN'S HCP		13	1	7	15	9	5	17	3	11			10	14	8	18	6	2	16	12	4		
PAR			4	4	4	3	5	4	3	4	4	35	4	4	5	3	4	5	3	4	4	36	71
RED	66.8	118	263	215	297	94	398	308	89	322	275	2261	293	285	356	115	237	345	120	268	296	2315	4576
WOMEN'S HCP		9	3	11	17	1	5	15	7	13			10	16	6	18	4	2	8	14	12		

Tees, the carry to the closest part of the putting surface is about 130 yards.

Number 17 is a moderate dogleg right par four with the same lake that fronts the 16th along its right length. It's a risk-reward hole in that the closer you play to the lake the closer your approach shot will be to the green. The perils are obvious if you bite off more of the water than you are capable of carrying. The finishing hole is a long, tight par-four dogleg left playing out of a forest to a landing area pinched on the left by a bunker and on the right by mounds and trees. The approach is uphill to a green that is bunkered on the left and mounded on the right.

Shot placement and course management will be rewarded on most holes at Timacuan, although length here is a benefit, too. My wife, Barbara, found the course challenging. "Women need two woods on a lot of the par-fours to be on in regulation," she observed. "And they'll need a wood, possibly even a driver, on at least two of the par threes."

Play this course once, and you'll want to play it again.

TOURNAMENT PLAYERS CLUB OF TAMPA BAY

5100 Terrain de Golf Dr., Lutz, Florida (From I-275 take exit 36 and turn west onto Bearss Ave.; go about 2 miles and turn right onto Dale Mabry Hwy.; go about 7 miles and turn left onto Lutz-Lake Fern Road; go about 5 miles to club entrance on the left.)
Phone: (813) 949-0091

Architect: Bobby Weed Year opened: 1990

Course rating/Slope rating:
TPC—73.4/130 Blue—71.9/126
White—69.1/119 Red—69.1/119

The Tournament Players Club of Tamps Bay is one of the first pro tournament venues you see on television each winter. If you happen to be a northerner, the lush green fairways, rolling greens, and the mild Gulf Coast temperatures probably look mighty tantalizing when your yard is still hip-deep in snow or the mountains of the stuff you've piled alongside your driveway have long since turned to impenetrable ice. The course is the home of the Senior PGA Tour's GTE Classic every February. And there's little wonder it's one of the favorite tournament stops on the senior circuit.

Architect Bobby Weed's par 71 design is a delight to play. It's not a monster in terms of length, but what it lacks in raw yardage it more than makes up for with shot-making demands. There's only one par five on the outgoing side, but Weed's assortment of par fours—from the short 5th, which measures only 332 yards from the back tees, to the huge 9th—created an interesting and memorable mosaic. The facility is extremely well maintained. They call it a "stadium" course because of the large number of hills positioned so that they are ideal places from which to watch a professional golf tournament.

This is a mature golf course, with dense forests, full-grown trees and shrubs, and well cared for plants. The greens tend to be big and receptive. Many have steep drop-offs at the back to discourage overly aggressive shots. There are abundant strategically places bunkers and water hazards. It is very much in keeping with the architectural style of Bobby Weed. Champion PGA player Chi Chi Rodriguez was Weed's player consultant.

The tightness of the golf course is evident from the moment you climb to the first tee. Your tee shot has to stay left of center to avoid catching a pair of fairway bunkers that guard the bend in the dogleg or being blocked out by a pair of stately old pines. The green is slightly elevated and drops off sharply at the rear. Go through the trees to find a solid par three with a big two-tiered green that's 40 yards from back to front. That's followed by a long, straight par four with a bunker placed squarely in the middle of the

A twosome of Sandhill Cranes playing through on the par-four 4th hole at the Tournament Players Club of Tampa Bay.

fairway. The smart money shot is to the right of the sand. Three bunkers protect the ample putting surface.

The long par-four 4th is a risk-reward hole playing around a lake that's in play along the right side to abut the 150-yard mark and with a second lake on the left coming into play from about 160 yards in. The long, thin green is pitched back toward the fairway and is loaded with contours and breaks.

Number 5 is a good scoring hole for everyone. It's a diminutive dogleg left and has one of the smaller greens on the course. After a short par three, you come to the only par five on the front, a long dogleg left. If you're a big hitter and plan to try for it in two, you have to avoid the lagoon to the left. A fairway bunker sits about driving distance down the left and trees and mounds are to the right. The entrance to the green is tightened severely by two big bunkers on the front left and one at greenside right.

Architect Weed has few constraints about putting sand in his fairways. The 8th is a lovely, difficult par four that features two bunkers in the fairway, a lake down the left, trees on the right, and a trio of bunkers protecting the green. The tough par-four 9th is rated the hardest hole on the course and is the longest of the par fours. A Precise tee shot must stay to the right-center of the fairway in order to open up the two-tiered green. For many women, the 349 yards from the red markers render it much more akin to a par five than a par four.

The back nine opens with a solid, straight par four and a par three that' less than 100 yards from the forward markers. Avoid the steep-faced kidney-shaped sand hazard to the left side of the green. A couple of local members with whom I played warned that getting your sand shot close from that bunker is nearly impossible, regardless of pin placement.

Two par fives on the incoming side are interrupted by a par four. The 12th is ribbon-thin from tee to green, with trees guarding the left and a pair of lakes along the right. The green is hooked behind the lake to the right and is difficult to approach; but even moderate hitters will think about going for this one in two shots. The short par four may require something less than a driver off the tee. The green is multi-tiered. Then set your jaw for the monstrously long par-five 14th. The hole has water down its entire left length. A think fairway bunker that measures more than 100 yards in length must be avoided on your second. The approach to the elevated two-tiered green is guarded by water and sand left and a trio of dangerously placed bunkers to the right. The green itself features drop-offs on all sides. When the pros play, this hole can set the stage for a win or something disappointingly less.

The next hole is rated the second toughest on the men's card. It's a long par four dogleg left around an expanse of lake and marsh that arcs along the left length of the hole. The green sits like a Hollywood set with bunkers right and left, water beyond the left side sand traps, and a backdrop of splendid old cypress trees.

The 16th is rated the second toughest hole on the course for women and at 332 yards from the red markers, it's a bear of a par four. The hole is extremely tight and plays to an elevated green guarded by big deep bunkers on the right side.

A very solid one-shot hole is the preamble to the finisher. It's visually intimidating with water along the right side and bunkers strategically placed around the enormous green. The putting surface covers some 11,000 square feet.

When you see the closing hole on television during the GTE Classic, the Senior Tour players make it look so easy. They play the risk-reward dogleg right with abandon, biting off enormous chunks of the lake that protect the right length of the hole. For us ragged amateurs, keeping our tee shots left avoids the water and the fairway bunkers. The veteran pros will have mid- to short-irons in to the flag. If we avoid the trouble, we hackers will have a long-iron or fairway wood to the green. The pros nail their approaches with ease. We who do not play the game for a living are chewing our fingernails until our ball is safely on the green and not in the water to the right or in the sand to the left.

The Tournament Players Club of Tampa Bay is not only fun to play once, it is the kind of top-notch course you want to play time and again. For those of us who will never experience the cheers of a huge gallery as we walk to the 18th green leading a pro tournament on Sunday afternoon, playing a course where it happens is the next best thing.

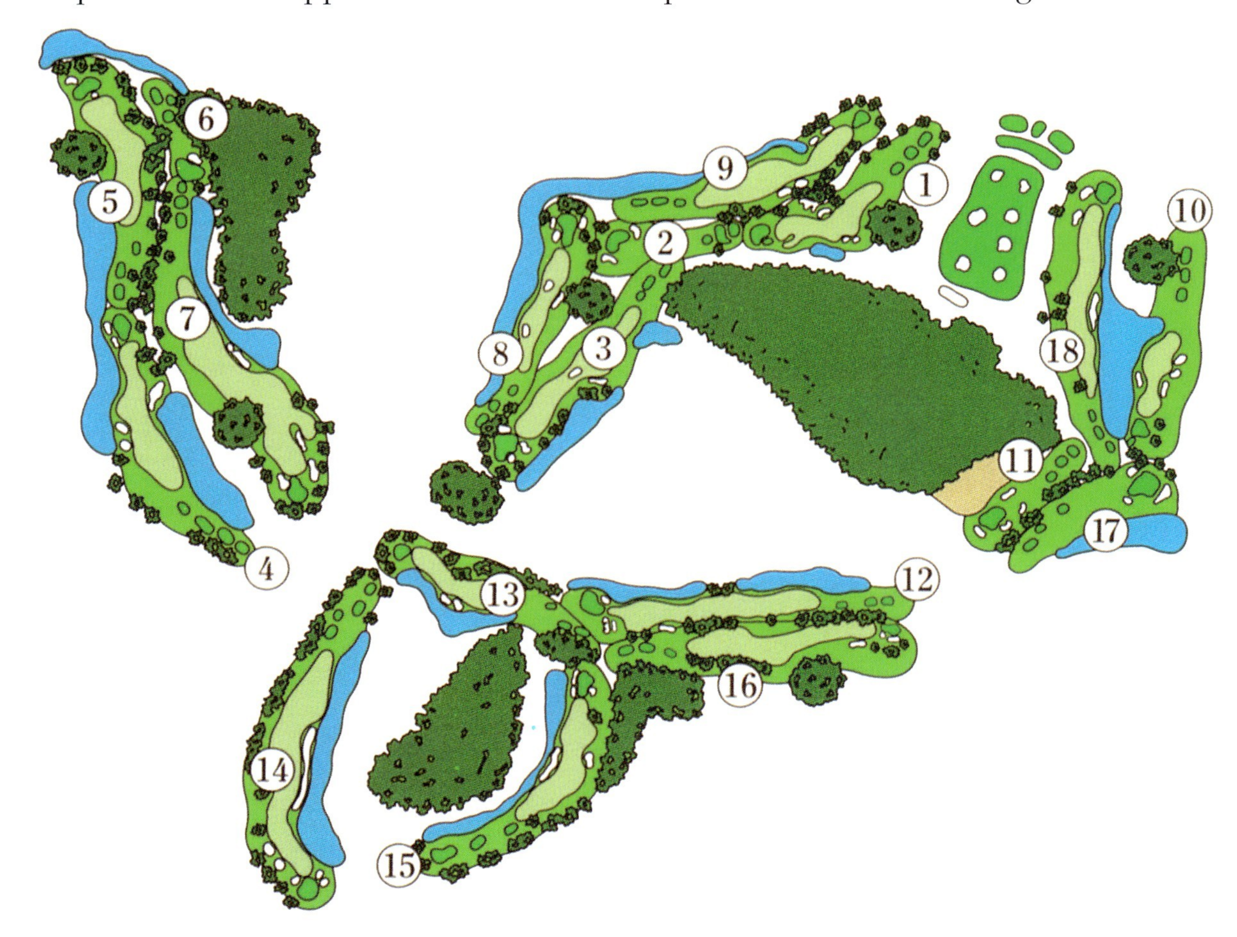

Tournament Players Club of Tampa Bay

HOLE	Ra	Sl	1	2	3	4	5	6	7	8	9	OUT	10	11	12	13	14	15	16	17	18	IN	TOT
TPC	73.4	130	395	191	425	427	332	144	541	414	472	3341	395	179	495	345	588	452	430	217	456	3557	6898
BLUE	71.9	126	372	179	404	408	322	133	533	391	435	3177	382	166	487	333	574	438	413	197	443	3433	6610
WHITE	69.1	121	347	161	351	373	293	116	505	363	406	2915	344	136	473	309	528	366	373	160	404	3093	6008
MEN'S HCP		11	13	7	3	15	17	9	5	1			10	18	14	16	6	2	8	12	4		
PAR			4	3	4	4	4	3	5	4	4	35	4	3	5	4	5	4	4	3	4	36	71
RED	69.1	119	309	124	310	304	236	94	422	316	349	2464	295	98	404	255	455	286	332	147	300	2572	5036
WOMEN'S HCP		11	15	7	9	13	17	5	3	1			10	18	12	14	4	6	2	16	8		

UNIVERSITY PARK COUNTRY CLUB

8301 Park Blvd., University Park, Florida (From I-75 take exit 40 and go west on University Parkway for just over 1« miles; turn right at the University Park entrance and follow the signs to the clubhouse.)
Phone: (941) 359-9999 or (800) 394-6325

Architect: Ron Garl   Year opened: 1991

Course rating/Slope rating for men:
Diamond—73.6/138   Emerald—71.4/132
Platinum—69.9/125

Course rating/Slope rating for women:
Silver—71.6/126   Bronze—68.3/118

University Park Country Club is a twenty-seven-hole golfer's delight. Architect Ron Garl, whose designs are famed for their wonderful use of natural topography, was hired to design the original eighteen which opened in 1991. And early in 1996, Garl's third nine holes opened for play. The original eighteen is carved out of a dense forest. "The third nine's a little bit different," said head pro Mike Clayton. "It's more of a pastureland, and so it feels a little more open. But the design is very similar to the original." My detailed profile is of the original eighteen holes, but a brief look at the new nine reveals a wonderful example of Architect Ron Garl's handiwork that is neither second class or second rate.

No matter which eighteen holes you play, it's guaranteed to be a superior golfing experience. The course is impeccably cared for; the staff is friendly and knowledgeable; the attitude is outstanding from the moment you arrive at the bag drop to the moment an attendant wipes down your clubs after your round.

The 1st hole is a gentle opener with woods to the right and a substantial waste bunker—which Architect Garl has studded generously with Pampas grass—to the front and right of the putting surface. Despite the obstacles, it presents a nice scoring opportunity with which to begin your round.

The next hole is a short par five that's reachable in two for many players. Your tee shot must avoid what they call "a transitional area" to the right, that's a waste bunker littered with pines, palmettos, and Pampas grass. The two-tiered, elevated green is guarded on the left by water and sand.

Two good par fours get you into the heart of the University Park course. One is a dogleg right and the other requires a drive that stays left of center. Drifting to the right will result in your approach being blocked by a huge old oak tree. The elevated green is protected on the right by one of Garl's transitional bunkers, this one containing palm trees and marsh grasses. (The transition in these bunkers, for the most part, seems to be from a place where you can hit your golf ball to a place where you can't.)

Number 5 is the signature hole. It's a lovely but dangerous par three that presents players with a long carry over a lake. A deep bunker lurks between the hillside and the green. A severe rolling contour

The signature hole at University Park Country Club—#5—is a beautiful but perilous par three that presents players with a long carry over a lake.

12
13
11
10
DRIVING RANGE
14
15
16
17
18
9
8
1
2
3
7
4
5
6
19
20
21
27
26
22
23
24
25

intersects the green front-to-back, making it a requirement that you get close to the pin on your tee shot if you want a run at birdie or par. There's no time to catch your breath. The 6th is a par four with a blind tee shot, the number one handicap hole on the side for men. (Unlike most courses, each of the three nines at University Park has handicap designations of one through nine.) The club's foremost expert says the 6th can't be taken lightly by anybody. "It's probably the toughest hole on the course," said head pro Mike Clayton. "It's a dogleg left. There are lateral water hazards on either side of the hole. It plays into a slightly elevated green." It's also extremely tight, with a mossy old oak on the left and a copse of pines and palmettos on the right working in tandem to tighten the entrance to the green.

A solid par five and a long par three with a two-tiered green take you to the 9th tees. You look out on a par-four dogleg left around a lake. Keep your tee shot far enough to the right that you take the water out of play on your approach to the two- tiered green.

The back side opens with a visually pleasing, shortish par four with trees to the left and another one of those Ron Garl signature transitional bunkers to the right. A long par three that plays to a small, well-protected green follows. Again there's one of those transition-to-nowhere bunkers with all manner of nasty vegetables in play right up to the elevated green. Two local members remarked that this is one of the toughest one-shot holes in the area.

A short par five presents a good scoring opportunity next. Even moderate hitters will want to try for the green in two. The 13th is a fine par four dogleg right with a transition bunker down most of the right side. If you try to cut too much of the corner, you stand a good chance of finding the waste area. That's followed by a long, straight par five that requires accuracy to stay within the bowling alley of fairway. That narrow runway is lined on both sides by trees, scrub brush, mounds, and sand traps. "Five wood. Four iron. Nice, high chip. And look at a birdie," said one local member by way of advice on the tees.

A dogleg left par four takes you to the 16th. It's a lovely, long par three over water to an elevated, multi-leveled green. For women, much of the visual intimidation and much of the challenge has been mitigated by the placement of the forward tees. They don't offer much lake that has to be cleared, so a lot of the danger is eliminated. Number 17 is a short par four, fairly straight, with water in play on your drive and as you get near the green. A crescent-shaped bunker wraps around the left side of the putting surface.

The finishing hole on the original eighteen is a delight for the eye and a challenge to your shot-making skills. The landing area is compact, with a lake to the right and a trio of fairway bunkers to the left. The hole provides a very satisfying conclusion to a wonderful round of golf.

"We're rated four stars by *Golf Digest,*" head pro Mike Clayton says with pride. "And we're rated number eight in the state by *Florida Golf News.*" The club's restaurant enjoys a fine reputation in the area and the well-stocked pro shop is a pleasure.

University Park Country Club

HOLE	Ra	Sl	1	2	3	4	5	6	7	8	9	OUT	10	11	12	13	14	15	16	17	18	IN	TOT
DIAMOND	73.6	138	390	493	458	411	193	441	533	207	422	3548	390	213	508	373	536	417	186	402	428	3453	7001
EMERALD	71.4	132	363	470	389	372	174	420	516	183	397	3284	351	186	485	337	502	375	160	367	394	3157	6441
PLATINUM	69.9	125	325	439	381	342	140	367	480	170	379	3023	342	176	471	329	495	362	154	359	379	3067	6090
MEN'S HCP		8	6	3	4	5	1	7	9	2			6	4	9	8	3	2	7	5	1		
PAR			4	5	4	4	3	4	5	3	4	36	4	3	5	4	5	4	3	4	4	36	72
SILVER	71.6	126	312	400	349	274	101	312	438	152	358	269	311	163	453	310	447	329	137	323	342	2815	5511
BRONZE	68.3	118	286	357	297	265	84	284	415	119	295	2402	268	142	417	276	424	300	119	272	294	2512	4914
WOMEN'S		6	5	1	7	8	4	2	9	3			5	7	2	8	1	4	9	3	6		

THE WESTIN INNISBROOK RESORT

36750 U.S. Highway 19 North, Palm Harbor, Florida (From I-275 near Tampa International Airport take route 60 west for about 12 miles; turn right onto U.S. Highway 19 and go north for about 9 miles to the entrance on the left.)
Phone: (727) 942-2000

Island Architect: Lawrence Packard   Year opened: 1970
Highlands North Architect: Lawrence Packard   Year opened: 1971
Copperhead Architect: Lawrence Packard   Year opened: 1972
Highlands South Architects: Lawrence Packard and Jay Overton   Year opened: 1998

Island rating/Slope rating:
Black—74.1/132   Gold—72.4/128
Silver—70.7/121   Jade—73.0/129

Highlands North rating/Slope rating:
Black—70.5/125   Gold—69.2/120
Silver—67.4/117   Jade—68.4/118

Copperhead rating/Slope rating:
Black—75.6/134   Gold—73.1/131
Silver—70.4/128   Jade—71.8/130

Highlands South rating/Slope rating:
Black—72.0/127   Gold—69.7/124
Silver—67.2/119   Jade—68.9/121

The Westin Innisbrook Resort was a favorite stop for golfers visiting the Tampa Bay area from the time the first ball was struck there in the early 1970s. By the early 1990s, however, the resort had fallen on hard times. Visitors complained that it had become "tired" and a little threadbare in places. Locals speculated ominously about what would become of it. Well, what's become of it is a full blown resurrection at the hands of Westin Hotels. They lavished money and imagination on the old place and what has emerged is what readers of *Conde Nast Traveller* magazine voted in 1999 one of the "best places to stay in the whole world."

The guest rooms have been upgraded to a standard of luxury and comfort that rivals any resort anywhere. The restaurants are first rate, led by DY's Steak House—offspring of former NFL coach Don Shula's famous Miami eatery. Non-golfers can enjoy tennis, a state of the art outdoor fitness course (including a rock-climbing tower), a health club and spa, and the multi-million dollar Loch Ness Pool with a 15-foot waterfall and two serpentine water slides.

Golfers all over the world have seen the pro tournaments played on Innisbrook's famed Copperhead. It's a 7,200 yard challenge that demands top performances from the world's top players. Until 1999 it was home to the J. C. Penney Classic which brought together stars from the PGA and LPGA Tours. John Daly and Laura Davies won the final Penney Classic. And starting in 2000, the course became home for the Tampa Bay Classic, one of the final stops on the PGA Tour.

But the golf doesn't stop there. The Island is every bit the equal of Copperhead, even though it's more than 200 yards shorter than the famous snake. The design is tight, treacherous, and demanding. "It's just a lovely golf course," said Ed Travis, Senior PGA Tour player and publisher of the *Florida Golf News.* He'd been visiting Innisbrook since the 1980s and shared his encyclopedic knowledge of the place as we played three of the four courses together.

The other two courses are a bit shorter than the two famous and demanding giants, but both are well worth playing, especially after a major facelift, completed in the fall of 2000; pleasant resort golf courses were redesigned and lengthened into championship tracks.

Highlands North has been there since the early days of Innisbrook and features many of the same Lawrence Packard design characteristics as the Island. Highlands North is tight, well-treed, and watery, placing a premium on accuracy. Highlands South combines one tight, treed nine designed by Packard and a second more open, but more highly contoured nine mostly designed by Innisbrook's long-time pro and Senior PGA Tour player Jay Overton.

Add to all that the Troon Golf Institute, one of the country's top teaching facilities and you have the whole Westin Innisbrook package—world class golf at a world class resort.

ISLAND

It's not easy growing up in the shadow of a famous younger sibling. There are always comparisons, often some jealousies, sometimes even a rivalry. If there is a rivalry between the Island and the famous Copperhead, let me weigh in. The Island is a spectacular golf course. It's extremely tight. It's also tough, beautiful, memorable, and a superior test of the game. And if it stood alone, away from its younger relation, it would enjoy a much greater level of recognition and adulation. As it is, I'm hard pressed to vote on which is the better track. Each has a tremendous amount to offer in that they present a different spectrum of challenges and rewards.

For women it's a brute, measuring just shy of 5,600 yards. Two of the par fours are in excess of 370 yards. Women's tee placement is exceptionally well considered, but difficult. Bring your *A* game when you come to play, or the course will leave you gasping.

The Island offers a wonderful mix of terrain and topography. The opening half dozen holes are fairly flat, with more water than Noah faced. The middle six are hilly and undulating—unusual for Florida golf courses. And the final six are a mix of rolling hills, trees, and lakes. Architect Packard varies the size of his greens. His bunkers—74 in all—are a demonstration of his design skill. He has a tendency to put a lot of space between his greenside bunkers and the putting surface, so without a precise sand game it's possible to get out of a trap and still be in the rough. If

Two lakes guard the front of the green on the finishing hole at Westin Innisbrook's Island Course.

Copperhead rewards raw power, the Island rewards accuracy and finesse.

Packard presents a gentle opening hole on the Island, a short par four, dogleg right. But the hole presages what is to come. You tee off through a chute of trees and must carry far enough to give you a clear look at the green around the moss-laden oak trees that line the right two-thirds of the hole. Water is in play down most of the left length and on the right from about 75 yards in to the green. The irregularly shaped green is sandwiched between a pair of bunkers.

The par-five 2nd offers a generous landing area, provided you avoid the lake along the left side. The hole then funnels into the green. The water hazard that sparkles among the cypress trees along the right, balloons into the fairway in front of the green, tightening the entrance to the putting surface against a left-side bunker.

Number 3 is a par four that requires a long drive between the big fairway bunker to the left and the cluster of bunkers to the right. Safely around the bend in the dogleg right and you'll still have a long- to mid-iron to the green. Many women will have to play two woods to get home in regulation.

The par three 4th is one of the most unique one-shot holes in Florida. Your tee shot is across water to a wishbone-shaped green that arcs around a long thin bunker. The bunker, with one tall cypress in it, is directly in front of the putting surface. The green is so severely arched that it is entirely possible to be on the putting surface and have to play a wedge to get across the sand and close to the flag. A tee shot that finds the sand and lodges anywhere near the tree can leave an impossible recovery shot. This is a hole you'll remember long after you've played it.

Number 7 is the Island's signature hole, the toughest hole on the course. It's a daunting *S*-shaped par five that's a three shot hole for virtually everybody. Water is in play on the right. Trouble lurks everywhere. Senior PGA Tour player Ed Travis said, "This is a hole where you just hitch up your socks and hit it as hard as you can—twice." The approach to the green is uphill and guarded by a quartet of big, menacing bunkers.

The long, uphill par-three 8th leads you to the spectacular 9th. It is one of my favorite holes in the entire Innisbrook complex. It's a solid par four with a blind tee shot down a hill. A water hazard sits at the base of the hill, where the hole turns to the left and heads back uphill to the large, two-tiered green. Women, whose tee is higher than the men's tee boxes, should aim at the bridge to open up the hole. Margaret Travis, Ed's wife, said that if it isn't *the* toughest hole on the course for women, it's certainly one of them. For all players, unless you leave your drive some 200 yards from the green, almost every lie you get will be downhill or downhill-sidehill, with the lake looming in front of you. Your approach is a test. If you get across the lake but come up short, there's a shelf of fairway below the green. The entire approach to the putting surface is an alley between dense forests of cypress and pine.

The back side opens with a long, uphill par four that leads to a short, down-hill par five with a small, plateaued green. The green is offset to the left, hooked behind a long bunker, and nestled against a stand of pines.

A pair of uphill holes follows. Number 12 is a short par four dogleg left with a blind tee shot. The landing area at the bend of the dogleg is compressed by giant oaks on the left and three fairway bunkers on the right. Number 13 is a long, uphill par three.

Your tee shot on the long par-four 14th must be kept right-center and be either long enough or right enough to keep from being blocked by the forest. The green is long (nearly 40 yards from front to back) and sits at the base of a depression between a pair of bunkered mounds. Number 15 is a long par five that tees off to the crest of a hill with a small, well-bunkered green.

Avoid the three big fairway bunkers on the 16th in order to set up an unobstructed approach. The dogleg right plays to a downhill green. There's a pond and a huge bunker on the left and a leafy, towering pair of oak trees on the right that makes your approach to the large green like threading a needle.

A long, watery par three sets the stage for the magnificent 18th. It's a short par four with a severe dogleg left. Two lakes are in play in front of the green. Precise shot making is required to score on this little devil. Your tee shot must be near the big fairway bunker on the right. If you're not long enough off the tees, your view of the green will be blocked by trees. Your approach is a forced carry across both lakes to an elevated, undulating green.

The Island is an absolute delight to the senses and a challenge to your shot-making skills. From the opening hole to the last, it's a course that will conjure up pleasant memories long after you've left the confines of the resort.

Island

HOLE	Ra	Sl	1	2	3	4	5	6	7	8	9	OUT	10	11	12	13	14	15	16	17	18	IN	TOT
BLACK	74.1	132	372	510	445	187	362	408	561	218	418	3481	440	523	355	203	435	543	456	211	370	3536	7017
GOLD	72.4	128	362	500	428	169	352	388	536	190	388	3313	403	495	337	185	423	523	435	185	355	3341	6654
SILVER	70.7	121	342	472	398	150	344	355	506	160	360	3087	360	456	319	156	403	481	415	161	328	3079	6166
MEN'S HCP		13	7	3	17	15	9	1	11	5			4	12	16	18	10	6	2	14	8		
PAR			4	5	4	3	4	4	5	3	4	36	4	5	4	3	4	5	4	3	4	36	72
JADE	73.0	129	322	442	349	130	309	326	467	132	329	2806	302	430	300	120	375	451	391	110	293	2772	5578
WOMEN'S HCP		11	7	3	17	13	9	1	15	5			4	14	12	16	10	6	2	18	8		

All of the trouble is in front of the green on the short par-four 14th on Highlands North at the Westin Innisbrook Resort.

HIGHLANDS NORTH

This newly lengthened and redesigned golf course was once a short, but pleasant, resort layout—nothing too arduous for the occasional player who only takes out the clubs during vacations. It was originally intended for the higher-handicap player, but architect Lawrence Packard had a marvelous piece of real estate to work with, and some wonderful holes sprang from his drawing board. While it is still not as demanding or intimidating as either the Island or Copperhead, Highlands North is a lovely, tight, treed, trapped, and watery golf course that will require shot-making skill and finesse to score. It's no pushover; it's a par 70, with two par-three holes and only one par five on the outward side. Three par threes and a pair of par fives face you on the back.

Two short par fours lead you into architect Packard's design. The opener is a short par four slight dogleg left with a downhill tee shot. Number 2 is a very short par four that's a severe dogleg left. The hole is cut around a bit of forest and while it's diminutive length might prompt some hotdogs to try for it in one shot, there's a lot of lumber between the tee boxes and the putting surface. A long-iron followed by a short-iron can set up a birdie for most players. The key it to be long enough off the tee that the two giant oaks that guard the left front of the green are taken out of play.

The 3rd hole used to be a short par five. It's now a long par four, one of the tightest holes on the outgoing side. A marshy water hazard plays down the left side and intersects the fairway in front of the green.

The next four holes have difficult greens to approach and putt. The short par four 5th features an island green. Your tee shot has to be far enough that you have a clear look at the green in order to score. Number 6 is a short, straight par four with water and bunkers down the left and right sides, forming a runway of fairway from tee to the very well protected, elevated green. The long par-three 7th plays to an elevated, well-bunkered green. And #8 is a solid, sinewy par five that plays to an elevated green, guarded by a stand of oaks on the right side.

You finish the outgoing side with a medium-length par four and start inward with an *S*-shaped par five. Number 11 is an uphill par four dogleg left with a blind tee shot and unless you really crank your drive, the putting surface may be blind on your approach as well. The 12th is an uphill par three with sand from tee to green. The long, thin putting surface is about 45 yards from front to back and is sloped from back to front.

A short par five that features a downhill tee shot and a short par four set up a good scoring opportunity as you move to the first of back-to-back par threes. The 15th is a fine one-shot hole. The water in play down the right side pinches against a bunker and trees to the left making the entrance to the green very tight. Number 16 is a short par three all downhill, with two big bunkers in front of the green.

A pair of solid par fours takes you back to the refurbished and remodeled Highlands Clubhouse shared by both Highlands Courses. Highlands North doesn't leave you gasping for air, but it is a fine example of Lawrence Packard's design skills and it is a most pleasant track.

Highlands North

HOLE	Ra	Sl	1	2	3	4	5	6	7	8	9	OUT	10	11	12	13	14	15	16	17	18	IN	TOT
BLACK	70.5	125	390	325	470	220	410	330	190	510	445	3290	530	415	195	500	400	205	170	375	435	3225	6515
GOLD	69.2	120	370	295	405	195	345	300	180	490	385	2965	495	380	160	475	365	160	155	350	420	2960	5925
SILVER	67.4	117	340	280	380	160	315	280	150	480	365	2750	475	360	140	455	345	145	135	325	405	2785	5535
MEN'S HCP		11	17	3	7	9	13	15	1	5			2	8	16	6	10	14	18	12	4		
PAR			4	4	4	3	4	4	3	5	4	35	5	4	3	5	4	3	3	4	4	35	70
JADE	68.4	118	320	255	345	145	300	230	110	425	330	2460	450	355	95	415	320	110	110	280	380	2515	4975
WOMEN'S HCP		11	17	5	9	7	13	15	1	3			4	8	16	6	10	14	18	12	2		

COPPERHEAD

This is a course you've seen on television. This is one of those tournament courses that tells you from the first tee that you are testing your skill on the same track as some of the world's greatest players. At 7,230 yards from the tournament markers, and only a par 71, it is a course that's given many a touring pro as much as he or she can handle. While it's longer than the Island, it's also more open, especially off the tees. It's less hilly than the Island, but you're often faced with longer approaches to the greens on Copperhead.

Whether Copperhead is better than it's older relative down the road will be debated for years among those players who have sampled both. Senior PGA Tour player Ed Travis calls Copperhead one of his favorite courses. "This is just a lot of golf course," he said standing on the first tee, pointing down the hill at the intimidating fairway. The opening hole is a long par five, dogleg right with three staggered bunkers intersecting the fairway. The approach is back up hill to a slightly elevated green.

Two par fours follow. Number 3 is a brute, featuring an almost 90 degree dogleg right. A pair of lakes right and left pinch the fairway down to minuscule width in front of the green. The medium-length par-three 4th is surrounded by sand, including one bunker directly in front of the putting surface. For women it's 130 yards from the forward markers and the lion's share of it is all carry.

Number 5 is a long, par five that plays to the crest of a hill and then down to a green that sits on a little dome at the base of the hill. Your drive is across a lake. Your second crests the hill and your approach must negotiate a huge pine tree that guards the left front of the green. That leads to a couple of fine par fours. One is a downhill, dogleg right with an elevated green that's protected by three staggered bunkers. The other is a short hole that plays over a hill on your drive and down to the small green. Your approach must avoid pines, oaks, and sand that squeeze the entrance to the putting surface.

Number 8 is a mammoth par three, made all the more challenging by the fact that the green is more than 45 yards from front to back. The side finishes with a splendid par four that tees off into a little valley and then plays back uphill to the green. Architect Lawrence Packard is fond of putting sand traps directly in front of his greens as well as letting trees create dangerous obstacles.

You start the back nine from a terraced set of tees. A towering pine sits on the left side of the fairway about driving distance. Your approach on this par four is back up the hill to a green that's in the shape of an inverted pear, with bunkers right and left.

Number 12 is a simply wonderful, difficult golf hole. It's a par four with a landing area between a pair of lakes. The second lake intersects the fairway about 120 yards from the slightly elevated green. The 13th is a medium-length par three that requires a forced carry over water to find the undulating green.

That leads you to Copperhead's signature hole, a serpentine par five that is a double-dogleg. "John Daly's the only player I know who's made it in two," said Ed Travis, golf pro and publisher of *Florida Golf News.* "Tiger can probably do it too, but for most of us it's a good three-shot hole." The landing zone is generous off the tees, but you have to keep your second shot left in order to avoid the lake right and below the green. The green is also guarded on the left by the biggest sand trap on the course.

Putting out on the signature hole—a long, serpentine par five—at Westin Innisbrook's famous Copperheard Course.

Number 16 is a long, tough par four dogleg right around a lake. A giant pine with a bald eagle's nest in it sits in the middle of the fairway in front of the tees. (Sometimes, if you're lucky, the eagle is at home and watching your tee shot.) The well-protected green is guarded by trees and bunkers.

The par-four 18th is an exhilarating way to finish the round at Copperhead. You drive into the flat between fairway bunkers right and left, and then climb to a hilltop green that's guarded by a huge bunker directly in front.

What more can I say? Copperhead is a wonderful, challenging, aesthetically pleasing golf course. It's worth a long trip out of your way to play it.

Copperhead

HOLE	Ra	Sl	1	2	3	4	5	6	7	8	9	OUT	10	11	12	13	14	15	16	17	18	IN	TOT
BLACK	75.6	134	560	410	455	195	605	465	380	235	425	3730	445	575	380	175	590	215	460	215	445	3500	7230
GOLD	73.1	131	535	380	435	165	570	440	360	195	400	3480	420	530	355	155	550	185	430	180	420	3225	6705
SILVER	70.4	128	500	360	400	135	530	400	330	170	370	3195	380	495	345	145	525	165	385	160	385	2985	6180
MEN'S HCP			5	11	7	17	1	3	13	15	9		8	6	12	18	2	14	4	16	10		
PAR			5	4	4	3	5	4	4	3	4	36	4	5	4	3	5	3	4	3	4	35	71
JADE	71.8	130	450	335	375	130	465	365	315	145	355	2935	350	430	320	105	510	150	340	140	325	2670	5605
WOMEN'S HCP			5	11	7	17	1	3	13	15	9		8	6	12	18	2	14	4	16	10		

HIGHLANDS SOUTH

Highlands South is a splendid hybrid golf course. Nine of the holes were part of a 27 hole layout called the Sandpiper Course designed by Lawrence Packard in the early 1970s. The other two nines are now incorporated into the other Highlands course—Highlands North. In the late 1990s after the Westin takeover of the property, it was determined that Innisbrook should have four 18-hole golf courses. Long time pro Jay Overton oversaw the addition of nine new holes and the melding of the old and the new nines into a fine little golf course. The 2000 lengthening and redesign of the lay- out to just under 6,800 yards has turned it into an excellent test of the game.

The old holes are tight and cut through dense forests, typical of architect Packard's other Innisbrook designs. The new nine is more open but plays among lakes and between rolling hills that present abundant changes in elevation. It's a par 71 with three par threes on the outward side. Don't harbor any illusions that it's an easy little golf course. Just consider the par fives—all are 500 yards or more from the back tees and for women all measure longer than 440 yards. That's big.

Highlands South opens with a couple of fine scoring holes. Number 1 is a very short par four that will require something other than a driver for most players. The 2nd is a short par five that features a blind

On Highlands South at the Westin Innisbrook Resort, the wide shallow green on the one-shot 3rd hole is a tough target to hit.

tee shot over a hill. At the crest of the hill, the hole bends to the left and plays downhill to a water hazard that crosses the fairway in front of the elevated green. You can't see it from the fairway, but there's a canal about 20 yards beyond the back of the small green that will catch an approach that's too aggressive. This is a tougher hole for women than for men. It's 445 yards from the Jade Tees and requires precision and length.

Number 3 is a fine par three. Everyone has a forced carry over water to a wide, shallow green squeezed between two bunkers. The green itself slopes severely from left to right. That's followed by a short, tight par four that plays over the crest of a hill. You can see the flag from the tees, but not the green. A lone pine sits at the left edge of the narrow fairway about 50 yards from the green with dense forest to the right.

Number 5 starts you into the new holes designed by Jay Overton. It's a medium par three with a half dozen bunkers staggered around the green. The 6th is a straight par four with a fairway plateaued between a drop off to the right and a water hazard to the left. The two-tiered putting surface sits behind a grassy trough. Number 7 is a long par four dogleg left. Your tee shot is blind, around a steep hill that contains a large waste bunker. The green is guarded by hillside bunkers above it to the left, and steep-faced sand traps to the right.

The 8th is the toughest hole on the course, a superior test of the game. It's a good three shot par five. You tee off from elevated tees and drive into a little valley. From there your second and approach shots are both uphill. A ridge intersects the fairway about 125 yards from the green and everything above the ridge slopes precariously from left to right. The green is on a shelf on the side of the hill.

The side finishes with a long par three with elevated tees. The green is guarded by water on both sides that creates a narrow, little neck to the putting surface. It's a very tough hole for women, playing 140 yards from the forward markers, and while there's enough of an opening to run the ball onto the green, it's a perilous shot at best.

The back side begins with a trio of par fours. The 12th is a dogleg right that plays from elevated tees into a valley that's littered with bunkers, including one in the middle of the fairway about 140 yards from the green. The approach is blind. The green is fronted by two big mounds that obscure the putting surface and create the optical illusion that it's closer than it really is.

Number 13 is the longest golf hole in the state of Florida. It is a whopping 650 yards from the back markers. The green is hooked to the right and from about 100 yards away, your approach must make its way through a minefield of bunkers and clumps of marsh grass.

Catch your breath on the next hole, a short par four and then get ready for another long par five. The hole narrows as you get closer to the green, which is hooked to the right behind water and a stand of oak trees.

Two par threes with a solid par four between them takes you back to the clubhouse. The 18th is a pretty par three with a forced carry over water.

Highlands South is a fine resort golf course with some exceptionally good golf holes. It would be well worth playing all by itself, but coupled with the rest of the wonderful golf at The Westin Innisbrook Resort, it's the icing on a very rich and tasty cake.

Highlands South

HOLE	Ra	Sl	1	2	3	4	5	6	7	8	9	OUT	10	11	12	13	14	15	16	17	18	IN	TOT
BLACK	72.0	127	335	500	180	350	170	410	410	545	210	3110	415	405	405	650	385	588	220	405	185	3658	6768
GOLD	69.7	124	300	475	145	300	160	380	390	535	185	2870	395	355	385	560	360	530	170	350	170	3275	6145
SILVER	67.2	119	265	460	130	280	145	350	370	510	160	2670	340	330	350	520	350	500	150	330	150	3020	5690
MEN'S HCP		11	3	15	9	17	7	5	1	13			6	14	12	4	8	2	16	10	18		
PAR			4	5	3	4	3	4	4	5	3	35	4	4	4	5	4	5	3	4	3	36	71
JADE	68.9	121	250	445	100	250	125	300	305	460	140	2375	260	300	275	450	310	470	135	310	90	2600	4975
WOMEN'S HCP		9	3	15	11	17	7	5	1	13			8	14	12	4	6	2	16	10	18		

The green on the par-five 11th at The Slammer & The Squire, with the short par-four 14th in the background.

WORLD GOLF VILLAGE

2 World Golf Place, St. Augustine, Florida (From I-95 take exit 95A and go west; turn right into the entrance of the complex and go about 3 miles, following the signs to the clubhouse.)
Phone: (904) 940-6100

The Slammer & The Squire Architect: Bobby Weed Year opened: 1998
The King & The Bear Architects: Jack Nicklaus and Arnold Palmer Year opened: 2000

The Slammer & The Squire rating/Slope rating for men:
Scratch—73.8/135 Black—72.5/128
Blue—69.7/123 White—67.9/119

The Slammer & The Squire rating/Slope rating for women:
Blue—74.9/131 White—72.5/124
Green—69.1/116

The King & The Bear rating/Slope rating:
Black—NA Gold—NA
Blue—NA White—NA
Red—NA

The complex that is the World Golf Village is an international shrine to the game of golf. It is home to the World Golf Hall of Fame—a spectacular tribute to the men and women who have made the game great—and the PGA Tour Shop—a multi-story department store for golfers featuring bags, clubs, clothes, accessories, gadgets, and gifts. There are also excellent accommodations, restaurants, an IMAX theater, and other boutiques and shops.

The complex is also home to a pair of championship golf courses. Put it all together and this is a fine stopping point if you're traveling the I-95 corridor and it is a worthy detour if you are anywhere in northeastern Florida.

THE SLAMMER & THE SQUIRE

Part of the concept of the World Golf Village from its inception was to honor the legends of the game of golf. Sam Snead and Gene Sarazan were brought in as consultants to architect Bobby Weed in the early stages of the design of the course that would bear the nicknames of the two champions. Snead was the original power hitter, knows as "The Slammer" or "Slammin' Sammy." Sarazan was the ever-dapper, debonair bon vivant of the pro golf world, knows as "The Squire." They offered their collective wisdom to Weed, who used it in creating a fine, playable golf course that is both challenging and fair to golfers of every level of ability.

The course is set in a pine forest, with plenty of water and wetland providing both aesthetic diversions and golfing perils. As home to the Senior PGA Tour's Liberty Mutual Legends of Golf, it's well known to TV golf fans. In addition, it provided the television stage for an episode of Shell's Wonderful World of Golf.

You are led gently into The Slammer & The Squire with a slight dogleg right par four. There is a series of bunkers along the right length of the hole. A tee shot center or left will provide a good look at the green. That takes you to a great one-shot hole tucked behind a corner of a lake with a big, well-bunkered green. There's a little bail-out room to the left front.

The 3rd offers a good par or birdie opportunity if your second shot stays on the plateau green. It's a par four that's only moderately long. The course's yardage book recommends playing your drive right over the bunker in front of the tee boxes. A shot to the flag that misses the putting surface is almost certain to cascade down the embankment that surrounds the green, leaving a recovery shot from one of several grassy collection areas.

Things get progressively tougher from here. Number 4 is a long par five that's a double- dogleg from the back tees and merely a lengthy dogleg left from the forward markers. The key is placement of your lay-up—it must stay to the right center in order to have a clear look at the well-guarded green. The 5th is a long, tight par four with water along the left from tee to green and forest along the right. The elevated fairway slopes down to the water and a shot that ventures from the short grass can easily finds itself in a watery grave.

Number 6 is a long, demanding par four that is a severe dogleg left with a blind tee shot, although you can occasionally glimpse the flag between the pines. A pair of enormous fairway bunkers on the left side of the hole at the point where the dogleg turns seem to dare you to try to carry them. The smarter shot is to play to the right of the bunkers and give yourself a clear look at the flag. Failure to clear the sand traps will probably leave you stymied on your approach. That takes you to a devilish par three that plays from elevated tees to an elevated green. The long, thin putting surface is treacherous, measuring more than 50 yards from back to front. It is intersected by a ridge that inclines the front of the putting surface back toward the tees and the back away from the players.

The par-five 8th hole features a generous landing area from the tees, but becomes tighter and narrower as you approach the small, round green. It's rated the toughest hole on the course. The side concludes with a pretty par four that plays to an elevated, well-protected green. Your approach shot must clear the big bunker in front of the green. That bunker creates an optical illusion, in that it appears to be greenside as you look at it on your approach. In reality, there are about 25 yards from the lip of the bunker to the apron of the green.

Number 10 is a pretty way to start the back nine. It's a gentle dogleg right with a green protected right and left by sand traps. A big bunker along the right needs to be avoided if you intend to bite off a bit of the dogleg. The next hole is a short par five that big hitters can consider going for in two. If you opt for a lay-up, play it well left-of-center. The green itself is not visible from the tees and can be obscured on your approach by a substantial hill out of which a gaping bunker has been scooped; this leads you to a long par four slight dogleg right. Don't miss the elevated

The Slammer & The Squire

HOLE	Ra	Sl	1	2	3	4	5	6	7	8	9	OUT	10	11	12	13	14	15	16	17	18	IN	TOT
SCRATCH	73.8	135	385	186	394	522	426	445	178	541	401	3478	379	517	442	205	311	147	576	459	425	3461	6939
BLACK	72.5	128	377	170	380	501	394	423	161	527	383	3316	365	510	421	192	300	135	561	448	412	3344	6660
BLUE	69.7(m)/74.9(w)	123(m)/131(w)	358	154	361	486	367	381	143	475	361	3086	343	472	373	161	284	128	527	387	371	3046	6132
WHITE	67.9(m)/72.5(w)	119(m)/124(w)	336	121	306	467	351	360	128	442	341	2852	295	448	361	148	273	122	481	372	359	2859	5711
HCP			13	17	9	3	7	5	15	1	11		12	4	8	18	14	16	2	6	10		
PAR			4	3	4	5	4	4	3	5	4	36	4	5	4	3	4	3	5	4	4	36	72
GREEN	69.1	116	271	94	280	417	315	321	107	424	259	2488	265	402	317	123	245	94	448	326	288	2508	4996

green to the right or you'll likely find one of a pair of bunkers or the bottom of a grassy basin into which stray shots flow.

The long par three 13th is bulldozed out of the side of a hill with a steep incline to the right and a drop off to the left that will reject imprecise shots into a long thin sand trap or, worse, into the lake. Take enough club as the *L*-shaped front bunker creates the illusion of a shorter hole. My wife, Barbara, noted that from the White or Green Tees—148 yards and 123 yards respectively—it's a very challenging one-shot hole for women. The day we played it the pin was well back on the 43-yard long green. She hit a solid seven wood and two-putted for a par.

Number 14 is a short par four that big hitters with a wind behind them might even consider going for in a single blow, but the long, thin green is one of the most difficult on The Slammer & The Squire to approach. Architect Bobby Weed has created a landscape of bunkers that makes missing the green a truly scary proposition. Sergio Garcia or Annika Sorenstam might take a rip at it. Average players like me will probably be content to play a four iron and a pitching wedge, and have a decent look at a birdie.

This takes you to the short par three 15th that requires a forced carry across a corner of a lake. There's bail-out room to the left. Pin placement and club selection are key as the big green is bisected by a substantial ridge. Number 16 is a tough par five, a dogleg right with a blind tee shot. The approach is to a wide, thin, highly-contoured green bunkered right and left. It's rated the second toughest hole on The Slammer & The Squire primarily because of length. It is the longest par five on the course, a monster from every set of tees. "Depending on the wind, a woman might even need three woods to get on in regulation," said Barbara.

Architect Weed's decision to challenge players with long holes at the end of the round continues as you head for home. The penultimate hole is the longest par four on the golf course, a dogleg left playing to a slightly elevated green. The 18th hole is a lovely dogleg left par four, with water along the entire left length of it. Aim your tee shot at the left edge of the huge fairway sand hazard visible from the tees. Avoid the sand and water to the left of the putting surface. The backdrop for the hole is the World Golf Hall of Fame with its distinctive tower. A Hollywood set designer could not have come up with a more perfect visual display against which to finish your round.

Architect Bobby Weed has provided ample greens with challenging contours and breaks. They tend to be receptive and true, with their speed ranging from moderate to lightening fast depending on the season and the amount of rain that's fallen. In the summer they can be blistering.

It's an exceptional design for women. The three sets of tees rated and sloped for female players offer a good, fair test. The forward most Green Tees give high handicappers a good workout playing just shy of 5,000 yards. My wife, Barbara, whose handicap is in the mid-teens, played it from the White Tees. She observed, "It's plenty long. I had to use two woods to reach most of the greens in regulation on the par fours." She noted that five of the par-four holes were in excess of 350 yards from the white markers and even for women who hit it well, that's hefty length.

In general, The Slammer & The Squire is enjoyable and challenging. Good shots are rewarded and bad shots are not so severely punished that it becomes disheartening. The course is kept in immaculate condition, with carefully tended fairways and bunkers. Abundant beds of flowering plants and attention to detail make this a premier facility.

THE KING & THE BEAR

"This course is quite different from The Slammer & The Squire," said Kevin Perrigo, the affable young head pro at The

King & The Bear. "It's longer. It plays harder. And where else do you have the product of a collaboration between Arnold Palmer and Jack Nicklaus?" In fact, The King & The Bear is the beneficiary of two of the world's best golf course designers combining their talents.

Palmer and Nicklaus golf courses each have distinctive characteristics. What you get here is a hybrid, with a fascinating introduction of new twists not common to either. For example, the design duo makes use of enormous coquina waste bunkers in which you can drive your golf cart, ground your club, and remove loose impediments. (Coquina is a composite of sand, shells, shell shards, and pebbles, indigenous to Florida's Atlantic coast.) On several holes, they have incorporated giant beach bunkers, sandy expanses that seem to rise out of lakes like golden strands.

The par fives are all long; the par threes, especially the two on the back nine are fabulous; the par fours present an interesting mix of long, medium and short holes that will stretch your shot-making ability. The greens vary in size, but are not generally huge or as severely contoured as some Palmer courses I've played. However, like many Palmer designs, The King has a preference for greens that are elevated, multi-tiered, or both. There's a lot of Nicklaus-style bunkering with deep faces and exaggerated scallops that define the boundaries between sand and grass. The use of hazards such as water and wetlands are pleasing to the eye and interesting to play, revealing bits of the design preferences of both men.

There are five sets of tees, the front two sets of markers rated and sloped for women, and the back four sets rated and sloped for men. The outward side is more open than the back, which has been carved through a dense forest. Both are designed to test average to good players and to provide a superior tournament venue for touring pros. It is something of a stadium course, with the finishing holes setting up nicely to accommodate a large gallery that might come to see a professional competition.

The King & The Bear opens with a pair of long par fours, the 1st a dogleg right with a lake on the right, the 2nd a dogleg left with a lake on the left. Both have elevated, well-bunkered greens. The starting hole provides your first glimpse of one of those beach bunkers at about driving distance. The third hole is the longest par three on the golf course and features a forced carry across an expanse of coquina waste area to an elevated green. From the back tees it's a massive 241 yards and for women playing the forward markers it's 159 yards the two legends give no quarter to anybody here.

Number 4 is a short par four with a large fairway bunker on the right and a line of towering ancient oaks along the left, leading up to the green. "You've got to challenge the bunker," said head pro Kevin Perrigo. "If you're too far left you'll be blocked out by the trees."

The next holes make up a par-three sandwich—two par fives with a one-shot hole in the middle. The 5th hole is the shortest par five on The King & The Bear. Unless you hit the ball like Tiger Woods or Sergio Garcia, it's the only par five the average player will contemplate trying to reach in two shots. A huge beach bunker rises from the lake on the right. That lake extends to a rocky embankment at greenside. A target bunker for your lay-up sits in the middle of the fairway about 70 yards in front of the putting surface.

Looking across the 12th green and across the lake at the long, tight par-four 13th on The King & The Bear, the unique World Golf Village Course designed by Arnold Palmer and Jack Nicklaus.

The following par three features another huge beach bunker on the right, and a sand hazard on the left that compress the entrance to the green. This takes you to the massive par five 7th, which plays 584 yards from the tips and well over 500 yards for all but women playing the Red Tees. The hole is a crescent-shaped dogleg left around a lake that just peeks between hills, providing only a glimpse of the hazard from the tees. The water extends all the way to the two-tiered green.

If you're not winded by now, the two closing holes on the outgoing side will leave you gasping for air. They are a pair of long, difficult par fours. Number 8 is a dogleg right with a blind tee shot. Your drive needs to be as close to the bunker on the right that defines the bend in the dogleg as you can place it. If you play into the flat left of the bunker you'll face well over 200 yards to the green which is at the base of a gentle hill. The 9th is an exercise in visual intimidation. All you see from the tees is the lake to the right. The fairway is a shelf between a hill on the left and the water. "It's wider than it looks," said Perrigo. It looks about as wide as my desk. The lake then protects the front and right of the green. Palmer and Nicklaus took pains with the forward markers on this. Women are presented with a lovely panorama of the hole from an elevated tee box.

A solid, straight par four takes you into the back nine. Drive straight down the trough of fairway between a ridge to the right and a coquina waste area to the left and this can offer a good scoring opportunity. The next hole is one of the prettiest par threes in the state. It's a short hole with a pond on the left, bunkers on the right, and a huge old oak tree shading the back of the smallish two-level green that's angled to the left.

The 12th is a long, straight par four with a lake in front of the putting surface that's hidden from view on the tees. The green is wide and shallow, with lots of contour. That takes you to the lovely par-five 13th. You drive from elevated tees to a fairly generous landing area. Head pro Perrigo recommends that your lay-up be into a little basin between the two fairway bunkers near the green.

Number 14 is the second gorgeous par three on the back side. There's a lake along the right. The elevated green looks down on one of those beach bunkers like an oasis above the desert. The design leaves an indelible image. The next hole takes you from picturesque to terrifying. As with the 9th, Palmer and Nicklaus have created a hole that is meant to intimidate you the moment you step onto the tee. While there's ample landing room to the left, the lake along the right looks big and oh, so dangerous. The lake arcs around the green and wedges in front of it on your approach, with the putting surface poised behind an embankment of boulders.

The long par four 16th leads you to the two marvelous finishers. The 17th requires a forced carry across a lake. The aim point on your tee shot is the fairway bunker visible from the tee boxes. Women, who do not have to clear the lake on their drive, should aim left of the bunker as it's reachable from the forward markers. The green is a feast for the eyes as you approach it. It's surrounded by bunkers and sits against a backdrop of towering ancient trees. The closer is a long par five with a coquina waste area in play on the left as you approach the elevated green.

As you head up the hill to the clubhouse and look back down the 18th fairway, you'll experience a pleasant glow of satisfaction at having played a unique golf course designed by two of the greatest players ever to have picked up a golf club. It's not hard to imagine the cheers of the gallery echoing through the trees on a Sunday afternoon after an exciting tournament finish. Long before ground was broken on this golf course, the corporate backers of the World Golf Village project envisioned something beyond the ordinary from a Palmer-Nicklaus partnership. They got their money's worth and more. The King & The Bear is a marvelous companion to The Slammer & The Squire, and makes the World Golf Village a superb stop on your golfing vacation.

The King & The Bear

HOLE	Ra	Sl	1	2	3	4	5	6	7	8	9	OUT	10	11	12	13	14	15	16	17	18	IN	TOT
BLACK	NA	NA	428	439	241	371	530	187	584	460	454	3694	432	155	411	543	196	361	460	440	555	3553	7247
GOLD	NA	NA	410	413	228	353	510	181	564	436	432	3527	412	139	395	533	183	342	433	422	538	3397	6924
BLUE	NA	NA	388	397	203	336	494	165	544	410	412	3349	391	125	377	514	171	325	408	399	525	3235	6584
WHITE	NA	NA	373	328	184	298	478	150	521	367	355	3054	350	115	336	488	151	287	365	351	501	2944	5998
PAR			4	4	3	4	5	3	5	4	4	36	4	3	4	5	3	4	4	4	5	36	72
RED	NA	NA	349	307	159	247	423	130	446	317	304	2682	300	98	287	423	127	234	321	305	418	2513	5195

(NOTE: Rating, slope, and handicaps not available.)

WORLD WOODS GOLF CLUB

17590 Ponce de Leon Boulevard, Brooksville, Florida (From I-75 take exit 61 and go west on State Road 98 for about 21 miles, entrance on right; from Highway 19 go east on State Road 98 for about 5 miles, entrance on left.)
Phone: (352) 796-5500

Pine Barrens Course Architect: Tom Fazio Year opened: 1993
Rolling Oaks Course Architect: Tom Fazio Year opened: 1993

Pine Barrens Course rating/Slope rating:
Tournament—73.7/140 Back—71.6/134
Middle—69.6/129 Forward—70.9/119

Rolling Oaks Course rating/Slope rating:
Tournament—73.5/136 Back—71.4/131
Middle—69.5/125 Forward—70.7/126

The head pro at my home course, Marsh Creek Country Club, has been around Florida golf for a long time. Jason Powell is both knowledgeable and articulate when it comes to the state's golf destinations. So in discussing golf courses for this book with him, I took heed when he lavished praise on World Woods Golf Club. "It's one of the finest facilities around," he said. "Wait 'til you see their practice facilities. And the golf courses are outstanding."

"They've even got a little par three course that will give you a test," said Kevin Perrigo, head pro at The King & The Bear. "Most people don't even know it's there."

The advance praise turned out to be understated. What I found was some of the best golf in the United States. Not only does World Woods have a pair of world class golf courses—some of architect Tom Fazio's best work—but there's a 2 acre practice green and a square practice range that covers 20 acres and features target greens, target fairways, chipping areas, and practice sand traps. In addition, there are three full-length warm-up holes—a par three, par four, and par five—and that nine-hole short course in case thirty-six regulation holes and a few hours of practice aren't quite enough.

Add in the fact that the staff is courteous and friendly and there's little wonder why World Woods constantly gets top ratings in such publications as *Golf Digest* and *Florida Golf News.*

PINE BARRENS COURSE

When you drive up to the starter at the first hole, he'll explain to you that all of the bunkers—fairway bunkers and greenside bunkers—are considered waste areas, which means you can ground your club, take practice swings, and remove loose impediments. It struck me as odd at first, but after playing the course it felt completely natural. It's part of architect Tom Fazio's design concept, an element that makes Pine Barrens so unique, challenging, and enjoyable.

The feel of the place is as unusual as the "local rule" about the sand; it feels as if

On architect Tom Fazio's Pine Barrens Course at World Woods Golf Club, the elevated 8th green is perched above a giant, steep-faced waste bunker.

the golf course has always been a part of the landscape. The abundant trees, sand, wild grasses, brush, and water all work together to create a unique tapestry on this par 71 course. Add some characteristic Tom Fazio trademarks such as large greens, well-contoured fairways, and interestingly designed greenside bunkers, and you have a winning combination all the way around. It's a long track—nearly 7,000 yards from the back tees and a breathtaking 5,301 yards from the forward markers. Women will find it a real test and most will end up using two woods on most of the par fours if they hope to get on in regulation.

The opening par fours set the table and provide a solid taste of what's to come. You begin the feast from elevated tees, driving into a little valley, and then approach an elevated green. Number 2 is a long dogleg left. Once again the tees are elevated. The key is to avoid the waste areas right and left that squeeze the fairway. These are just the appetizers.

The 3rd starts the main course. It's a pretty one-shot hole with a forced carry over water. Pine trees ring the two-tiered putting surface. That takes you to a difficult and dangerous par five. It's a dogleg right that plays around a gigantic waste area that looks like it could have been an old surface mine or quarry. "Nope," said head pro Scott Wyckoff when asked about it. "Tom Fazio just dug all that out to create that look." The look is like some place Moses could spend 40 years wandering. And it reaches right up to the front of the elevated green, creating an intimidating approach shot.

Number 5 is a fairly straight par four with elevated tees and an elevated green. Fazio gives you a generous landing area here, but the approach to the green is tight. The green itself is long, thin, and multi-tiered, with a false front that will reject short approaches back down the hill toward the fairway.

Number 6 plays over a little valley from elevated tees. You then play over a hill and down to a green that's hooked to the right behind a waste area studded with pine trees. It's important to keep your lay-up second far enough left that you're not blocked out by the trees. Big hitters trying to make it in two will have to hit a long, precisely controlled left-to-right shot to find the green. The 7th is a long par three, especially long for women. It's 142 yards from the forward markers to the green. There's a big waste bunker to the right and a small one about 20 yards from the putting surface on the left.

The nine finishes with a pair of par fours one short, with the green offset to the right behind a steep-faced waste area, and the other huge with a highly compressed approach to the green.

The back side opens with a lovely long par three that plays to a Fazio trademark huge, rippling green. "It looks like a potato chip," quipped my playing partner, Charles Schmitt of New York, an architect with an eye for detail.

Number 11 is a short par four dogleg right, with the elevated green guarded at the left front by a large waste area. This is followed by a most memorable golf hole. It's a long, difficult par four with two small greens. It's rated the most difficult hole on the course for both men and women. The left green is slightly elevated and fairly open, inviting a run-up approach. The right green is tucked behind a cavernous wasteland. They are played on alternate days.

A solid par four takes you to the only par five on the inward side. It's a long hole with a generous landing area off the tees.

The approach to the green narrows dangerously with steep mounds and forest to the left. A large waste bunker splits the fairway in front of the green giving you the option of approaching it above the bunker to the left or below it to the right.

I especially like the 15th. It's a tiny par four, severe dogleg right, with a small green down in a well-guarded bowl. Some big hitters could consider going for it from the tees, but it's a risky option. The percentage play is to use less than a driver and put your tee shot in the fairway about 100 yards from the flag. A high, soft short-iron approach will yield dividends.

Pine Barrens finishes with a long par three that looks shorter than it really is and a pair of par fours. Number 17 is medium length with elevated tees. It's a tight hole with a waste area to the right and menacing stands of trees to the left. Your final drive is again from terraced tees across a waste bunker. It's a dogleg left, the identical length of #17, except from the Tournament Tees. The elevated 18th green is guarded left and right by waste areas.

"A spectacular golf course," said Charles Schmitt, the architect from New York, who assured me he would be thinking fondly about his round when the snows fly and the winter winds howl up north. The fact is that there's not a weak hole on the golf course. Take your scoring opportunities where you can because there's more than enough trouble to take you into the realm of bogeys and worse. And take in the glory of the place itself, the natural beauty and the extraordinary playing experience of Pine Barrens. It's worth a long detour or a special trip.

Pine Barrens Course

HOLE	Ra	Sl	1	2	3	4	5	6	7	8	9	OUT	10	11	12	13	14	15	16	17	18	IN	TOT
TOURNAMENT	73.7	140	406	453	157	494	383	532	207	402	424	3458	191	403	470	429	547	330	224	404	446	3444	6902
BACK	71.6	134	371	428	146	480	362	518	185	361	395	3246	158	379	457	421	527	313	205	376	376	3212	6458
MIDDLE	69.6	129	351	373	127	429	351	486	156	361	395	3029	158	379	417	398	485	292	176	349	349	3003	6032
MEN'S HCP		16	4	18	2	8	14	12	10	6			17	15	1	7	9	13	5	11	3		
PAR			4	4	3	5	4	5	3	4	4	36	3	4	4	4	5	4	3	4	4	35	71
FORWARD	70.9	119	328	312	93	406	325	448	142	307	344	2705	131	329	368	345	454	260	93	308	308	2596	5301
WOMEN'S HCP		16	10	18	2	4	12	14	6	8			15	11	1	13	7	5	17	9	3		

ROLLING OAKS COURSE

Architect Tom Fazio is quoted in World Woods' promotional literature as saying that he didn't start by designing holes, but rather by looking at the "land mass" as a whole. By doing so he created the concept, "suggesting the styles of the courses." In this case it isn't difficult to describe the difference in temperament between these two neighboring tracks. Where the Pine Barrens Course is aggressive, Rolling Oaks is laid-back; where Pine Barrens is a type-A personality, Rolling Oaks is a type-B; where Pine Barrens is rugged and raw, Rolling Oaks is urbane and sophisticated. The Pine Barrens Course feels like it belongs in the hills of Virginia or West Virginia, maybe at the Homestead or Greenbrier; the Rolling Oaks Course feels as if it could be in New York's Westchester County, maybe next door to Winged Foot.

The fact that the same architect designed them both bespeaks the talent of Tom Fazio. In the case of Rolling Oaks, he has used a marvelous piece of land to sculpt and mold a golf course that fits its surroundings. The course is loaded with subtle surprises. The big greens are full of obvious contours as well as nuances that require all your short game skills. The sand here—unlike Pine Barrens where it's all waste area—is all traditional bunkering in which you may not ground your club or remove loose impediments. It looks more open than Pine Barrens, but you'll quickly discover that the sophisticated twists and turns of the holes demand focus and concentration from the first drive to the last putt.

A long par four followed by a medium-length par three get you into the golf course. The 3rd is a long par five, a double-dogleg that bends to the right at first. It offers an extremely tight landing area down a fairway that's lined right and left by bunkers. The green is then hooked back to the left protected by a pair of bunkers.

I like the next hole because it is more complex than it's length would indicate. It is a short par four with a severe dogleg left. It's considered an easy hole on the scorecard, but if you fail to keep your tee shot far enough to the right to open up the green or if you catch the fairway bunkers that define the bend in the dogleg, it can produce some frightening results. It's only 227 yards from the forward markers and offers a good scoring opportunity for women who play it carefully. A regular from Tampa said, "Length doesn't help you as much as accuracy."

Number 5 is a short par five, dogleg right. The green sits down in a little basin and is tucked back to the right behind a big bunker. It's reachable in two for the big hitters, but even a big drive along the left side of the fairway will require a substantial left-to-right approach to find the green. The 6th is a short, difficult par four, made a little longer because the hole plays uphill with a bend to the left about midway from tee to green. Put your tee shot over the two big bunkers along the left side of the fairway and you'll have a perfect shot at the pin. The entrance to the green is tricky, with a bunker dead center and a pair of ancient oaks on either side, their canopies almost forming an interrupted arch in front of the putting surface.

The next hole is a par-four slight dogleg right. You drive into a little valley and play back uphill to the green. For men, it's a long hole; architect Fazio gave women a substantial break on distance—it's only 294 yards from the forward markers—but he put the women's tee box on the

Large bunkers minimize the fairway and create a testing approach to the par-four 4th green on World Wood's Rolling Oaks Course.

hillside, exacerbating the dogleg and bringing the right fairway bunker dangerously into play off the tee.

The outward side finishes with beauty and the beast. Number 8 is one of the prettiest par threes around. An elevated set of terraced tees give you a look at a long, thin, tiny green that sits across a lovely little pond. A steep hill and bunker guard the right. The water extends around the left length of the green. The target is small; the risks are great; the sheer artistry of it is immense.

Number 9 is a long grueling par four that plays slightly uphill and requires a pair of big accurate shots to be on in regulation. (It's 410 yards from the forward tees and for most women, plays like a par five.) It's a slight dogleg right, with a two-tiered and highly contoured green.

The back nine opens with a long downhill par five. Your lay-up is back up the hill to a big green protected by giant sand traps right and left front. Number 11 is a par four that plays into a valley and back uphill to a wide, shallow, elevated green. Tom Fazio has a brilliant touch with short par fours. The 12th funnels down a hill with the green canted to the right in a small basin, guarded by a trio of bunkers. The front sand hazard is designed to prevent a run-up approach to the putting surface.

That takes you to a splendid par three that requires your tee shot to pass through a chute of trees and across a rocky field. The green is guarded by bunkers to the right and there's a little rocky chasm to the left. Number 14 is a very tight par four, dogleg left across a valley and uphill to the green. Trees line the right and left, some so close to the fairway that their branches shade the short grass. The green itself is divided front to back by a ridge that will cause shots to roll sharply right or left depending on which side of the ridge you hit. This is rated the toughest hole for women on Rolling Oaks.

Number 15 is the toughest hole for men. It's a breathtakingly long par four. You drive into a valley to about the point where the hole turns to the left. Your second shot is back up the hill to an elevated green that's offset to the left behind a pair of gaping bunkers. That's followed by a long par three that plays from hillside tees down to a green at the base of the hill. Number 17 is a lovely short par four with a blind tee shot. You drive over the crest of a hill. It's a dogleg left with a well-bunkered green.

The finishing hole is a fine par five. It's not a tremendously long hole but the gentle dogleg right is mostly uphill to an elevated, well-protected multi-level green. Looking back down the hole as you wait to play your final stroke is a feast for the eye. Play Rolling Oaks to your handicap and you can leave World Woods well satisfied.

Rolling Oaks Course

HOLE	Ra	Sl	1	2	3	4	5	6	7	8	9	OUT	10	11	12	13	14	15	16	17	18	IN	TOT
TOURNAMENT	73.5	136	422	204	542	374	503	341	440	174	458	3458	566	409	378	208	412	457	234	360	503	3527	6985
BACK	71.4	131	395	172	519	341	458	322	409	148	437	3201	547	394	356	186	370	434	209	333	490	3319	6520
MIDDLE	69.5	125	395	149	492	341	458	300	351	121	412	3019	517	366	329	159	327	408	177	303	464	3050	6069
MEN'S HCP		8	16	6	18	10	12	4	14	2			11	5	9	17	3	1	13	15	7		
PAR			4	3	5	4	5	4	4	3	4	36	5	4	4	3	4	4	3	4	5	36	72
FORWARD	70.7	126	346	114	450	277	403	234	294	98	410	2626	404	336	296	97	289	363	152	288	394	2619	5245
WOMEN'S HCP		14	16	2	18	8	12	4	10	6			7	11	9	13	1	5	17	15	3		

COURSES BY REGION

Northeast Florida (Amelia Island to Daytona)	Eagle Harbor Golf Club Grand Haven LPGA International Radisson Ponce de Leon Resort Ravines Inn & Golf Club The Golf Club at South Hampton World Golf Village
Southeast Florida (Daytona south)	Alantis Country Club & Inn Baytree National Golf Links Doral Golf Resort and Spa Emerald Dunes PGA Golf Club
Southwest Florida (Tampa south)	Legacy Golf Club at Lakewood Ranch Riverwood University Park Country Club
Central Gulf Coast (Tampa to Tallahassee)	El Diablo Golf and Country Club Saddlebrook Resort Tournament Players Club at Tampa Bay The Westin Innisbrook Resort World Woods Golf Club
Florida Panhandle	Bay Point Yacht & Country Club Emerald Bay Kelly Plantation Golf Club Sandestin
Central Florida (Orlando area)	Black Bear Golf Club Diamond Players Club Clermont Mission Inn Golf & Tennis Resort Orange County National Golf Center Southern Dunes Golf and Country Club Timacuan Golf and Country Club

COURSES BY ARCHITECT

Aoki, Isao	Crooked Cat (at Orange County National Golf Center, with Dave Harman and Phil Ritson) Panther Lake (at Orange County National Golf Center with Dave Harman and Phil Ritson)
Bates, Gene	Riverwood
Byrd, Willard	Club Meadows (at Bay Point)
Clarke, Charles	El Campion (at Mission Inn)
Couples, Fred	Kelly Plantation Golf Club
Cupp, Robert	Emerald Bay
Devlin, Bruce	Gold Course (at Doral, with Robert von Hagge) Lagoon Legend (at Bay Point, with Robert von Hagge) Red Course (at Doral, with Robert von Hagge) Silver Course (at Doral, with Robert von Hagge)
Dye, P. B.	Black Bear Golf Club
Dye, Pete	Dye Course (at PGA Golf Club)
Fazio, Jim	El Diablo Golf and Country Club
Fazio, Tom	Emerald Dunes North Course (at PGA Golf Club) Pine Barrens Course (at World Woods Golf Club) Rolling Oaks Course (at World Woods Golf Club) South Course (at PGA Golf Club)

Garl, Ron	Ravines Inn & Golf Club (with Mark McCumber) Timacuan Golf and Country Club (with Bobby Weed) University Park Country Club
Harman, Dave	Crooked Cat (at Orange County National Golf Center, with Isao Aoki and Phil Ritson) Panther Lake (at Orange County National Golf Center, with Isao Aoki and Phil Ritson)
Hills, Arthur	Legends Course (at LPGA International)
Jackson, Tom	Baytowne Golf Club (at Sandestin Golf and Beach Resort) Links Course (at Sandestin Golf and Beach Resort)
Johnson, Clyde	Eagle Harbor
Jones, Rees	Burnt Pine Golf Club (at Sandestin Golf and Beach Resort) Champions Course (at LPGA International)
Jones, Robert Trent, Jr.	Raven Golf Club (at Sandestin Golf and Beach Resort)
Koch, Gary	Las Colinas (at Mission Inn)
Lee, Joe	Diamondback Golf Club
LaGree, Terry	Diamond Players Club Clermont
McCumber, Mark	Ravines Inn & Golf Club (with Ron Garl) The Golf Club at South Hampton
Nicklaus, Jack	Grand Haven The King & The Bear (at World Golf Village, with Arnold Palmer)
Norman, Greg	Great White Course (at Doral)

Overton, Jay	Highlands South (at Westin Innisbrook Resort, with Lawrence Packard)
Packard, Lawrence	Copperhead Course (at Westin Innisbrook Resort) Highlands North (at Westin Innisbrook Resort) Highlands South (at Westin Innisbrook Resort, with Jay Overton) Island Course (at Westin Innisbrook Resort)
Palmer, Arnold	The King & The Bear (at World Golf Village, with Jack Nicklaus) Legacy Golf Club at Lakewood Ranch Palmer Course (at Saddlebrook Resort, with Ed Seay)
Player, Gary	Baytree National Golf Links
Refram, Dean	Saddlebrook Course (at Saddlebrook Resort)
Ritson, Phil	Crooked Cat (at Orange County National Golf Center, with Isao Aoki and Dave Harman) Panther Lake (at Orange County National Golf Center, with Isao Aoki and Dave Harman)
Ross, Donald	Radisson Ponce de Leon Golf & Conference Resort
Seay, Ed	Palmer Course (at Saddlebrook Resort, with Arnold Palmer)
Smyers, Steve	Southern Dunes Golf and Country Club
Simmons, Robert	Atlantis Country Club & Inn
von Hagge, Robert	Gold Course (at Doral, with Bruce Devlin) Lagoon Legend (at Bay Point, with Bruce Devlin) Red Course (at Doral) Silver Course (at Doral, with Bruce Devlin)

Weed, Bobby	The Slammer & The Squire (at World Golf Village) Timacuan Golf and Country Club (with Ron Garl) Tournament Players Club of Tampa Bay
Wilson, Dick	Blue Course (at Doral)

FIFTY MORE COURSES THAT YOU CAN PLAY

Abacoa Golf Club
Jupiter (north of Palm Beach)
(561) 622-0036

Palms, pines, and water. The course has gotten a lot of very favorable local press.

Ballantrae Golf and Yacht Club
Port St. Lucie
(561) 337-5315

Long Jack Nicklaus course.

Bardmoor Golf Club
Largo (southwest of Tampa)
(727) 392-1234

Much praise in the local golf press for redesigned greens and new clubhouse.

Binks Forest Golf Club
Wellington (near West Palm Beach)
(561) 795-0595

Pleasant par 72 cut through forests.

Bobby Jones Golf Complex
Sarasota
(941) 365-4653

36 holes plus an executive-length course designed by Donald Ross. History and a bargain.

The Breakers Club
Palm Beach
(561) 659-8407

Opened in 1897 in conjunction with Henry Flagler's Breakers Hotel.

Celebration Golf Club
Celebration (west of Orlando)
(407) 566-4653

The design of the father-son team of Robert Trent Jones Sr. and Jr.

Champions Club at Julington Creek
Duval County (southwest of Jacksonville)
(904) 287-4653

Well-maintained course with fast greens.

Champions Club at Summerfield
Stuart (north of Palm Beach)
(561) 283-1500

Tom Fazio design with lots of marsh and water.

Cimarrone Golf & Country Club
Duval County (south of Jacksonville)
(904) 287-2000

Lots of hills and water in a pleasant residen tial community.

Crandon Park Golf Course
Key Biscayne
(305) 361-9120

Senior PGA Tour tournament course with nice views of Biscayne Bay.

Deer Creek Golf Club
Deerfield Beach (north of Ft. Lauderdale)
(954) 421-5550

Pleasant, popular course in metro Miami area.

Diamond Players Club Wekiva
Longwood (northeast of Orlando)
(407) 862-5113

Another in a group of golf properties owned by several Major League baseball players.

Fairwinds Golf Club
Ft. Pierce (north of Palm Beach)
(561) 462-4653

St. Lucie County course designed by Jim Fazio. A bargain.

Falcon's Fire Golf Club
Kissimmee
(407) 239-5445

Lots of mounding and sand on this Rees Jones course.

Foxfire Golf Club
Sarasota
(941) 921-7757

Very popular, mature layout with 27 holes.

Fox Hollow Golf Club
New Port Ritchie (north of Tampa)
(727) 376-6333 or (800) 943-1902

Good, long, fair design by Robert Trent Jones Sr.

Gateway Golf & Country Club
Fort Myers
(941) 561-1010

Architect Tom Fazio's mature layout. Popular with locals and visitors alike.

Golden Bear at Hammock Creek
Palm City (north of Palm Beach)
(561) 220-2599

Only course in Florida designed by father and son, Jack Nicklaus and Jack Nicklaus II.

Grand Palms Golf and Country Club
Pembroke Pines (northwest of Miami)
(954) 437-3334

27 good holes at affordable prices in the Miami area.

Grenelefe Golf & Tennis Resort
Haines City (southwest of Orlando)
(863) 422-7511 or (800) 237-9549

54 holes in rolling and wooded terrain.

Halifax Plantation Golf Club
Ormond Beach (south of Daytona)
(904) 676-9600

Picturesque and popular course.

Hawk's Landing Golf Club
Orlando
(407) 238-8660

Robert Cupp redesign of Joe Lee's lovely and popular course.

Hidden Creek, The Club at
Navarre (east of Pensacola)
(850) 939-4604

Mature Ron Garl design.

Hombre
Panama City Beach
(850) 234-3673

Water in play on 15 holes. PGA Tour qualifying school course.

Indigo Lakes Golf Club
Daytona Beach
(904) 254-3607

Mature Lloyd Clifton course with small, fast greens.

Jacaranda Golf Club
Plantation (just west of Ft. Lauderdale)
(954) 472-5836

36-hole facility. U.S. Amateur qualifying course in 2000.

The Legacy Club at Alaqua Lakes
Longwood (northeast of Orlando)
(407) 444-9995

Scenic, difficult, well-maintained Tom Fazio course.

Lost Key
Perdido Key (southwest of Pensacola)
(850) 492-1300

Challenging Arnold Palmer course with big bunkers and undulating greens.

Matanzas Woods Golf Club
Palm Coast (south of Daytona)
(904) 446-6330 or (800) 874-2101

Lovely, challenging course that's popular with area players.

Metrowest Country Club
Orlando
(407) 299-1099

Hilly, mature golf course by the legendary Robert Trent Jones Sr.

The Moors
Pensacola
(850) 995-GOLF or (800) 727-1010

Senior PGA Tour tournament venue.

Naples Beach Hotel & Golf Club
Naples
(941) 435-2475

Traditional golf course re-designed by Ron Garl, originally opened in 1930.

Palisades Golf Club
Clermont (west of Orlando)
(352) 394-0085

A local favorite with some interesting holes.

Pelican Pointe Golf and Country Club Venice (941) 496-4653	Long, watery, and scenic.
Pelican's Nest Golf Club Bonita Springs (south of Fort Myers) (941) 947-6378	A mature, watery layout with 36 holes.
Regata Bay Destin (850) 650-7800	Water, woods, and sand.
River Bend Golf Course Ormond Beach (south of Daytona) (904) 673-6000	Manatees at play in the Tomoka add to a unique natural atmosphere.
River Hills Country Club Tampa (813) 653-3323	Tough, well-maintained Joe Lee design.
Rock Springs Ridge Golf Club Apopka (northwest of Orlando) (407) 814-7474	Long course through unusually hilly terrain.
Royal Amelia Golf Links Amelia Island (north of Jacksonville) (904) 491-8500	Lovely setting along the Amelia River.
Scenic Hills Country Club Pensacola (850) 476-0611	Much improved by Jerry Pate's redesign.
St. Johns County Golf Club Elkton (southwest of St. Augustine) (904) 825-4900	Great layout at bargain prices. Just expanded to 27 holes.
Tournament Players Club at Heron Bay Coral Springs (north of Miami) (954) 796-2000	Championship Mark McCumber design with lots of sand and water.
Waterlefe Golf & River Club Bradenton (941) 744-9771	The Manatee River forms the backdrop for this scenic and tough track.